# The Masonic Book Club

## Vol. 23

### *The Folger Manuscript*
S. Brent Morris

## Westphalia Press
An Imprint of the Policy Studies Organization
Washington, DC

THE FOLGER MANUSCRIPT

All Rights Reserved © 2026 by Policy Studies Organization

Westphalia Press
An imprint of Policy Studies Organization
1367 Connecticut Avenue NW
Washington, D.C. 20036
info@ipsonet.org

ISBN: 978-1-63723-664-2

Daniel Gutierrez-Sandoval, Executive Director
PSO and Westphalia Press

Updated material and comments on this edition
can be found at the Westphalia Press website:
www.westphaliapress.org

# The Masonic Book Club

The *Masonic Book Club* (MBC) was formed in 1970 by two Illinois Masons, Alphonse Cerza, 33°, and Louis L. Williams, 33°. The MBC primarily reprinted out-of-print Masonic books with scholarly introductions; occasionally they would print additional texts as "bonuses" (though none were marked specifically as such on the title pages); sometimes a reprint would be marked "Masonic Book Club Edition"; often an unnumbered bonus was published jointly with the Illinois Lodge of Research or the Supreme Council, 33°, NMJ, USA.

Most of the MBC volumes indicated on the title page, "Volume [*Number*] of the Publications of the Masonic Book Club," some were misnumbered, and some were unnumbered. Indeed, the numbering of the early volumes was inconsistent. For example, *A Serious and Impartial Enquiry* is "Volume Five" (1974) but *Masonic Membership of the Founding Fathers* is "The Masonic Book Club Edition" (1974). Then, *Masonry Dissected* is "Volume Eight" (1977), *The Trestleboard* is "Volume 8A" (1978), and *Anderson's Constitutions of 1738* is "Volume Nine" (1978). If nothing else, MBC books keep bibliophiles on their toes.

The first volumes had deckle-edged paper and pages of slightly different sizes, though eventually the MBC settled into a 6"×9" trimmed-page format for their books. The books were bound in a dark blue fabric with gold lettering. Listed below are the fifty-nine MBC volumes published 1970–2010 with bonuses. N.B.: A number and letter, e.g. "Volume 8A," is a numbering for this reprint series.

The club originally was limited to 333 members, but the number grew to nearly 2,000, with 1,083 members when it dissolved in 2010. In 2017 MW Barry Weer, 33°, the last president of the MBC, transferred the MBC name and assets to the Supreme Council, 33°, SJ, USA. Under the editorship of Arturo de Hoyos, 33°, G∴C∴, and S. Brent Morris, 33°, G∴C∴, the revived Masonic Book Club has the goal of publishing classic Masonic books while supporting Scottish Rite, SJ, USA philanthropies.

## Publications of the Masonic Book Club, 1970–2010

| | | | |
|---|---|---|---|
| 1 | 1970 | *The Regius Poem* | Masonic Book Club |
| 2 | 1971 | *The Constitutions of the Free-Masons* | Benjamin Franklin |
| 3 | 1972 | *Ahiman Rezon* | Laurence Dermott |
| 4 | 1973 | *Illustrations of Masonry* | William Preston |
| 5 | 1974 | *A Serious and Impartial Enquiry into the Cause of the Present Decay of Free-Masonry in the Kingdom of Ireland* | Fifield D'Assigny |
| 5A | 1974* | *Masonic Membership of the Founding Fathers* | Ronald E. Heaton |

| | | | |
|---|---|---|---|
| 6 | 1975 | *The Signers of the Declaration of Independence* | David C. Whitney |
| 7 | 1976 | *The Signers of the Constitution of the United States* | David C. Whitney |
| 7A | 1976* | *Masonic Symbols in American Decorative Art* | Louis L. Williams & Alphonse Cerza |
| 8 | 1977 | *Samuel Prichard's Masonry Dissected, 1730* | Harry Carr |
| 8A | 1978* | *Trestle-Board (A facsimile of the original Trestle Board by the Baltimore Masonic Convention of 1843)* | Dwight L. Smith |
| 9 | 1978 | *Anderson's Constitutions of 1738* | Lewis Edward & W. J. Hughan |
| 10 | 1979 | *Sufferings of John Coustos* | Wallace McLeod |
| 11 | 1980 | *The Revelations of a Square* | George Oliver |
| 11A | 1980 | *Biblical Characters in Freemasonry* | John H. Van Gorden |
| 11B | 1980* | *A Masonic Reader's Guide* | Alphonse Cerza & Thomas Warden |
| 12 | 1981 | *Three Distinct Knocks and Jachin and Boaz* | Harry Carr |
| 13 | 1982 | *Masonic Almanacs and Anti-Masonic Almanacs* | Plez A. Transou |
| 13A | 1982* | *Stephen A. Douglas: Freemason* | Wayne C. Temple |
| 14 | 1983 | *The Beginnings of Freemasonry in America* | Melvin M. Johnson |
| 14A | 1983* | *Bespangled, Painted & Embroidered: Decorated Masonic Aprons in America, 1790–1850* | Scottish Rite Masonic Museum & Library |
| 14B | 1983* | *Making a Mason at Sight* | Louis L. Williams |
| 15 | 1984 | *Masonic Concordance of the Holy Bible* | Charles Clyde Hunt |
| 15A | 1984* | *By Square and Compasses: The Building of Lincoln's Home and Its Saga* | Wayne C. Temple |
| 16 | 1985 | *The Old Gothic Constitutions* | Wallace McLeod |

| | | | |
|---|---|---|---|
| 16A | 1985* | Modern Historical Characters in Freemasonry | John H. Van Gorden |
| 17 | 1986 | The Rise and Development of Organised Freemasonry | Roy A. Wells |
| 17A | 1986* | Ancient and Early Medieval Historical Characters in Freemasonry | John H. Van Gorden |
| 18 | 1987 | The Lodge in Friendship Village and Other Stories | P. W. George |
| 18A | 1987* | Masonic Charities | John H. Van Gorden & Stewart M. L. Pollard |
| 18B | 1987* | Medieval Historical Characters in Freemasonry | John H. Van Gorden |
| 18C | 1987* | George Washington in New York | Allan Boudreau & Alexander Bleimann |
| 19 | 1988 | Records of the Hole Crafte and Fellowship of Masons | Edward Conder, Jr. |
| 20 | 1989 | A Candid Disquisition of the Principles and Practices of the Most Ancient and Honourable Society of Free and Accepted Masons | Wellins Calcott |
| 20A | 1989* | Freemasonry and Nauvoo, 1839–1846 | Robin L. Carr |
| 21 | 1990 | Masonic Odes and Poems | Rob Morris |
| 22 | 1991 | Lessing's Masonic Dialogues | Gotthold Lessing |
| 22A | 1991* | ABC of Freemasonry: A Book for Beginners | Delmar D. Darrah |
| 23 | 1992 | The Folger Manuscript | S. Brent Morris |
| 24 | 1993 | Freemasonry and Christianity: Lectures from Two Ages | T. De Witt Peake & John J. Murchison |
| 25 | 1994 | The Constitutions of St. John's Lodge | Robin L. Carr |
| 25A | 1994* | The Mystic Tie and Men of Letters | Robin L. Carr |
| 26 | 1995 | Recollections of a Masonic Veteran | S. Brent Morris |
| 27 | 1996 | The Freemason's Monitor or Illustrations of Masonry in Two Parts | Thomas Smith Webb |

| | | | |
|---|---|---|---|
| 28 | 1997 | *The Masonic Ladder or the Nine Steps to Ancient Freemasonry* | John Sherer |
| 28A | 1997* | *Freemasonry and Democracy: Its Evolution in North America* | Allen E. Roberts & Wallace McLeod |
| 29 | 1998 | *The Masonic Harp: Collection of Masonic Odes, Hymns, Songs* | George Wingate Chase |
| 30 | 1999 | *Symbolic Teachings of Masonry and Its Message* | Thomas Milton Stewart |
| 31 | 2000 | *Freemasonry Its Meaning and Significance, An Exposition of its Ethics, Religion and Philosophy* | Otto Caspari |
| 32 | 2001 | *K. R. Cama Masonic Jubilee Volume* | Jivanji Jamshedji Modi |
| 33 | 2002 | *Caementaria Hibernica* | W. J. Chetwode Crawley |
| 34 | 2003 | *A Daily Advancement in Masonic Knowledge* | Wallace McLeod & S. Brent Morris |
| 35 | 2004 | *The Craftsman, and Templar's Textbook and, also, Melodies for the Craft* | Cornelius Moore |
| 36 | 2005 | *The Text Book of Freemasonry* | Retired Member of the Craft |
| 37 | 2006 | *Orations of the Illustrious Brother Frederick Dalcho Esq., M.D.* | Frederick Dalcho |
| 38 | 2007 | *Antiquities of Freemasonry Comprising Illustrations of the Five Grand Periods of Masonry from the Creation of the World to the Dedication of King Solomon's Temple* | George Oliver |
| 39 | 2008 | *Diogenes' Lamp or an Examination of our Present-Day Morality and Enlightenment* | Adam Weishaupt |
| 40 | 2009 | *Proofs of Conspiracy Against All the Governments of Europe* | John Robison |
| 41 | 2010 | *The Evolution of Freemasonry* | Delmar Darrah |

\* indicates a bonus book

# The Folger Manuscript

# THE FOLGER MANUSCRIPT

VOLUME TWENTY-THREE
of the publications of
The Masonic Book Club

Published by
The Masonic Book Club
A Not-for-Profit Corporation of Illinois
Bloomington, Illinois
1992

[This text appeared in the original printing]

This volume has been published

for members of

The Masonic Book Club

in an edition of 1600 copies,

this being

No._____888_____

# THE FOLGER MANUSCRIPT

**Robert Benjamin Folger**

From *The Masonic Chronicle*, Vol. VI, No. 10, September 1884

# THE FOLGER MANUSCRIPT

*The Cryptanalysis and Interpretation
of an
American Masonic Manuscript*

S. BRENT MORRIS

Ft. George G. Meade, Maryland
1992

*To Harold D. Thomas*

*Friend, Magician, Master Mason*

# Contents

Illustrations .................................................... xi
Acknowledgements ............................................. xiii
Preface ......................................................... xv

**Introduction** .................................................. xix
    New York Freemasonry in the early 1800s .................... xix
        Civic respectability ..................................... xix
        Additional degrees ....................................... xx
    Scottish Rite Freemasonry ................................... xxi
        Ramsay's oration ......................................... xxi
        Stephen Morin .......................................... xxii
        The Mother Supreme Council ............................ xxiii
    Cerneauism ................................................ xxiii
        Opportunists in New York .............................. xxiii
        Legitimacy in the north .................................. xxv
        The Cerneau Supreme Council(s) revived ................ xxvi
    The American antimasonic movement ....................... xxvi
        The abduction of William Morgan ...................... xxvii
        The birth of a movement .............................. xxvii
    A glossary of Masonic terms ................................ xxix

**1. The Mystery of the Folger Manuscript** ........................ 1
    Setting the scene ............................................. 2
    Identifying the Rituals ....................................... 3
        Emblems of the degrees .................................... 5
        Plan of the lodge .......................................... 8
        History of Freemasonry ................................... 11
    Locating the source ......................................... 15
    Inferring its use ............................................. 18
        A second copy ............................................ 18
        Elmira Consistory ........................................ 25
        Zorobabel Lodge ......................................... 26
        John the Forerunner Lodge ............................... 27
        Revocation of the preface ................................. 29
    Reviewing the solution ..................................... 30

**2. The Cryptanalysis of the Folger Cipher** ..................... 33
    Assumptions ................................................ 35

Table of Contents

    Analysis .................................................. 37
        Boxed-in symbols ..................................... 38
        The mystery digraph .................................. 39
        Words 1–4 ............................................ 40
        Words 5, 6 and 7 ..................................... 41
        Synthesis ............................................. 42
        Words 8–13 .......................................... 42
        Other interesting words .............................. 43
        The solution ......................................... 43

    Summary ................................................. 44

## 3. The Coadjutors of Robert B. Folger .......................... 47

    Hans Burch Gram ......................................... 47
        From Boston to Copenhagen .......................... 48
        Zerubbabel Lodge .................................... 48
        From Copenhagen to New York City .................. 50
        Folger and Wilsey .................................... 50
        Professional activities ............................... 51

    Ferdinand Little Wilsey .................................. 53
        Folger and Gram ..................................... 53
        From manufacturing to medicine .................... 54

    Henry Clinton Atwood ................................... 55
        Mystic Lodge and the Cross work ..................... 56
        Abraham Jacobs and the 32° ......................... 58
        James Cushman and the 33° ......................... 59
        The St. John's Day parade ........................... 60
        St. John's Grand Lodge .............................. 62
        The Cerneau Supreme Council revived ............... 63
        The Supreme Council for the Northern Hemisphere .. 64
        The Supreme Council for the State of New York ..... 67
        Scottish Rite symbolic lodges ........................ 69
        St. John's Grand Lodge revived ...................... 72
        The grand plan ...................................... 73
        The crumbling empire ............................... 76
        The final years ...................................... 80

## 4. The Biography of a Remarkable Mason ....................... 83

    Early life ................................................ 84
        Light in Masonry .................................... 84
        More light in Masonry ............................... 85
        Further light in Masonry ............................ 86
        Medicine and Masonry from Denmark ............... 87
        The Cipher Manuscripts ............................. 88

    Return to New York ..................................... 89
        The Dutcher affair .................................. 90
        Suspended from Masonry ............................ 91
        Masonic, medical, and mercantile pursuits .......... 92
        The Revival of the Supreme Council ................. 94
        Scottish Rite symbolic lodges ........................ 95

*Table of Contents*

|  |  |
|---|---|
| *Further controversy* | 96 |
| *Suspended again from Masonry* | 97 |
| *Revocation of the preface* | 99 |
| *Return to the fold* | 100 |
| *Resignation as Grand Secretary General* | 101 |
| Later Years | 102 |
| *Defending the Cerneau Supreme Council* | 102-A |
| *The Union of 1867 and temporary peace* | 102-B |
| *The reprinted history* | 102-D |
| *The final controversy* | 102-E |

## 5. The Manuscript and its Translation .......... 103

| The Manuscript | 103 |
|---|---|
| *General comments* | 103 |
| *The cipher* | 104 |
| *Hebrew* | 105 |
| *Stick figures* | 108 |
| *Unknown symbols* | 109 |
| The translation | 110 |

## 6. The Rituals and the History .......... 179

| Observations | 179 |
|---|---|
| *The obligations* | 179 |
| *Words* | 180 |
| *The cord* | 181 |
| *Ode to a skull* | 182 |
| *The ablution* | 182 |
| Disciple's Grade | 184 |
| *First section* | 184 |
| *Disciple's obligation* | 190 |
| *Second section* | 192 |
| *Lecture* | 194 |
| *Opening the Disciple's Lodge* | 199 |
| *Closing the Disciple's Lodge* | 201 |
| *Disciple's catechism* | 203 |
| Fellow's Grade | 206 |
| *First section* | 206 |
| *Address from the Master* | 207 |
| *Lecture* | 214 |
| *Opening of the Fellow's Lodge* | 217 |
| *Closing of the Fellow's Grade* | 219 |
| Master's Grade | 222 |
| *Preparation* | 222 |
| *Address from the Master* | 223 |
| *Lecture and instructions* | 226 |
| *Opening or closing of the Master's Lodge* | 232 |
| Prayers | 233 |
| Scottish obligations | 234 |

*Page ix*

## Table of Contents

    The History ................................................. 235
References ................................................. 241
Index ................................................. 247

# Illustrations

Robert Benjamin Folger .................................................................. ii

**1. The Mystery of the Folger Manuscript**

    1. Square stone ...................................................... 6
    2. Pencil sketch of a ship ........................................ 6
    3. Emblems of the Strict Observance ........................... 7
    4. Triangular monument ......................................... 7
    5. Lodge floor plan ................................................ 9
    6. Second degree R.E.R. tracing board ........................ 10
    7. Similar cipher letters ......................................... 20
    8. Single page from the *Supreme Council Book* .................... 21
    9. Extracts from several pages of the *Macoy Book* ............... 21

**2. The Cryptanalysis of the Folger Cipher**

    1. Page 84 from the *Macoy Book* ................................. 34
    2. Page 21 from the *Macoy Book* ................................. 36
    3. Possible elemental cipher symbols ........................... 37
    4. Boxes in cipher text .......................................... 38
        The mystery digraph ......................................... 39
    5. The thirteen words with the mystery digraph ................ 39
        Word 1 ........................................................ 40
        Word 2 ........................................................ 40
        Word 3 ........................................................ 40
        Word 4 ........................................................ 41
        Word 5 ........................................................ 41
        Word 6 ........................................................ 41
        Word 7 ........................................................ 41
    6. Tentative cipher characters ................................... 41
        "Our" .......................................................... 42
    7. Synthesizing short words ..................................... 42
        Word 8 ........................................................ 42
        Word 13 ....................................................... 43

Illustrations

    "Rules" .................................................... 43
    "Efforts" .................................................. 43
  8. Folger's cipher alphabet ................................ 44

## 3. The Coadjutors of Robert B. Folger

  1. Hans Burch Gram, M.D. ................................. 49
     Gram's gravestone ....................................... 52
  2. Henry Clinton Atwood .................................. 57

## 5. The Manuscript and its Translation

    Typical punctuation marks ............................... 104
  1. Representative Masonic ciphers ........................ 105
  2. Linear and non-linear writing ......................... 106
  3. The "key" ............................................. 106
     Hebrew from page 84 ..................................... 107
  4. Representative stick figures .......................... 108
     Unknown symbols ......................................... 109
     Altar and cross ......................................... 109
     Steps, carpet, sword, and gavel ......................... 109
  5. The key to Folger's cipher ............................ 111
     The cord ................................................ 181
     A skull ................................................. 182

# ACKNOWLEDGEMENTS

This study of the *Folger Manuscript* has continued off-and-on since 1978. Portions of the research have been presented at various times, something like dress rehearsals, and are now all gathered together for the opening night. The research first produced a biography of Robert B. Folger which was presented to Independent Royal Arch Lodge No. 2 on September 20, 1979. Additional material on Folger plus information on Henry C. Atwood were combined for the first Wendall K. Walker Lecture at I.R.A. No. 2 on October 8, 1991, "Henry C. Atwood and Robert B. Folger: Faithful Followers or Wild-eyed Fanatics?" These papers yielded Chapter 4, "The Biography of a Remarkable Freemason," and the Atwood portion of Chapter 3, "The Coadjutors of Robert B. Folger." Chapter 2, "The Cryptanalysis of the Folger Cipher," was originally presented to the American Lodge of Research on October 29, 1990. Chapter 1, "The Mystery of the Folger Manuscript," is revised and expanded from a presentation made at Quatuor Coronati Lodge No. 2076 on September 10, 1992.

Over these years, many people have contributed to the research; so many that there is a danger of overlooking someone in any listing. There is a greater problem, however, in producing no list – failing to recognize the tremendous help and support that made this book possible.

Two people must be singled out for their exceptional, continuous support: •Prof. Wallace McLeod, University of Toronto, for his linguistic, grammatical, and textual advice; and •Mrs. Nancy T. Morris, my wife, for her cryptanalytic, grammatical, and general all-around support.

Others who have given many hours assistance in unravelling this mystery are Dr. William T. Anton; •Mr. Keith Arrington, Librarian, Grand Lodge of Iowa, A. F. & A. M.; •Mr. Wil Baden;

Acknowledgements

•Ms. Jennifer Barlow, Assistant Librarian of the Supreme Council, 33°, N.M.J.; •Mrs. Inge Baum, Librarian of the Supreme Council, 33°, S.J.; •Mr. Donald H. Bennett; •Mr. Christian D. Besson; •Dr. John W. Boettjer, Editor, *The Scottish Rite Journal*; •Dr. Allan Boudreau, Librarian, Chancellor Livingston Library, Grand Lodge of New York, F. & A. M.; Mr. Michel Brodsky; •Mr. Barry Carleen; •Mr. Henry Emmerson; •Mr. Alfred Engel; •Mr. Herbert A. Fisher; •Mr. David Gaddy; •Mr. R. A. Gilbert; •Ms. V. Hansen, Secretary, Macoy Publishing and Masonic Supply Co., Inc.; •Ms. Gloria Jackson, Assistant Librarian of the Supreme Council, 33°, N.M.J.; •Mr. Jørgen Vagn Jørgensen, Præses, Informationsdirektoriet, Den Danske Frimurerorden; •Mr. Reynolds J. Matthews, Archivist, Supreme Council, 33°, S.J.; •Mr. Stephen Patrick, Curator, George Washington National Masonic Memorial; •Dr. William G. Peacher; •Mr. Norman D. Peterson; •Mr. Aemil Pouler, Editor, *The New Age*; •Mr. H. Paul Scholte, President, Macoy Publishing and Masonic Supply Co., Inc.; •Mr. Eric Serejeski; •Dr. Clemente Silvestro, Director, Scottish Rite Museum of our National Heritage; •Ms. Nola Skousen, Archivist/Librarian of the Supreme Council, 33°, N.M.J.; •Mr. Harold van Buren Voorhis; •Prof. Julian Winston; •Mr. David Ward; •Prof. Ralph Weber, Marquette University.

S. BRENT MORRIS

Columbia, Maryland
July 12, 1992

# Preface

ULIKELY AS IT MAY SEEM AT FIRST GLANCE, this book is really a detective story. Let me try to outline the mystery, without spoiling the impact of the investigation too much. A few years ago a strange manuscript, dated at New York, in 1827, and written in a curious hieroglyphic characters, was discovered, or rediscovered. It turns out that the text was a substitution cipher, a sort of private code devised expressly for this document. And the text is a ritual for three Masonic degrees, written out in full. The scribe was a medical doctor named Robert B. Folger. His particular version of the ritual, it appears, is not used any more by American Freemasons, and it was never very common here.

Many questions leap to mind. How can one read a manuscript that is written in code? (Those who are familiar with Edgar Allan Poe's story "The Gold-Bug" may have some idea, but read on.) Where did the text come from? Is it made up, as it were, out of whole cloth? Or was it brought in from somewhere else? When was it ever used? Did Folger work along, or did he have helpers? Obviously there is a broad field for investigation! We have good reason to thank Dr. S. Brent Morris, who has applied his considerable skills of research and deduction to solving these riddles. He guides us expertly through a perplexing maze, and makes us feel that we are a part of the team that eventually finds the solutions.

He offers us a facsimile of the original manuscript. He clearly explains how it was possible to decipher it. He gives us a line-by-line transliteration. Then, since the original writer (in order to make his text even more obscure) had abbreviated it, broken it up and shuffled it about, Dr. Morris reconstructs the continuous version, and offers explanatory comments. He provides a plausible line of descent, and shows that the rituals almost certainly was brought over from continental Europe, probably from Denmark. He tells us about the lives of the four men who worked together in

Preface

transporting it to America, and in translating and adapting it for local use. In short, the book will be of interest not only to cryptanalysts, and to Freemasons, but also to students who are interested in nineteenth century American history, and to those who simply like to see problems unfolded and then solved.

Let me try to offer a bit of background, in order to suggest how Folger's ritual fits into Masonic history. Historians always say that the era of Modern Freemasonry began on June 24, 1717, when four Lodges in London met together and formed themselves into a Grand Lodge. (We may note with interest that 1992 marks the 275$^{th}$ anniversary of this event.) Evidently these four lodges must have existed before that date. It is clear also that, in some sense, they were the successors of men called Masons who were organized into groups in Britain from about 1350 on.

There is some dispute about what these groups did, and why they were formed. In the present writer's view, the evidence suggests that they were made up of operative stonemasons, the cathedral builders of the later Middle Ages. In the course of time these groups took the name "lodges," from the lodge or shelter that was built on the south side of the project. The organization served the function of a union, not so much to protect the welfare of the laborers as to maintain the quality of their stonework. These lodges had a set of written regulations and a traditional history, of which over a hundred copies have survived to our time; they are usually written on a scroll of paper or parchment. Apparently they were read to each new member at his admission. The operative lodges also had a rudimentary ceremony of admission, including an invocation and a promise to obey the regulations. It seems also that, as time passed, the lodges adopted signs of recognition. When the members moved to a new job in a different location, they would use the signs to show that they were regular skilled workmen.

Gradually, in England, Scotland, and Ireland, for reasons that are obscure to us, the operative lodges began to admit men who were not practising stonemasons. Among he earliest were Sir Robert Moray, the first president of the Royal Society (1641), and

Elias Ashmole, the founder of the Ashmolean Museum in Oxford (1646). In due course, some of the lodges came to be composed mainly of "accepted" or non-operative Masons. It was four of these new lodges that formed the first Grand Lodge in 1717.

The notion of a grand lodge was contagious; about 1725 the Grand Lodge of Ireland was founded, and in 1736, the Grand Lodge of Scotland. These three bodies are the sources from which Freemasonry spread across the globe. It reached France (Paris) from England in 1725, Spain (Madrid) and India (Calcutta) in 1728, Russia in 1731, Italy (Florence) and America (Boston) in 1733, Sweden in 1735, Germany (Hamburg) from France in 1737, and Denmark in 1744. And wherever it went, it eventually came to have its own independent grand lodge, to govern it.

Enough documents survive to show that the ritual was constantly growing, evolving, expanding, becoming more elaborate, adopting new symbols, abandoning former practices. And all over the world, the ritual has continued to develop. That is why distinctive rituals are used today in various parts of the British Isles, of Europe, and of America.

We can trace some of the stages in the evolution. Let us simply give a few examples to indicate how Folger's ritual fits into this development. In his Grade of Fellow, in the Lecture, there is mention of the Liberal Arts and Sciences, and the Building of Solomon's Temple; both topics appear in the Cooke Manuscript of the Old Charges, written about the year 1410.[1] The *Folger Manuscript* has a vow or oath for each degree, in which the candidate promises not to disclose the secrets to any unqualified person; and such an oath is found in six versions of the Old Charges, and was used as early as 1650.[2] In the Second Section of Folger's Grade of Disciple, the presiding officer presents the new member with a pair

---

[1] Douglas Knoop, G. P. Jones, and Douglas Hamer, eds., *The Two Earliest Masonic Manuscripts* (Manchester: Manchester University Press, 1938), p. 71, lines 40ff., and p. 99 lines 548ff.

[2] *The Collected Prestonian Lectures 1975-1987* (Shepperton, England: Lewis Masonic, 1988), p. 274.

Preface

of gloves, to be given to the woman who merits his esteem; the practice is associated with the Masons as early as 1686, by Robert Plot in his *Natural History of Stafford-shire*.[3] One of the words mentioned in the Opening of the Fellow's Lodge according to Folger is *Giblem*; this goes back ultimately to the Hebrew text of 1 Kings 5:18, and first turns up in a Masonic context in 1713.[4] In Folger's Grade of Disciple, just before the obligation is administered, the Master refers to God as the "Architect of the Universe"; this term was regularly used by John Calvin, and was introduced into Freemasonry by the Calvinist Presbyterian minister, Rev. James Anderson, in his first book of *Constitutions* in 1723.[5] In Folger's Lecture for the Fellow Lodge, the working tools of the degree are the square, plumb, and level – three implements which appear together in Prichard's *Masonry Dissected* of 1730.[6] In the Disciple's Catechism, there is mention of the broken pillar bearing the motto *Adhuc stat*; this is, as Dr. Morris, demonstrates, taken over from Hund's Strict Observance, and must go back to about 1750.

But there is no excuse for delaying the patient reader any further. Read on, and share in the excitement of learning about this fascinating document.

WALLACE McLEOD

University of Toronto
June 24, 1992

---

[3] Douglas Knoop, G. P. Jones, and Douglas Hamer, eds., *Early Masonic Pamphlets* (Manchester: Manchester University Press, 1945), p. 32.

[4] G. W. Speth, *Ars Quatuor Coronatorum*, Vol. 1, 1886-1888, pp. 128-129; H. Poole and F. R. Worts, *The "Yorkshire" Old Charges of Masons* (York: 1935), p. 170.

[5] *Ars Quatuor Coronatorum* Vol.101, 1988, p. 147; James Anderson, *The Constitutions of the Free-Masons* (London: 1723), p. 1.

[6] Douglas Knoop, G. P. Jones, and Douglas Hamer, eds., *The Early Masonic Catechisms*, 2nd ed., ed. Harry Carr (London: Quatuor Coronati Lodge No. 2076, 1975), p. 162.

# INTRODUCTION

THE STORY OF THE *FOLGER MANUSCRIPT* is an intriguing tale set in the middle of nineteenth-century New York Freemasonry. It is almost impossible to appreciate all the influences on the manuscript's author, Robert B. Folger, without understanding the milieu in which the story unfolds. The following paragraphs should give a sufficient overview of the Byzantine complexities of New York Freemasonry to help the reader appreciate his tale.

## NEW YORK FREEMASONRY IN THE EARLY 1800s

The earliest record of Freemasonry in the United States is the account book of a St. John's Lodge in Philadelphia, known as "Libre B"; its first entry is dated June 24, 1731. A year earlier on June 5, 1730, Daniel Coxe had been appointed Provincial Grand Master for New York, New Jersey, and Pennsylvania, but he seems not to have exercised his authority. The first reference to Masonry operating in New York City is an oblique notice in January 1737/38, stating the Master of a Lodge had resigned because of his removal from the city. The formal chartering of Lodges started with St. John's Lodge No. 2 (now No. 1) on December 7, 1757, and continued with Temple Lodge ca. 1758, La Parfait Union on November 1, 1760, and St. John's Independent Royal Arch Lodge No. 8 (now No. 2) on December 15, 1760. The Grand Lodge which governs all subordinate Lodges in the state was formed in 1787.[1]

## CIVIC RESPECTABILITY

By the early 1800s Freemasonry had become a large, influential organization throughout New York state, attracting many prominent citizens. During the War of 1812 De Witt Clinton, Mayor of New York

---

[1] Henry W. Coil, et al., eds., *Coil's Masonic Encyclopedia* (New York: Macoy Masonic Publishing and Supply Co., 1961), s.v. "New York."

Introduction

City and Grand Master of the Grand Lodge of New York, assembled the Grand Officers and members of two local Lodges to construct fortifications in Brooklyn that became known as "Fort Masonic." By 1826 there were 480 Lodges throughout the state and a total membership of 20,000, making it one of the largest Grand Lodges in the world. New York City Masonry was particularly cosmopolitan, with Lodges working in several languages, including French and German.

> As an organization with the discretion to choose its members from among the applicants, Masonry was exclusive by definition. Nevertheless, the diversity of its membership suggests that neither wealth, politics, nor religion governed admission.... Men who otherwise were prominent in their communities also, though not always, tended to be rewarded for Masonic merit.... The membership seems best explained as an association of like-minded men who were attracted to Masonry because of its exotic qualities and its personal or social usefulness.[2]

### ADDITIONAL DEGREES

Masons in New York, and particularly in New York City, had many opportunities for involvement. They first joined a Lodge and received the degrees of Entered Apprentice, Fellowcraft, and Master Mason. If they sought further "light" and involvement in the fraternity, they could join a Chapter of Royal Arch Masons and receive four more degrees, culminating in Royal Arch Mason. The first Chapter of Royal Arch Masons was formed about 1791 and the Grand Chapter followed in 1798. Royal Arch Masons could join a Council of Royal and Select Masters (also called Cryptic Masonry), and those who were Christian could join an Encampment (now Commandery) of Knights Templar. Cryptic Councils began in New York about 1810 and Templary started there as early as 1783. The Knights Templar became the elite of New York Masonry, not only because of their greater Masonic "knowledge" but also because of the expense of multiple dues and initiation fees.

[2] Dorothy Ann Lipson, *Freemasonry in Federalist Connecticut, 1789–1835* (Princeton: Princeton University Press, 1977), p. 238.

Introduction

Providing yet another source of Masonic light was the Scottish Rite with its thirty-three degrees and two competing bodies in New York City. One grew from a Consistory of the 32° established without authority by Antoine Bideaud on August 6, 1806. The other was started by Joseph Cerneau in 1807, who illegitimately extended his authority under the Rite of Perfection to create a Consistory in New York City and later extended his degrees to thirty-three to compete with the Scottish Rite. The conflicts of these two groups plagued New York Masonry for nearly a century, at times threatening to destroy it.

## SCOTTISH RITE FREEMASONRY

Like nearly every major Masonic Rite, the Scottish Rite is not really sure of its earliest origins. The Scottish Rite confers thirty-three degrees—thirty beyond the first three, which are under the control of Grand Lodges. Its origins can be traced to the rise of *hauts grades* in France, which in turn are believed to have started with the celebrated oration of Chevalier Andrew Michael Ramsay in 1737 in Paris.

**RAMSAY'S ORATION**

Ramsay put forward the original (and unsubstantiated) theory that the Crusaders were the originators of Freemasonry. Ramsay wove a romantic story about the knightly origins of Freemasonry that resonated with continental Masons, especially those in France.

> Our ancestors, the Crusaders, gathered together from all parts of Christendom in the Holy Land, desired thus to reunite into one sole Fraternity the individuals of all nations. . . .
>
> We have secrets; they are figurative signs and sacred words, composing a language sometimes mute, sometimes very eloquent, in order to communicate with one another at the greatest distance, and to recognize our brothers of whatsoever tongue. These were words of war which the Crusaders gave each other in order to guarantee them from the surprises of the Saracens, who often crept in amongst them to kill them. . . .
>
> The word Freemason must therefore not be taken in a literal, gross, and material sense, as if our founders had been simple work-

ers in stone, or merely curious geniuses who wished to perfect the arts. They were not only skillful architects, desirous of consecrating their talents and goods to the construction of material temples; but also religious and warrior princes who designed to enlighten, edify, and protect the living Temples of the Most High. . . .[3]

Apparently inspired by Ramsay, a whole succession of Masonic degrees was created on the continent. Those taking these degrees seemed most interested in discovering prestigious Masonic pedigrees for themselves. Each Degree claimed to be of higher importance or authority than any other, hence the name *hauts grades*. During the eighteenth century these degrees waxed, waned, and were gathered together into "Rites" or systems of interrelated ceremonies.

**STEPHEN MORIN**

These Rites in turn competed for influence and power in the chaotic swirl of continental Freemasonry. The Emperors of the East and West, formed in 1758, gained momentary ascendency in the battle for control of the *hauts grades*; the degrees they controlled were known as the Rite of Perfection. The most significant action of the Emperors was the 1761 deputation of Stephen Morin as a Grand Inspector of the Rite of Perfection in America, ". . . authorizing and empowering him to establish perfect and sublime Masonry in all parts of the world, . . . with full and entire power to create Inspectors in all places where the sublime degrees shall not already be established. . . ."[4]

Morin lived in Saint Domingue (now Haiti) and Jamaica, where he established bodies of the Rite of Perfection and created dozens of other Inspectors. These Inspectors were often itinerant degree peddlers, supplementing their incomes with the sale of Masonic titles, but they spread the Rite to the United States and eventually around the world. Henry Andrew Francken established the first American Lodge

---

[3] Robert Freke Gould, et al., *The History of Freemasonry*, 3 vols. (New York: John C. Yorston & Co., 1889), Vol. III, p. 339.

[4] Coil, s.v. "Scottish Rite Masonry," "Stephen Morin."

of Perfection in Albany, New York, in 1767. Others soon followed in Philadelphia, Charleston, Baltimore, and New York City.

**THE MOTHER SUPREME COUNCIL**

On May 31, 1801, the Rite of Perfection was effectively replaced by the establishment of the Supreme Council, 33°, Ancient and Accepted Scottish Rite of Freemasonry. The Mother Supreme Council was created on the basis of the "Constitutions of 1786," attributed to Frederick the Great of Prussia for reorganizing the Rite of Perfection. All the degrees of the Rite of Perfection are contained in the Scottish Rite plus eight additional ones, including the 33°, Sovereign Grand Inspector General. It is not known when or where any of the founders of the first Supreme Council received their 33° or how they came into possession of the Constitutions of 1786, but the organization they created stretches around the world today.

**CERNEAUISM**

The Mother Supreme Council was created to bring order to the chaotic world of high-grade Masonry, but its early effects were just the opposite. The Constitutions of 1786 authorized two Supreme Councils in the United States, and the Charleston Supreme Council seemed intent on waiting until just the right moment to divide its territory and share it with a sister Supreme Council. The right moment came sooner than expected.

**OPPORTUNISTS IN NEW YORK**

In August 1806, Antoine Bideaud, a member of the Supreme Council of the "French West India Islands," visited New York City and found an opportunity to make a little extra money. He conferred the Scottish Rite degrees on J. J. J. Gourgas and four other Frenchmen for $46 each and then created a "Sublime Grand Consistory 30°, 31°, and 32°." Bideaud's authority was for the islands only and certainly did not extend into New York, which was under the jurisdiction of

Introduction

the Charleston Supreme Council. Principal officers of the Bideaud Supreme Council were J. J. J. Gourgas, Daniel D. Tompkins, Sampson Simpson, and Richard Riker.[5]

In New York City in October 1807, Joseph Cerneau, a jeweler from Cuba, constituted a "Sovereign Grand Consistory of Sublime Princes of the Royal Secret." Cerneau was a "Deputy Grand Inspector, for the Northern part of the Island of Cuba" under the Rite of Perfection. His patent limited him to confer the 4° through 24° on Lodge officers, and the 25° once a year. Early records are sufficiently vague that it cannot be determined if the original members of Cerneau's Sovereign Grand Consistory thought they had the 25° or the 32°. With even less authority than Bideaud, Cerneau launched his foray into high-grade Masonry in New York. Principal officers of the Cerneau Grand Consistory included Cerneau, De Witt Clinton, John W. Mulligan, and Cadwallader D. Colden.[6]

Complicating the situation of the rival and equally illegitimate Supreme Councils were the personal, political, and Masonic rivalries of their principal officers. Tompkins as governor of New York was succeeded in office by Clinton, his lieutenant governor; Clinton as Grand Master of New York was succeeded by Tompkins. Simson and Mulligan opposed each other in Grand Lodge; Mulligan defeated Simson as Grand Treasurer in 1814, but Simson regained the office in 1815. Colden was assistant attorney general in 1798 and replaced Riker as district attorney in 1811; Riker regained the position in 1812.[7]

> [N]either Clinton nor Tompkins cared one whit for the honors conferred upon him by his Supreme Council. Both of them were first, last and always, politicians, bending every effort and every agency they could to secure for themselves political preferment. . . . [Each was] perfectly willing to permit Freemasonry to use itself in his service. . . . Mulligan and Simson were adversaries in the Grand Lodge of New York. The professional paths of Colden and Riker

[5] Samuel H. Baynard, Jr., *History of the Supreme Council, 33°* (Boston: Supreme Council, 33°, N.M.J., 1938), p. 152.

[6] Baynard, pp. 155–156; Joseph Cerneau, Patent of Authority, July 15, 1806, Baracoa, Cuba, Manuscript in the hand of Mathieu Dupotet(?), Archives, Supreme Council, 33°, S.J., Washington, D.C.

[7] Baynard, pp. 181–183.

were continually crossing and soon we find their political reactions antagonistic.[8]

## LEGITIMACY IN THE NORTH

In 1813 Emmanuel de la Motta, Grand Treasurer of the Mother Supreme Council, travelled to New York City for his health. While there he discovered the two competing "Supreme Councils," each created without authorization from Charleston. He examined the two groups and "healed" the Bideaud organization, making it legitimate. His actions were confirmed by the Mother Supreme Council on December 24, 1813, which issued letters of Constitution for the Bideaud Supreme Council on January 7, 1815.

The Cerneau Grand Consistory ignored de la Motta's actions, but it was aware the competition had thirty-two degrees.

> To the minds of Clinton and his colleagues something had to be done to put their Grand Consistory at least on the same level as the Bideaud Sublime Grand Consistory, and they wheedled Joseph Cerneau into taking a step which in all probability he otherwise would not have taken.
>
> In 1813 Cerneau... claimed jurisdiction over thirty-two degrees [for his Sovereign Grand Consistory] and announced the formation of what he called a Supreme Council of Grand Inspectors General of the Thirty-third Degree for the United States of America.... In this body both Clinton and Colden were given high official posts.[9]

The two Supreme Councils continued side-by-side for years, usually as bitter rivals, each having their ups and downs, though the Cerneau faction had the more irregular existence. Neither side was diplomatic in language, and each seemed to delight in bold, public condemnations of the other. Finally in 1867, after years of feuding, the two sides peacefully united to form the Supreme Council, 33°, for the Northern Masonic Jurisdiction of the United States.

The peace was short-lived.

[8] Baynard, p. 183.
[9] Baynard, pp. 155–156.

Introduction

**THE CERNEAU SUPREME COUNCIL(S) REVIVED**

Harry Seymour, expelled from the Cerneau Supreme Council in 1865, started the Ancient and Primitive Rite of Freemasonry, an outgrowth of the Rite of Memphis of about ninety degrees. By 1872 Seymour had reduced the rite to thirty-three degrees and was claiming to confer Scottish Rite degrees as the only legitimate successor to Joseph Cerneau. Robert Folger and others, angered by the position of the United Supreme Council towards the old Cerneau Supreme Council, revived the Cerneau Supreme Council in 1881. Both of these Supreme Councils proudly traced their origins to Joseph Cerneau, and about this time the term *Cerneauism* was coined to describe their movement.

Cerneauism finally died when the corrosive rivalry of the groups spilled over into the activities of other Masonic organizations. Grand Lodges began asserting their authority as the ultimate arbiters of Masonic regularity within their jurisdictions. Masons in state after state were forbidden to join a Cerneau body under pain of expulsion. Several suits were brought by Cerneaus challenging the authority of Grand Lodges to declare them forbidden, but each case eventually was lost. The Cerneau movement ended in 1919 when M. W. Bayliss died; he was the head of Folger's revived Cerneau Supreme Council and probably the last Cerneau officer.

**THE AMERICAN ANTIMASONIC MOVEMENT**

As Freemasonry grew in prestige and importance in America during the eighteenth and early nineteenth centuries, many citizens became increasingly concerned about its effect on the Republic. Some disliked private meetings of wealthy and important men in Lodges. Others objected to Masonic toasting, drinking, and singing after meetings, while still others found the Masonic ideal of religious tolerance blasphemous, especially when applied to non-Christians. In short, the growing respectability of Masonry was matched by the increasing suspicions of antimasons.

## THE ABDUCTION OF WILLIAM MORGAN

In 1826 in Batavia, New York, William Morgan, a disgruntled Mason, announced plans to publish the rituals of Freemasonry. This created a great deal of excitement in the community—Masons were outraged their "secrets" would be divulged and citizens were eager to know what the Masons were hiding. Neither group seemed to be aware that nearly thirty Masonic exposés had been published in English since 1723. A fire in the printer's office was blamed on the Masons, while the Masons blamed the printer for staging a publicity stunt. On September 11, Morgan was arrested for a debt and was jailed in Canandaigua, New York. The next day four Masons appeared at the jail, discharged the debt, and escorted Morgan to an awaiting carriage. He was driven to Ft. Niagara, held in the old Powder Magazine for five days, and never seen after September 19, 1826.[10]

The public was shocked by the charges that Morgan had been murdered by the Masons.

> In February, April, and August of 1827, various participants in Morgan's abduction were tried; but the choice of Masonic jurors, the silence of the local press, and the circumspection of law enforcement officers who were also Masons outraged some people. The sentences were light, ranging from a few months to two years.[11]

## THE BIRTH OF A MOVEMENT

Fueled by the outrage of Morgan's abduction and by a general sense of helplessness in the face of huge social changes of the time, many people found Masonry convenient to blame for all of society's ills.

> The Antimasons quickly developed a conspiracy theory with respect to Masonry, "suddenly" uncovering a group of unscrupulous leaders plotting to overthrow the American social order.... Many Antimasons believed that Masonic secrecy concealed the members' "unconditional loyalty" to an autonomous state, and this allegiance far exceeded any loyalty to the nation.[12]

[10] Coil, s.v. "Morgan Affair."
[11] Lipson, *Freemasonry in Federalist Connecticut*, p. 268.

Introduction

In the decade after William Morgan's disappearance, Antimasonry raged like a brushfire, spreading into politics and giving birth to the first third party in American history. It expanded from western New York in an arc that stretched from Pennsylvania to Maine. The flames of Antimasonry burned especially brightly in New England. In Vermont, Antimasons became the largest political party in the early 1830s; in Massachusetts they edged aside the Democrats to become the second strongest party; in Rhode Island they captured the balance of power between Democrats and National Republicans and ruled in coalition with the Jacksonians. In Connecticut they polled at their peak almost a quarter of the vote.[13]

The high water mark of political antimasonry came in the 1832 presidential election when William Wirt ran on the Antimasonic ticket against two Masons, Andrew Jackson and Henry Clay. The political movement soon died after Wirt's defeat, but the effects of social antimasonry lingered much longer.

Many churches banned Masons and argued that

[u]nless it was destroyed, Masonry as a tool of Satan would overthrow the church and its moral code along with the American system of justice and other republican institutions. Antimasons, using the religious argument, therefore condemned Masonry as an evil and dealt with it as they would with any other form of "flagrant sin."[14]

New York went from 480 Lodges in 1826 to 75 in 1835; Massachusetts dropped from 108 Lodges in 1830 to 56 Lodges in 1840. The Grand Lodge of Vermont simply went out of existence. The antimasonic movement was strongest in the Northeast, but its effects were felt throughout all the United States. The low point for Masonry came in 1840, after which the fraternity slowly regained members and prominence. It was not until 1860 that American Freemasonry fully recovered from the Morgan Affair.[15]

[12] William Preston Vaughn, *The Antimasonic Party in the United States* (Lexington, Ky.: University Press of Kentucky, 1983), p. 14.

[13] Paul Goodman, *Towards a Christian Republic* (New York: Oxford University Press, 1988), p. 4.

[14] Vaughn, p. 16.

[15] Coil, s.v. "Anti-Masonry."

Introduction

## A GLOSSARY OF MASONIC TERMS

*A.F.&A.M.*: Ancient, Free and Accepted Masons.

*A.&A.S.R.*: Ancient and Accepted Scottish Rite.

*Blue Lodge*: The basic organizational unit of Masons. (see *Lodge*)

*Brother*: The general term applied to any Freemason, especially a member of a Lodge.

*Capitular*: Concerning Royal Arch Masonry.

*Captain General*: Third officer of a Knights Templar Encampment or Commandery, roughly corresponding to second vice-president.

*Chapter*: The basic organizational unit of Royal Arch Masons which confers the degrees of Mark Master, Past Master, Most Excellent Master, and Royal Arch Mason.

*Chapter of Rose Croix:* An organizational unit of the Scottish Rite which confers the 17° and 18°, and sometimes the 15° and 16°.

*Commander*: Presiding officer of an Encampment or Commandery of Knights Templar.

*Companion*: The general term applied to Royal Arch Masons and Royal and Select Masters.

*Consistory*: An organizational unit of the Scottish Rite which confers the 19° through 32° degrees. It is the highest body of the Scottish Rite outside of the Supreme Council. In the Southern Jurisdiction today, Consistories confer only the 31° and the 32°.

*Council*: The basic organizational unit of several Masonic organizations, usually Royal and Select Masters which are sometimes called Cryptic Masons. Princes of Jerusalem, 16° of the Scottish Rite, meet in a Council of Princes of Jerusalem. (A *Supreme* Council is the supreme governing body of the Scottish Rite, and a *Grand* Council is the supreme governing body of Royal and Select Masters).

*Craft Lodge*: The basic organizational unit of Masons. (see *Lodge*)

*Cryptic*: Concerning the Royal and Select Masters Degrees.

## Introduction

*Encampment*: The basic organizational unit of Knights Templar (now known as a Commandery) which confers the orders of Knight of the Red Cross, Knight of Malta, and Knight Templar.

*Exalt*: To confer the Royal Arch Mason Degree.

*F.&A.M.*: Free and Accepted Masons.

*Generalissimo*: Second officer of a Knights Templar Encampment or Commandery, roughly corresponding to first vice-president.

*Grand*: When used to describe a Masonic organization, it usually indicates the supreme organization for a branch of Masonry within a jurisdiction, composed of representatives from all of the subordinate bodies. *Grand* Officers preside over *Grand* Bodies.

*Grand Commander*: The presiding officer of a Scottish Rite Supreme Council is the *Sovereign* Grand Commander, the presiding officer of a Grand Encampment of Knights Templar is the *Right Eminent* Grand Commander.

*Grand Council*: The supreme organization for Cryptic Masonry, Councils of Royal and Select Masters. Not to be confused with a Supreme Council of the Scottish Rite.

*Grand Lodge*: The supreme Masonic organization for a jurisdiction, usually a state in the U.S.A., composed of representatives from all Lodges. Since all other Masonic organizations limit their membership to Master Masons, the Grand Lodge effectively controls them by saying which groups Master Masons may or may not join. There is no national Grand Lodge in the U. S.

*Grand Master*: The presiding officer of a Grand Lodge.

*Greet*: To confer the Select Master Degree.

*Hauts Grades*: French term meaning "high grades" and referring to degrees that evolved in France often with a numerical designator greater than 3°, Master Mason. Some of these degrees eventually coalesced into the Scottish Rite and other rites.

*High Priest*: The presiding officer of a Chapter of Royal Arch Masons in the U.S. (known as the First Principal in England).

*Ineffable*: Concerning the 4° through 14° of the Scottish Rite conferred in a Lodge of Perfection.

*Initiate*: To confer the 1° or Entered Apprentice Degree.

*Inspector General*: A 33° Mason and member of a Supreme Council with authority to create and govern Scottish Rite Masons and Bodies of lesser degree; also Sovereign Grand Inspector General, Deputy Inspector General, etc.

*Inspector General Honorary*: A 33° Mason, not a member of a Supreme Council, without any special authority.

*K.T.*: Knights Templar.

*Lodge*: The basic organizational unit of all Freemasonry which confers the three fundamental degrees of Entered Apprentice, Fellowcraft, and Master Mason. These degrees are common to all Masonic rites. Sometimes called a "Symbolic Lodge," "Craft Lodge," "Ancient Craft Lodge," or "Blue Lodge."

*Lodge of Perfection*: An organizational unit of the Scottish Rite which confers the 4° through 14° or the ineffable degrees.

*Master*: The presiding officer of a Lodge.

*N.M.J.*: Northern Masonic Jurisdiction.

*Pass*: To confer the 2° or Fellowcraft Degree.

*Profane*: Literally "before the temple" or one who has not yet entered the temple, hence a non-Mason.

*Raise*: To confer the 3° or Master Mason Degree.

*R.A.M.*: Royal Arch Masons.

*R.&S.M.*: Royal and Select Masters.

*Receive*: To confer the Royal Master's Degree.

*Rectified Scottish Rite*: A system developed by J. B. Willermoz which replaced the Rite of Strict Observance in 1782. The degrees of the Lodge are considered part of this and all other Masonic Rites.

*R.E.R.*: Regime Ecossais Rectifié or Rectified Scottish Rite.

Introduction

*Rite*: A system of Masonic degrees, usually with a unified theme and teaching, controlled by one central authority, e.g., Scottish Rite, Rite of Perfection, York Rite, Rectified Scottish Rite, etc. The degrees of the Lodge are considered part of all Masonic Rites.

*Rite of Perfection*: A system of twenty-five degrees, originating in France that evolved into the Scottish Rite. The degrees of the Lodge are considered part of this and all other Masonic Rites.

*Rose Croix*: The 18° of the Scottish Rite, conferred in a Chapter of Rose Croix.

*Scottish Rite*: A system of thirty-three degrees, originating in France, that evolved out of the Rite of Perfection. The degrees of the Lodge are considered part of this and all other Masonic Rites.

*S.J.*: Southern Jurisdiction.

*Sovereign Grand Commander*: Presiding officer of a Scottish Rite Supreme Council.

*Strict Observance*: A rite of Masonic Knighthood started by Baron von Hund in Germany ca. 1750 which promoted the theory that Masonry originated with the Knights Templar. The Rite of Strict Observance was replaced by the Rectified Scottish Rite in 1782.

*Supreme Council*: The Supreme organization of the Scottish Rite within a jurisdiction, composed of 33°, Inspectors General. Not to be confused with a *Grand* Council of Royal and Select Masters.

*Symbolic Lodge*: The basic organizational unit of Masons. (see *Lodge*)

*Templar*: Concerning the Orders of Masonic Knighthood conferred in an Encampment or Commandery of Knights Templar.

*Wardens*: Two officers of a Lodge, Senior and Junior, roughly corresponding to first and second vice-presidents.

*York Rite*: The sequence of Masonic degrees conferred in Royal Arch Chapters, Royal and Select Councils, and Knights Templar Encampments or Commanderies. Sometimes called the American Rite. The degrees of the Lodge are considered part of this and all other Masonic Rites.

# THE MYSTERY OF
# THE FOLGER MANUSCRIPT

THE *FOLGER MANUSCRIPT* is a curious enigma in Masonic literature. Its author, Robert Benjamin Folger, M.D., (1803-1892) lived during some of the most turbulent yearsof Freemasonry. He experienced the American antimasonic movement first hand, witnessed at least six different Grand Lodges for the state of New York, lived through the American Civil War, and saw more than fourteen Supreme Councils for the Scottish Rite come and go. Through all of this, he was seldom an idle bystander, but was actively involved in many of the controversies. He is today viewed as a schismatic, a troublemaker, and one of the most ardent proponents of the Cerneau faction of the Scottish Rite.

Among his legacies to the Craft is a small book, written in a cipher, with a plaintext preface and bequest dated July 12, 1827; the book contains the rituals for the first three degrees of the Rectified Scottish Rite from Copenhagen. The preface and bequest were subsequently revoked on September 25, 1854. Folger was a new and active Mason in 1827, having been Raised to the Sublime Degree of Master Mason only seventeen months before. In the short space between his Raising and the dating of the manuscript, he joined additional masonic groups, including the Chapter, Council, Commandery, and Consistory; helped found a Royal Arch Chapter; and served as charter Senior Warden of a Lodge.

Follow here the mystery of the *Folger Manuscript;* the reader will be shown the evidence and deductions that led to a solution. The steps for solving the mystery will include identifying the rituals, locating their source, and inferring their use. These puzzles are interesting in their own right, but solving them gives us a glimpse of early Rectified Scottish Rite workings and insight into the tumultous world of nineteenth century American Masonry.

## SETTING THE SCENE

Robert Benjamin Folger was born on December 16, 1803 in Hudson, New York. His education began in the Quaker Schools there and then was continued at a boarding school in Lenox, Massachusetts, some 35 miles from Hudson. He moved to New York City and became a Master Mason on February 10, 1826, in Fireman's Lodge No. 368. Three months later, on May 25, he met Dr. Hans Burch Gram in Jerusalem Chapter No. 8, R.A.M., when Gram officiated at his Exaltation, and "the acquaintance there formed soon ripened into very close intimacy...."[1]

Folger had entered the College of Physicians and Surgeons (later with Columbia University) in 1821,[2] and probably graduated in 1824; he is listed in the 1825 *New York City Directory* as a physician. His new friend, Hans Gram, son of the secretary to the Governor of the Danish West Indies, was born in Boston in 1787 and died in New York City on February 26, 1840. He began studying medicine in 1808 at the Danish Royal Academy of Surgery[3] and became a convert in 1823 to Samuel Hahnemann's theory of homeopathy, new at the time. Gram returned to America in 1825, began a medical practice, and is known today as the "Father of American Homeopathy." He and Folger became fast friends apparently because of their Masonic and medical interests, and through Gram's influence, Folger eventually became a convert to homeopathy.

The *Folger Manuscript* was written in a strange hieroglyphic-like cipher in a black leather-bound book on thirty-three of eighty-eight $4\frac{3}{4}$-by-$7\frac{1}{2}$-inch pages. It appears to be a blank book from a

---

[1] Robert Folger, "Recollections of a Masonic Veteran," Part 11, *New York Dispatch*, Sept. 28, 1873.

[2] *Columbia University Alumni Register: 1754-1931*, (New York: Columbia University Press, 1932), p. 285.

[3] "The Late Dr. Gram," *The Homeopathic Examiner*, Vol. I, No. 2, Feb. 1840, p. 101; "Hans B. Gram, M.D.," *The U. S. Medical and Surgical Journal*, Vol. II, July 1867, pp. 449-452.

stationery store, the pages are watermarked "Lathrop & Willard" with yellow fore edges, and the front and back covers are bordered in gold with a large gold cross embossed in the center. The cipher looks like Chinese ideographs, and some pages are decorated with pen sketches that have a Masonic tone. Representative illustrations include blazing stars, a cubical stone with a square resting on it, a carpet with an hourglass and cross between a square and compasses, and a sketch of what seems to be the layout of a Lodge room.

The cipher is first known to have been broken in the 1950s by Wil Baden, Past Master of Henry Clay Lodge, No. 277 in New York (now merged with George Washington Lodge, No. 287), who had a photocopy of the manuscript *plus* a page from a second book (neither the single page nor a second book can now be found, though a translation of the single page survives).[4] He used the cryptanalytic technique of "matched plain and cipher" to break the code. Some thirty years later, Mr. Donald H. Bennett independently broke the cipher from a single page using a "ciphertext only" attack. Macoy Publishing and Masonic Supply Co., Inc. of Richmond, Virginia owns the copy of the *Folger Manuscript* analyzed here, referred to as the *Macoy Book*, as well as the Baden decryption.

Beyond this basic, descriptive information lurk several intriguing mysteries. What does the cipher conceal? Why did Folger so painstakingly write this book? Who, if anyone, helped him prepare it? Where did the text originate?

## IDENTIFYING THE RITUALS

The *Folger Manuscript* contains the Rituals for the "Blue" Degrees or grades of Disciple, Fellow, and Master Mason from a Masonic system unlike any widely known in the United States. It can be inferred from a note on the cover page of the Baden translation that Ward K. St. Clair (1899–1966), a noted student of Masonic Ritual, identified the manuscript as a "French Blue Lodge

---

[4] Wil Baden, Decryption of the Folger Manuscript, ca. 1955, Typescript, Archives, Macoy Publishing and Masonic Supply Co., Inc., Richmond, Va.

Ritual." A detailed examination of the text shows that it is a very good interpretation of the first three Degrees of the Rectified Scottish Rite [*Régime Ecossais Rectifié* or R.E.R.], whose six Degrees are Apprentice, Fellow, Master Mason, Scottish Master, Squire Novice, and Knight Beneficent of the Holy City [*Chevalier Bienfaisant de la Cité Sainte* or C.B.C.S.].

In fact, the *Folger Manuscript* represents the earliest evidence of the Rectified Scottish Rite or R.E.R. in the United States. While the R.E.R. Degrees still are worked actively in several other countries, including France, Belgium, and Switzerland, the R.E.R. has never been a significant force in American Masonry, though it has surfaced at least two other times. On May 16, 1900, the Great Priory of Helvetia granted Edouard Blitz a charter to establish the R.E.R. in the United States. The American Metropolitan College of the Grand Professed was founded on June 16, 1901, in Pentwater, Michigan, with Blitz as Great Prior of America. There were few members, and it was active only a short time.[5] Then William Moseley Brown (1894–1966) and J. Raymond Shute II (1909–1988) reestablished the rite on August 8, 1934, in Raleigh, North Carolina, again with a Swiss Charter; it continues today as an exclusive group with an annual meeting and a limit of eighty-one members.

An *hauts grades* connection is suggested within the document by several references to what could be the R.E.R. Fourth Degree, *Maître Ecossais* or Scottish Master. "Vow of the Anc[ient] Scotch Master: I promise" appears on page 83 (with the rest of the page maddeningly blank). Page 16 has the "Obligation for all members, also all candidates for Scots Ritus, and visiting Masons"; and the "Covenant before entering a Scotch Lodge" is on page 86.

This evidence could support a connection with the *Ancient and Accepted* Scottish Rite as well as the *Rectified* Scottish Rite; but when Folger was Grand Secretary General and Atwood was Grand Commander of the Cerneau Supreme Council, they sought

---

[5] R. A. Gilbert, "The Masonic Career of A. E. Waite," *Ars Quatuor Coronatorum*, Vol. 99, 1986, pp. 96, 97; William G. Peacher, M.D., Great Prior, C.B.C.S., Riverside Calif., Jan. 15, 1991, to S. Brent Morris, Columbia, Md., Typescript, In the possession of the author.

Scottish Rite Rituals for the first three Degrees. In a letter of ca. July, 1853, to James Foulhouze, Sovereign Grand Commander of the clandestine Supreme Grand Council for the Sovereign and Independent State of Louisiana, Henry Atwood requested assistance for his Supreme Council.

> And now my brother permit me to remind you of some things about which we conversed while together.... We should be glad to obtain the Scottish ritual of the 3 first or symbolic Degrees in English–or if not possible–then French, as I can get them translated...
>
> The above are sufficient to trouble you with & you can reply to them as you may find leisure, as there is no pressing haste in the case.[6]

Whatever origin Folger may have ascribed to his Masonic Rituals, he obviously did not think they were from the Scottish Rite, else he would have offered them to his Supreme Council.

## EMBLEMS OF THE DEGREES

The strongest connection to the R.E.R. is given by certain emblems of the three Degrees, unique since about 1782 to that Rite. (The references that follow are to the *Macoy Book* as annotated in Chapter 3.) For the First Degree, the following question and answer appear on page 8, line 5: "**Q:** What is the emblem of a Disciple? **A:** A broken pillar with the inscription *Adhoc [sic] stat.*" The Ritual of the Belgian R.E.R. requires among the "Decorations and Accessories Particular to the First Grade, ... a picture representing a column ruined and broken, but standing on its base, with the motto: *Adhuc stat* [Thus far it stands]."[7]

Further evidence comes from the Second Degree. The Fellow's Catechism, page 10, lines 28,29, has the following question and answer: "**Q:** What is the symbol of a Fellow? **A:** The square

---

[6] [Henry C. Atwood] to [James Foulhouze], New Orleans, [ca. July, 1853], Transcript in the hand of Robert B. Folger, Archives, Supreme Council, A.A.S.R., N.M.J., Lexington, Mass.

[7] *Rituel de Loge de Saint-Jean, 3e Grade* (Brussels: Grande Loge Régulière de Belgique, n.d.), p. 61.

stone with the inscription *DO*." Then on the right of page 11, which has the heading "Fellow," is a drawing of a square stone on which is resting a Mason's square and on which is written *DO* ( □ ∩ ) in cipher (see Figure 1). The decorations of the Lodge for the R.E.R. Second Degree include "a picture of a cubical stone, on which is resting a square, with the motto: *Dirigit Obliqua* [He makes the crooked straight]."⁸

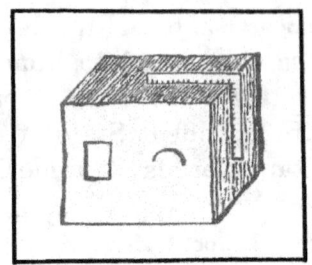

**FIGURE 1.** Square Stone, Page 11

Finally, there is a pencil sketch on page 77 of a ship with its three masts broken off (see Figure 2). This researcher initially

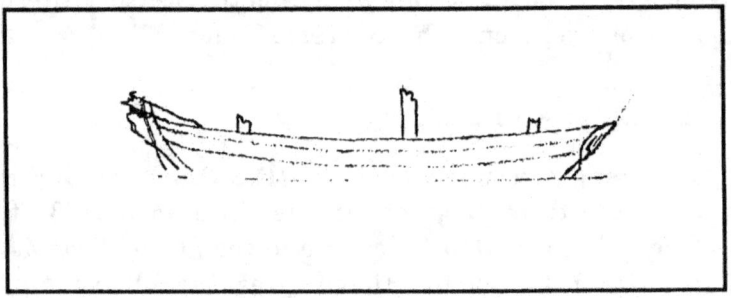

**FIGURE 2.** Pencil Sketch of a Ship, Page 77

identified this as a drawing made by a child sometime after Folger finished the manuscript; there was no apparent connection to Masonry. However, part of the decorations for the R.E.R. Third Degree is "a picture representing a dismasted vessel, without sails and without oars, tranquil on a calm sea, with the motto: *In silentio et spe fortitudo mea* [In silence and hope is my strength]."⁹

---

⁸ *Rituel, 3ᵉ Grade*, p. 62; F. Amez-Droz trans., "Ritual of the Second Degree (Companion), Decreed at the Convent General of the Order in 5782 [1782]," n.d., p. 1, Archives, Iowa Masonic Library, Cedar Rapids.

⁹ *Rituel, 3ᵉ Grade*, p. 63; F. Amez-Droz trans., "Ritual of the Third Degree (Master Mason), Decreed at the Convent General of the Order in 5782 [1782]," n.d., p. 1, Archives, Iowa Masonic Library, Cedar Rapids.

The Mystery

FIGURE 3. Emblems of the Strict Observance
From Ferdinand Runkel, *Geschichte der Freimaurerei in Deutschland*, 3 vols. (Berlin: Verlag von Reimar Hobbing, 1931), vol 1, pp. 192, 193.

These emblems are also found in the first three Degrees of Baron von Hund's Rite of Strict Observance (see Figure 3), but a succession of Masonic congresses, Kohlo in 1772, Lyons in 1773, and finally Wilhelmsbad in 1782, modified its organization and ceremonies to produce the Rectified Scottish Rite. For all practical purposes, the Strict Observance ceased to exist after the Congress of Wilhemsbad when its transformation into the R.E.R. was completed. Other evidence, discussed later, leaves little possibility that Folger's Rituals are from the Strict Observance, and thus the R.E.R. remains the major candidate as the ultimate source.

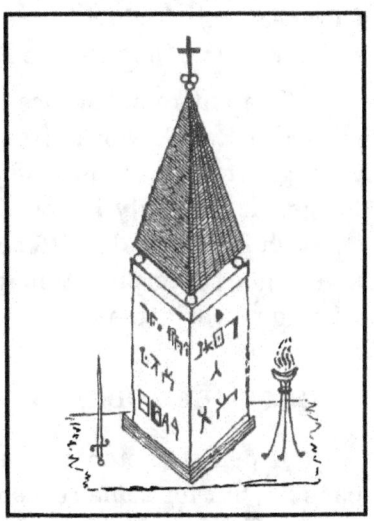

FIGURE 4. Triangular Monument, Page 19

On page 19 of the manuscript a triangular monument is drawn, carrying an inscription (in very poor Latin): *Tria formant alienum deponent et ascendit in unum* [Three things form an alien thing, they set it aside, and it rises into one(?)] (see Figure 4). This is very similar to a decoration of the R.E.R. third degree:

> A picture representing a triangular mausoleum sitting on three steps. At each of the three corners of the mausoleum are shown three small balls, colored yellow or gold, joined together, for a total of nine balls. The mausoleum is topped by a funeral urn, over which is a blazing flame detached from the opening of the urn. The picture has the following mottoes, on the upper part: "Deponens aliena ascendit unus" [Setting aside alien things, he rises as one] and on the lower part: "Ternario formatur, novenario dissolvitur" [It is formed by three, dissolved by nine].[10]

On page 13, lines 2–5, the candidate for the Fellow's Grade draws aside a veil over a mirror to behold his reflection and is then told, "Know thyself." It is important to note Lachmann, in his *Geschichte und Gebräuche*, claims the R.E.R. was the first system to use the mirror in the Second Degree, not the Strict Observance.[11] Today this ceremony is still in the Rectified Scottish Rite as well as the Scottish Rite and the French Modern Rite.

The entire substance and tone of Folger's work harmonizes with the R.E.R. work, from the introduction of the candidate, through the broad flow of the ceremonies, to the closing of the Lodge. It certainly is not a translation of contemporary Rectified Scottish Rite Rituals, differing as it does in so many places, but it is a very good interpretation, preserving the substance of the R.E.R. with some variations.

**PLAN OF THE LODGE**

A pencil sketch of the symbolic floor plan of a Lodge is on page 25, but for some reason it was not finished with ink (see Figure 5). The drawing has a large rectangle in the center composed of four Mason's squares with a knotted cord bordering the interior. Inside the top or east of the rectangle is a sun, a blazing star, and a

---

[10] *Rituel, 3e Grade*, p. 63; F. Amez-Droz, trans., "Third Degree," p. 1.

[11] Heinrich Lachmann, *Geschichte und Gebräuche der maurerischen Hochgrade und Hochgrad-Systeme* (Braunschweig: Herzoglich Waisenhaus-Buchdruckerei, 1866), p. 36.

FIGURE 5. The Lodge Floor Plan, Page 25
(redrawn for clarity)

moon with stars. In the center are seven steps surmounted by a large locked door, possibly with a curtain across the bottom step. At the bottom is a rough stone, an opened book, and a square stone. At the top of the large rectangle is a smaller one, representing the Master's seat with two seats on either side for other officers, perhaps the Secretary and Orator. In the center of these three stations is what appears to be a draped rectangle, probably the Altar; at the

The Mystery

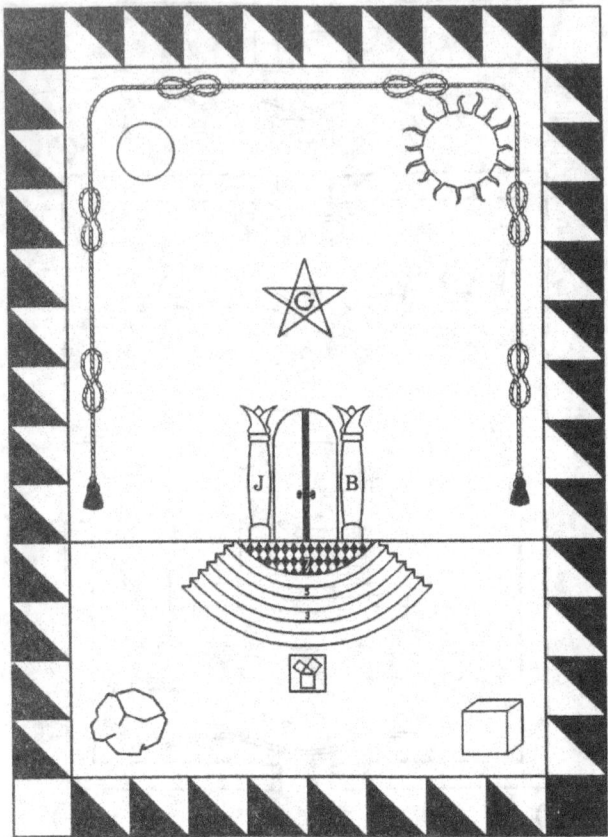

FIGURE 6. Second Degree R.E.R. Tracing Board
From *Rituel de Loge de Saint-Jean, 2e Grade*, (Brussels: Grand Loge Régulière de Belgique, n.d.), p. 9.

bottom or west are the Wardens' seats. This seating arrangement follows several eighteenth century French exposés and is used today in the Scottish Rite, the French Modern Rite, and the R.E.R. Three small circles, probably representing candles, are at the northwestern, southwestern, and southeastern corners of the central rectangle and two small double circles, perhaps representing more candles, are at the north and south of the central rectangle.

This layout is similar to plans for Apprentice-Fellow Lodges found in eighteenth century French exposés: *Catéchisme des Francs-Maçons*, 1744; *L'Ordre des Francs-Maçons Trahi*, 1746; *Les Francs-Maçons Ecrasés*, 1747; *La Desolation des Entrepreneurs Modernes*, 1747; and *Le Maçon Démasqué*, 1751. All of these plans show "Steps of the Temple," and *Les Francs-Maçons Ecrasés* and *L'Ordre des Francs-Maçons Trahi* show locked doors at the top of their steps. The placement of the officers is also supported by these texts. The only features prominent in the other plans and left out by Folger are the pillars Boaz and Jachin. Folger's plan, however, seems to be an unfinished pencil sketch (perhaps being prepared for redrawing in ink), and what may be a pillar is partially drawn to the right of the steps.

More significant, Folger's floor plan is nearly identical to the Tracing Board of the Second Degree from the Belgian R.E.R. (see Figure 6). The Belgian design shows no officers' positions nor candles and has a drawing of the forty-seventh problem of Euclid in place of Folger's open book. The only major difference is the absence of pillars, as noted above. Allowing for these few variations, perhaps from more than 150 years between the interpretations, the drawings are the same.

## HISTORY OF FREEMASONRY

On pages 81 and 82, Folger has written (or paraphrased or transcribed) a curiously distorted history of Freemasonry. Part of it explains that Oliver Cromwell altered the doctrines of Masonry to suit "his republican and later despotical views." Albert Mackey wrote about the Cromwell theory in his *History of Freemasonry*.

> The theory that Freemasonry was instituted by Oliver Cromwell was ... the invention of a single mind and was first made public in the year 1746 [sic], by the Abbé Larudan, who presented his views in a work entitled *Les Francs-Maçons Ecrasés*–a book which Kloß, the bibliographer, says is the armory from which all the enemies of Masonry have since derived their weapons of abuse.

The Mystery

> The propositions of Larudan are distinguished for their absolute independence of all historical authority and for the bold assumptions which are presented to the reader in place of facts.[12]

Larudan was the first writer to present this bizarre theory, and Folger's history on page 82, lines 17 to 31, seems to have come directly from *Les Francs-Maçons Ecrasés*. These lines are printed below beside the appropriate text from a 1778 edition of Larudan and its translation. Because of the extent and detail of the rest of the history, there must have been some additional intermediate text, that itself may have been based in part on Larudan.

Further supporting some intermediary is Folger's lack of knowledge of French. In 1889 while giving a deposition for a lawsuit, Folger was asked if he had ever met or talked with Joseph Cerneau. He answered: "No, sir. I have never conversed with him; he was a Frenchman and he did not understand the language very well. John W. Mulligan was his interpreter."[13] Regardless of Folger's answer, there was no one living to contradict it, and it would have increased his prestige in the eyes of the Cerneau Supreme Council to say "Yes." The clear implication is that Folger knew no French and could not have translated any French text.

| FOLGER | ECRASÉS | TRANSLATION |
|---|---|---|
| In England about this time, the Order had many names one after the other as Freemasons – then **Nivelleurs** –then members of the 5th Monarchy and finally were again called Freemasons. | La Société a souvent changé de nom dans ses premieres années: celui qu'elle porte aujourd'hui a été le premier; ensuite ses Partisans ont été apellés **Nivelleurs**, après cela Indépendants de la Politique, depuis Membres de la cinquieme Monarchie; enfin ils ont repris leur premier nom de Francs-Maçons, qu'ils conservent encore aujourd'hui. | The Society changed names often in its first years: that which it carries today was the first; afterwards its members were called **Levellers**, after that Independents of Politics, then Members of the fifth Monarchy; finally they again took their first name of Freemasons, which they still retain today. |

[12] Albert Gallatin Mackey and William R. Singleton, *The History of Freemasonry* (New York: The Masonic History Co., 1906), Vol II, p. 293.

[13] "Scottish Rite Testimony," *Masonic Chronicle*, Vol. XV, No. 7, June, 1893, p. 196.

# The Mystery

Here is evidence that one of the intermediate texts that led to Folger's History was French and probably *Ecrasés*. The translator (possibly Gram) did not know the meaning of *Nivelleurs* or thought this was actually an accepted name for the *Levellers*, one of a group of radicals arising in the Parliamentary army during the English Civil War and advocating a program of constitutional reform.

| FOLGER | ECRASÉS | TRANSLATION |
| --- | --- | --- |
| Cromwell appointed [**priests**] for Secretaries for the four Quarters of the Globe, etc. **General Rainsborough** was the Master of the Nivelleurs. *Page 82, lines 19–20* | Ils rendoient quelques raisons plausibles de chacun des différents titres qu'ils ont portés: celui de Nivelleurs étoit destiné à exprimer le dessein qu'ils avoient de mettre tous les Membres de niveau, c'est-à-dire, dans l'égalité; leur Chef étoit le **Général Rainsborough**, grand ami de Cromwel. | They gave several plausible reasons for each of the different titles that they have had: that of Levellers was intended to express the plan that they had of putting all the Members on the same level, that is to say, making them equal; their Leader was **General Rainsborough**, a great friend of Cromwell. |

Folger wrote that "Cromwell appointed † for Secretaries for the 4 Quarters of the Globe, etc.," with the cross probably meaning priests; this passage does not occur in Larudan. Thomas Rainborow or Rainsborough (?–1648) was an English soldier, a leader of the republican officers, and a supporter of the Leveller document, *Agreement of the People*, which called for manhood suffrage and religious toleration.

| FOLGER | ECRASÉS | TRANSLATION |
| --- | --- | --- |
| Some of his Companions were concerned in the death of the King. *Page 82, line 20–21* | Les Nivelleurs étoient les plus hardis & les plus puissants de tous les Républicains; ils furent les principaux auteurs de la mort du Roi, & se piquerent si fort du changement que Cromwel voulut faire de leur nom en celui de Francs-Maçons, qu'ils conspirerent contre sa vie. | The Levellers were the boldest and the most powerful of all the Republicans; they were the principal authors of the death of the King and were so severely offended by the fact that Cromwell wanted to change their name to Freemasons, that they conspired against his life. |

The Mystery

| FOLGER | ECRASÉS | TRANSLATION |
|---|---|---|
| Their ostensible object was as a society to the establishment of Freedom, etc. **Harrington** was Master of the 5th Monarchy and a friend and connection of Cromwell. Their professed object was freedom and equality and not to acknowledge any other Regent than Jesus.<br>*Page 82, lines 21-24* | Leur Chef, ou du moins un des principaux, étoit **Harrison**, à qui Cromwel avoit communiqué une bonne partie de son enthousiasme & de son fanatisme. Ils se proposoient d'établir la Liberté & l'Egalité, & de ne plus obéir qu'à Jesus-Christ; ce qui leur faisoit dire, qu'ils attendoient d'un jour à l'autre l'arrivée du Roi Jesus. | Their Leader, or at least one of the leading members, was **Harrison**, to whom Cromwell had communicated a good part of his enthusiasm and his fanaticism. They intended to establish Liberty and Equality, and no longer to obey any but Jesus Christ; which led them to say that they were waiting for the arrival of King Jesus from one day to the next. |

Thomas Harrison (**1616-1660**), an English Parliamentarian General and a leader of the Fifth Monarchy, appears to have been confused with James Harrington (**1611-1677**), a republican sympathizer but devoted friend of King Charles I.

| FOLGER | ECRASÉS | TRANSLATION |
|---|---|---|
| They had the form of a flag with a Lion **sleeping** with this motto – "Who will wake him?"<br>*Page 82, lines 24-25* | Ils avoient un étendard, sur lequel étoit un Lion **couchant**, tel qu'est celui de la Tribe de Juda, avec cette devise: Qui est-ce qui le réveillera?<br>*Page 112* | They had a flag, on which was a Lion **couchant**, like that of the Tribe of Judah, with this motto: Who will wake him? |

This is further evidence that one of the intermediate texts was French (and that the translator, possibly Gram, did not have a perfect command of the languages). He did not realize that *couchant*, while derived from the verb *coucher*, meaning to sleep, has a specific meaning in heraldry: lying down with the head up. Clearly the latter meaning is more appropriate when describing a device on a flag.

The Mystery

| FOLGER | ECRASÉS | TRANSLATION |
|---|---|---|
| They conspired, however, against Cromwell and were persecuted afterwards by him. Hereafter Cromwell sought to give to Free Masonry in England a more religious tendency than it had before had in that land, and it is said that the oath now has received quite another form and a more political one than before.<br>*Page 82, lines 25 – 29* | Ainsi *Harrison* n'ajoutant point de foi aux raisons ni à la dissimulation de Cromwel, forma une conspiration contre lui, souleva presque tous le Membres de la Société, & les rassembla dans un maison qui n'étoit pas loin du Shoneditch, afin de mettre le Roi Jesus à sa place, c'est-à-dire, de se procurer une parfaite liberté, en secouant le joug de Cromwel.<br>*Page 111* | In this way Harrison, putting no faith in the reasoning or the deceit of Cromwell, formed a conspiracy against him, stirred up almost all the Members of the Society, and gathered them in a house not far from Shoneditch, in order to put King Jesus in his place, that is to say, to procure perfect liberty by throwing off the yoke of |
| And several Nivelleurs were during this alteration severely punished, even with death (see Parchards History, 1736, when the Order had got a more fearsome(?) oath, etc.)<br>*Page 82, lines 29 – 31* | L'une de ces infortunées victimes de la colere de l'Ordre, a été un Anglois, appellé *Pichard*, qui, l'an 1736, si je ne me trompe, fit imprimer en François, à Liege, un Ouvrage *in-douze*, que l'on a dans le suite traduit in Allemand, en Anglois, & en Italien.<br>*Page 114* | One of these unfortunate victims of the anger of the Order was an Englishman named Pichard, who, in 1736, if I am not mistaken, printed in French, at Liege, a work in duodecimo, that was subsequently translated into German, English, and Italian. |

## LOCATING THE SOURCE

Folger had been a Master Mason only 17 months when he dated his manuscript, and the ceremonies seem too sophisticated and too much at variance with standard American workings to have been created by so recent a Mason without some guidance or inspiration. It is possible that he was inspired by the ceremonies of some New York Lodge working a French or R.E.R. Ritual. In his "Recollections of a Masonic Veteran," Folger wrote about visiting Lodge L'Union Française during his early years in the Craft.

> The Lodge was a French Lodge, their members were French, the usages were French, as also the language.... [During the reception of a *Profane*] the Nature of Fire, Air, Earth, and Water were fully demonstrated and developed.... [T]he French recipient

would, though perspiring at every pore, view the whole with the most perfect nonchalance, and bow with a gracious smile, with the hand upon the breast, when it was finished, although it had taken the whole of two or three hours to pass the rugged way.[14]

The ceremony "demonstrating" the four elements and the length of the Degree are enough to eliminate L'Union Française as the source of the Rituals. Folger's first Degree is a rather straightforward ceremony that might last an hour or so, but nothing like the grueling two or three hours at L'Union Française which left the candidate "perspiring at every pore." Ceremonies with fire, air, earth, and water are characteristic of the French Rite and Scottish Rite Blue Degrees, but most other distinctive Scottish Rite features are completely absent from the manuscript.[15] While the possibility of some local Lodge serving as the source cannot be eliminated, a much more satisfying solution can be found.

The solution to this mystery begins on the first page, Folger's dedication or bequest (underlining in original).

Dr. Hans B. Gram, No. 296 Pearl St.
Mr. Ferdinand L. Wilsey, Fulton Slip near Fulton Bank.   R.B.F.

New York July 12th 1827.

It is my earnest prayer that this book, if it be found among my earthly remains after my decease, may be handed over to my dearly beloved Friend and Brother, Dr. Hans B. Gram to whom I bequeath it with my thanks for the constant and untired kindness which he has shewed me from the first hour of my acquaintance with him to the present–to whom I feel that I never can be too grateful and whose good will I desire to seek to my latest breath. If he is not in America at the time of my dissolution–it may be given to Mr. Ferdinand L. Wilsey who will know what it contains and also how to preserve the substance in his mind while he commits the manuscript to the <u>flames</u>. This he will do for the sake of one who loves him with a Brothers [sic] love and who has desired during his life to merit his esteem.

<u>Robert B. Folger</u>

---

[14] Robert Folger, "Recollections," Part 3, May 18, 1873.

[15] Norman D. Peterson, "Broad Characteristics of the A.&A.S.R. Blue Degrees" (typescript, Portland, Oreg., N. D. Peterson, Aug. 1990 draft), p. 3; N. D. Peterson, *A Documentary Notebook on the Latin Craft* (Portland, Oreg.: N. D. Peterson, 1975), passim.

The critical piece of the puzzle comes in September 1826, four months after Folger's Exaltation in Jerusalem Chapter. The following event was detailed in 1871 in *The New England Medical Gazette* by Henry M. Smith, M.D., (emphasis added).

> From conversations with Drs. Wilsey, ... , Folger, ... , and others, I have obtained many of the facts herein mentioned. ....
> In September, 1826, Dr. Gram was introduced to Mr. Ferdinand L. Wilsey by Dr. Folger, who had made his acquaintance the year before. Mr. Wilsey, then a merchant and comb-manufacturer, was a master of a masonic Lodge, and *Dr. Folger having received from Dr. Gram some important information in Masonry, desired that his friend should also receive the benefit of it.*[16]

Folger dated his manuscript on July 12, 1827, ten months after he introduced Gram to Wilsey for the purpose of sharing "important information in Masonry." On November 3, 1819, while living in Copenhagen, Hans Gram had entered one of the predecessor Lodges of Zerubbabel and Frederick of the Crowned Hope.[17] Belonging to this Lodge in Copenhagen from 1819 to 1826, Gram must have been familiar with the R.E.R. Rituals, and his presiding over Jerusalem Chapter in New York shortly after returning to America indicates more than a passing enthusiasm for Masonry.

The solution is now at hand! Hans Gram joined a Danish Lodge working the R.E.R., and a familiarity with its Rituals would be consistent with his Masonic activity in New York in 1826. In May of that year he met fellow physician Robert Folger, and sometime after this Folger received "important information in Masonry" from Gram. In September 1826 Folger introduced Gram to Ferdinand Wilsey so that he too could benefit from this information, and ten months later the manuscript with R.E.R. Rituals was prepared. The timing of these events, the reason for Wilsey's introduction to Gram, and the dedication page strongly point to the scholarly and worldly Gram as the source, to the established and

---

[16] Henry M. Smith, "Homeopathic Directory: New York Historical Sketch," *The New England Medical Gazette*, Vol. VI, No. 2, Feb. 1871, pp. 91-94.

[17] Jørgen Vagn Jørgensen, Præses, Den Danske Frimurerorden Informationsdirektoriet, Copenhagen, to S. Brent Morris, Columbia, Md., Nov. 8, 1990, Typescript, In the possession of the author.

The Mystery

successful Wilsey as a participant, and to the young and eager Folger as the scribe.

## INFERRING ITS USE

The meticulously prepared cipher manuscript shows an intent to preserve information of great value, but there is no direct evidence that it was ever used. There is only one clue pointing to a definite use of the Ritual, and a few hints as to other places it may have been employed. Internal, textual evidence indicates strongly that the extant book, the *Macoy Book*, was copied from another.

### A SECOND COPY

The *Macoy Book* is one of at least two cipher Rituals prepared by Robert Folger. Harold Voorhis wrote about the volumes, "My copy was found in Macoy safe & so far as I know is still there but not to be removed."[18] Later he expanded on this: "The first one of the code books I found in an ancient safe in 1946. The second I found in the library of the Supreme Council (S.J.) a dozen or more years ago."[19] Henry Emmerson, who worked with Voorhis and Wil Baden on the manuscript in the early 1950s, confirmed the existence of two books when he wrote, "The copy in the House of the Temple [headquarters of the Southern Jurisdiction] I have never seen, only the Macoy copy."[20] There is the further corroboration for two books from Wil Baden who wrote to Emmerson about breaking the cipher, "The Rosetta stone was [the phrase] 'contains great treasures,' which is in code in Voorhis' copy but not in the Supreme Council's."[21]

---

[18] Harold Voorhis, Summit, N.J., to S. Brent Morris, Columbia, Md., Aug. 2, 1979, Manuscript, In the possession of the author.

[19] Voorhis to Morris, [Aug. 29, 1979], Typescript, In the possession of the author.

[20] Henry Emmerson, Cresskill, N.J., to S. Brent Morris, Columbia, Md., Sept. 22, 1980, Typescript, In the possession of the author.

[21] Wil Baden, [New York], to Henry Emmerson, New York, [1955], Typescript, In the possession of Herbert A. Fisher, Virginia Beach, Va.

Macoy Publishing and Masonic Supply Co., Inc. has carefully preserved its copy to this day; the Supreme Council, S.J., has apparently misplaced or misfiled theirs. To distinguish the two, they are referred to as the *Macoy Book*, the version reproduced in Chapter 3, and the *Supreme Council Book*. Two questions about the books come to mind: Why are there two copies, and which was written first? The first question is easy: it makes sense to have two or possibly more copies of a Ritual book, both for security from loss and for convenience. The question of primogeniture, however, is more subtle.

The vows of the Master Mason and the Ancient Scotch Master in the *Macoy Book* are incomplete. The former, on page 17, consists of only the few words: "Master's vow begins in the same way as the Fellow's, with the following additions." The latter, on page 83, is even more tantalizing: "I promise." The drawing of the Lodge Room on page 25 is an incomplete pencil sketch, apparently awaiting completion before being inked. The sketch of the dismasted ship on page 77 also awaits inking. It could be that Folger was waiting to confer with Gram before finishing the Rituals. It is more likely a first book had been finished and was in use; Folger was completing the *Macoy Book* at his leisure; and something, probably the snowballing antimasonic movement in New York, prevented him from finishing it.

The *Macoy Book* is a marvel of penmanship. The intricate cipher words are carefully formed with little crowding of letters and are precisely written; there are virtually no mistakes. The few errors are usually confusions of similar cipher letters: $b$, $d$, $p$, and $q$; or $l$, $r$, $s$, and $t$ (see Figure 7). This near perfection shows Folger was experienced with writing in the cipher, much more than could have come from preliminary practice or even from making a draft before final lettering. The nearly flawless cipher words suggest that the *Macoy Book* was not Folger's first attempt at this writing. While supporting neither version as the earlier, it is interesting to note how Folger began introducing abbreviations and increasingly

The Mystery

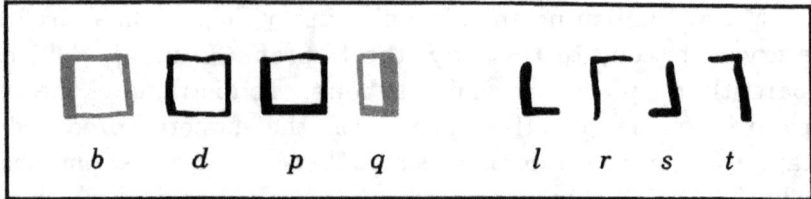

FIGURE 7. Similar Cipher Letters

elaborate illustrations after about page 8. This could be explained by a growing familiarity with the cipher as he wrote the book.

The *Supreme Council Book* is unavailable, except for a single page preserved in a letter. After breaking the cipher sometime in 1955, Wil Baden excitedly dashed off a note to Henry Emmerson which included the translation of one page from the *Supreme Council Book*. This one page, Figure 8, can be compared with the corresponding text from the *Macoy Book*, Figure 9. The spelling of the passages is exactly as written; punctuation and capitalization have been added for clarity. For the comparisons that follow, an abbreviated notation will be used to refer to the texts (e.g., SC.2-3 for lines 2-3 from the page from *Supreme Council Book* and M.17 for line 17 from the pages from the *Macoy Book*). Note that Baden must have confused *m*, ⊓, for *d*, ☐, in *miuneull*, SC.23. Since ∪ can represent *u*, *v*, or *w*, the correct reading should be *divne wll*.

The spelling differences between the two pages are enough to show that neither is an exact copy of the other. Fifteen mostly short words on the Supreme Council page are abbreviations of Macoy words, while forty-one longer Macoy words are abbreviations (e.g., compare SC.3 with M.3 and SC.14 with M.13). This could be explained by the abbreviation of long words as they were copied from the *Supreme Council Book* into the *Macoy Book*.

The pages differ by several words in a few places, but only the *Macoy Book* has missing words that make for ungrammatical text. Again, this could have happened with omissions from sentences as they were copied from the *Supreme Council Book*. The three ungrammatical passages are compared below.

| | |
|---|---|
| 1 | The guide introduces the candidate, seats him, then says: |
| 2 | Hither we have come. Lt us now rest for a short tme. I beg of you |
| 3 | to abstract yourself frm wll worldy thoughts fr a little period of tme to |
| 4 | devote this season to the consideration of yourslf, and those thngs wh |
| 5 | may ocr to you. |
| 6 | To the place of whi ths is a symbol we must all soonr or later |
| 7 | come. |
| 8 | The rules of our order hve made me bring you hither. Let me |
| 9 | mak you acquaintd with these things. |
| 10 | Here is the mblm of time. Turns it. Behold how rpdly the |
| 11 | particles of sand run. It wll soon run out. Once/Since(?) no external |
| 12 | power set it in motion agn its movements wll never be rnud. Forget |
| 13 | this not. |
| 14 | Here is water for your refreshment. |
| 15 | Here is the image of death, mblm of mortality. No human |
| 16 | phlsphy or thnkng can devise what lies on the other side of this veil or |
| 17 | what shall hapn to us there yet is is certain we shal all go thither to |
| 18 | return no more. It is certain that duration byond the grave in |
| 19 | comparison to the period of human lfe is infnte. This sbject then is to |
| 20 | you, is to us all an nteresting one, of great moment. |
| 21 | See. Here is the only light by wh we cn learn how to anter the |
| 22 | grave so as to njoy hapnss hereafter. It is the Bk of Wisdom, and |
| 23 | contans a revelation of the miuneull (millenium?). |
| 24 | Goes out. Candidate here studies the tablets and so forth. Then |
| 25 | it is pruper to carry the answer to the Master by the guide. |
| 26 | KNOW THYSELF |
| 27 | Consider thyself. This is shewed, that thou often shouldest think |
| 28 | upon this duty. Remember that whh you here see, (apparently at the |
| 29 | bottom of a vault), is the image of the receptacle that |

**FIGURE 8. Single page from the Supreme Council Book**
From a letter from Wil Baden to Henry Emmerson, ca. 1955.

The Mystery

| |
|---|
| *Page 4, line 1* |
| 1   Discpulus. |
| 2       Hihr we have come. Lt us nw rest for a short tm. I beg to abstract |
| 3   yrself fm all worldy thghts for a shrt space of time and to devote this |
| 4   tme to the cnsdrtn of yourslf and such things as may her occr to you. |
| 5       To the place f wh this is a symbol we must all snr or later come. It |
| 6   is dark dlack seperated from the world. |
| 7       The ruls f r rder have made me brng you hr. Let me make you |
| 8   acquntd with these things. |
| 9       The [hourglass]. An mblm f tme. Turns it. Bhold how rapidly |
| 10  the particles of sand run. It wil soon run out and then if no externl |
| 11  pwer set it in motion agin its movemnts will never renewed. Forgt this |
| 12  not. |
| 13       Here is watr f your refrshmnt. |
| 14       Her is an imag of death and mblm f mortality. No human |
| 15  philoshy or thinkng can divne what lies on the other side of this veil or |
| 16  what shll hpn to us there yet it is crtain we shall all thence and it is |
| 17  certn that duration beyond the grave in comparison to the period of |
| 18  hmn life is infinite. This subjct is intrsting then. |
| 19       See. Here is the only light by whh we can learn how to ntr the g |
| 20  so as to enjo hapns herft. It is the bk of wsdm and cntns a rvltion of the |
| 21  dn will. |
| *Page 2, line 3* |
| 22  Here it is proper f a depty to retrn to the Master the aspirants answer |
| *Page 84, line 12* |
| 23                    KNOW THYSELF |
| 24       Consider thyself. This is shewn and that thou shouldst often |
| 25  think upon this duty and remember that wh you here see, (aparently |
| 26  at the bottom of a vault), is the image of the receptacle that contains |
| 27  great treasures. |

FIGURE 9. Extracts from Several Pages of the Macoy Book

| | |
|---|---|
| M.2-3 | I beg to abstract yrself |
| SC.2-3 | I beg **of you** to abstract yourself |
| | |
| M.11 | its movemnts will never renewed. |
| SC.12 | its movements wll never **be** rnued. |
| | |
| M.16 | we shall all **thence** and it is |
| SC.17-18 | we shal all **go thither to return no more**. It is |

One other passage from the *Macoy Book*, while not ungrammatical, is dramatically shortened from the *Supreme Council Book*, as if a large body of text were dropped in transcription.

| | |
|---|---|
| M.18 | This subjct is intrsting then. |
| SC.19-20 | This sbject **then is to you, is to us all**, an nteresting one, **of great moment**. |

The *Supreme Council Book* has the Guide return the candidate's questions to the Master, SC.24-25, while the *Macoy Book* has a Deputy do the work, M.22. Only one sentence, M.5-6, is found on the Macoy pages but not on the Supreme Council page. It was inserted with an asterisk after the line was completed, as if correcting or improving the original. The other differences are minor, either conscious corrections or unconscious rewordings.

These differences taken as a whole, however, point slightly to the *Macoy Book* being copied from the *Supreme Council Book* or from its ancestor, with Folger or his source still editing the *Macoy Book* as it was written. Professor Wallace McLeod has lent his considerable textual analysis skills to this comparison.[22] He has noted several interesting passages in the texts, which are given below with his opinions.

•*Macoy* "right" and *Supreme Council* "wrong:"

| | |
|---|---|
| M.15 | philoshy or thinkng can divne what lies |
| SC.16 | phlsphy or thnkng can devise what lies |

---

[22] Wallace McLeod, Victoria College, University of Toronto, to S. Brent Morris, Columbia, Md., Jan. 22, 1991, Typescript, In the possession of the author.

The Mystery

- *Supreme Council* "right" and *Macoy* "wrong:"

    | M.1 | Discpulus |
    | SC.1 | The guide introduces the candidate, seats him, then says: |
    | | |
    | M.23 | This is shewn and that thou |
    | SC.27 | This is shewed, that thou |

- Both intelligible, but *Macoy* preferred:

    | M.3 | for a shrt space of time |
    | SC.3 | fr a little period of tme |
    | | |
    | M.4 | such things as may her occr to you. |
    | SC.4-5 | those thngs wh may ocr to you. |
    | | |
    | M.9 | The [hourglass]. An mblm f tme. |
    | SC.10. | Here is the mblm of time. |
    | | |
    | M.14 | Her is an imag of death and mblm f mortality. |
    | SC.15 | Here is the image of death, mblm of mortality. |
    | | |
    | M.24-25 | that thou shouldst often think |
    | SC.27 | that thou often shouldest think |

- Both intelligible, but *Supreme Council* preferred:

    NONE

- No preference:

    | M.3-4 | this tme |
    | SC.4 | this season |
    | | |
    | M.22 | Here it is proper f a depty to retrn to the Master the aspirants answer |
    | SC.24-25 | Then it is pruper to carry the answer to the Master by the guide. |
    | | |
    | M.25 | think upon this duty and remember that wh |
    | SC.28 | think upon this duty. Remember that whh |

Professor McLeod notes the evidence is not watertight, but with two exceptions he does prefer the passages from the *Macoy*

*Book*. The evidence is subtle but suggestive. The unfinished text and drawings, precise lettering, and textual comparisons point faintly to a verdict: the *Macoy Book* was written after if not copied from the *Supreme Council Book* or its ancestor.

## ELMIRA CONSISTORY

The only indication of a direct use comes from February 26, 1883, fifty-six years after the manuscript was dated. Folger, then eighty years old, was at a Reunion of 200 candidates at Elmira Consistory, New York, a Cerneau Body. He was introduced as the oldest American 33° Mason, having received the Degree in 1827. At the end of his talk, recorded in the Elmira *Daily Advertiser* for February 27, 1883, he proposed a toast which must have been taken from the Disciple's catechism of his Ritual, page 8, lines 5-10.

### DISCIPLE'S CATECHISM

Q: What is the emblem of a Disciple?

A: A broken pillar with the inscription "Adhoc [sic] stat."

Q: How is it explained?

A: *As by the remnant of the pillar that is yet standing we can ascertain to what order it belongs and determine what its proportions and ornaments were when it was entire,* and thus *be enabled to form another pillar in likeness of the broken one,* so from what we know relative to man we hope and believe that he may be restored to a state approaching to that first pristine purity and happiness.

### FOLGER'S TOAST

And now, in closing, let me offer this toast:

OUR INSTITUTION

Though adverse circumstances have likened it to the broken pillar of our order with its beautiful capital buried at its base, it is consolatory to us to know that it is not entirely cast down or destroyed. *As by the remnant of the pillar that is yet standing we can ascertain to what order it belongs, and determine what its proportions and ornaments were when it was entire,* may we *be enabled* by diligence and perseverance *to form another pillar in the likeness of the broken one,* more perfect and beautiful than that which adverse circumstances have destroyed.

Folger could have been reviewing his manuscript before the Elmira meeting, but the difficulty in reading the cipher, even for someone familiar with it, makes this seem remote. It is more likely he memorized portions of the Ritual earlier in his Masonic career and called on them when needed.

## ZOROBABEL LODGE

Other possible uses of the Rituals by Folger are more speculative. On June 8, 1827, one month before the manuscript was dated, a charter was granted to Zorobabel Lodge No. 498 of New York City with Hans B. Gram, Master; Robert B. Folger, Senior Warden; and Lewis Saynisch, Junior Warden.[23] The Lodge had a brief existence and then apparently closed during the antimasonic excitement. Beyond the presence of Gram and Folger as the top two officers, the name of the Lodge is significant to the mystery.

Dr. Gram is listed in the 1871 register of the Copenhagen Lodge Zerubbabel and Frederick of the Crowned Hope [*Zorobabel og Frederik til det kronede Håb*] as having entered November 3, 1819. Zerubbabel and Frederick Lodge was formed in 1855 by the merger of two Lodges, Zerubbabel of the North Star [*Zorobabel til Nordstjernen*] and Frederick of the Crowned Hope [*Frederik til det kronede Håb*].[24] The 1871 register does not indicate in which Gram was Initiated, but it is a striking coincidence that the Lodge over which he presided in 1827 chose the name *Zorobabel*, selecting the Greek form of the name used by the Danish Lodge.

Perhaps Gram was Initiated in *Zorobabel til Nordstjernen* and honored his Mother Lodge in naming the new Lodge, and perhaps Zorobabel Lodge No. 498 worked the R.E.R. Degrees? Certainly the dating of the manuscript on July 12 coincides nicely with the chartering of the Lodge on June 8. Masonic Ritual in New York at that time was in a state of flux, and the Grand Lodge exercised little control. There were German and French Lodges, and the Ritual system taught by Jeremy Ladd Cross (now nearly

---

[23] *Transactions of the Grand Lodge of Free and Accepted Masons of New York, 1816–1827* (New York: Masonic Publishing and Furnishing Co., 1880), p. 477.

[24] Vagn Jørgensen, to Morris, Nov. 8, 1990. Typescript, In the posession of the Author.

universal in the United States) was just beginning to challenge the "old style" of work. Thus one more Lodge working one more variant of the Degrees would not have caused particular notice. However, Folger had just learned the Cross system from Henry C. Atwood during his first classes in 1826, and it is also possible Zorobabel joined those Lodges working this version of the Ritual, which Folger said were "overrun with candidates and members."[25]

## JOHN THE FORERUNNER LODGE

A much better candidate for use of the Rituals comes from the Cerneau faction of the Scottish Rite, of which Folger was a lifelong, ardent supporter. Around 1853 the Supreme Council in and for the Sovereign and Independent State of New York, with Henry C. Atwood as Grand Commander and Folger as Grand Secretary General, began plans to charter symbolic Lodges in New York City, which is the exclusive right of the Grand Lodge. The minutes for March 8, 1853, detail the only two such charters.

> The Ill∴ Bro∴ Folger then proceeded to lay before the Council the following Petitions for the constituting and establishing Symbolic Lodges of the Ancient Free and Accepted Scottish Rite.
>
> From Bro. Robert B. Folger and others for a Lodge of St∴ John by the distinctive title of "John the Fore-runner" and by Number 1 (See document on file) which petition was granted and the Patent ordered to be made and executed bearing date March 8th 1853 of the Christian Era.
>
> From Bro. Deszelus, Roullier, Vatet, Ploquin & others, in all 14, for a Lodge of St. John, the ritual &c in the French Language, by the distinctive title of "La Sincérité," and by number 2 (see documents in French and English on file) which petition was granted and the Patent ordered to be made out and executed, bearing date March 8th 1853 of the Christian Era.[26]

---

[25] Robert B. Folger, "Recollections," Part 4, June 1, 1873.

[26] Minutes, Supreme Council in and for the Sovereign and Independent State of New York, Mar. 8, 1853, Transcript in the hand of Robert B. Folger, Collection Number SC012, Archives, Supreme Council, A.A.S.R., N.M.J., Lexington, Mass.

The Mystery

Twenty-one years later in 1874 Folger gave some details on this ultimately unsuccessful action, unprecedented by an American Supreme Council (emphasis added).

> The petition for [a charter for John the Forerunner Lodge] is believed to have been the first effort made in this country to establish the French system in the English language. *And for this purpose a very beautiful and minute translation of the French ritual into the English, together with the consecration, the installation, and the table rituals and ceremonials, with abundant and minute directions, had been procured,* and everything was in readiness to go forward. But at this juncture there was some misgivings on the part of the founders–although the ritual was entirely and essentially different from the York Rite–so much so that it could not be taken for Masonry, as practiced at the present day; yet there were certain things about it which led to the determination, on the part of the founders, to abandon the project altogether–and it proved to be a wise course. The lodge was never constituted, and *the rituals, etc., are now in our possession.*[27]

Recall that around July, 1853, a few months after chartering John the Forerunner and La Sincérité Lodges, Henry Atwood wrote to James Foulhouze requesting "the Scottish Ritual of the 3 first or Symbolic Degrees in English." The founders of La Sincérité Lodge apparently had no written Ritual then, even though they had been members of the French Scottish Rite.[28] Foulhouze was told to reply as he found leisure, "as there [was] no pressing haste in the case" (see page 3). Since there was "no pressing haste" in sending the Rituals, John the Forerunner must have worked some French ceremonies that could be passed off for Scottish Rite Rituals.

Five years later on September 14, 1858, Atwood wrote again to Foulhouze repeating his request for Rituals of the first three Degrees (emphasis added).

> We find ourselves embarassed with the Scottish Rituals that we have; *they are translations teeming with considerable variations.* If you have at your disposal an English copy of the Ritual of

[27] Robert B. Folger, "Recollections," Part 34, July 19, 1874.
[28] [E. Diterlé], *Précis Historique de La Sincérité No. 373*, ([New York]: [1955]), p. 26.

these Degrees such as you work, I beg of you to send it to me so that we can compare them.[29]

Atwood gave a perfect description of the *Folger Manuscript* in this letter: a translation that varies considerably from Scottish Rite Rituals. Here is yet further circumstantial evidence that Folger offered Gram's R.E.R. Rituals for use in Scottish Rite Blue Lodges.

Gram may have thought *Rectified* Scottish Rite Rituals were the same as those of the *Ancient and Accepted* Scottish Rite. He may have told Folger these Rituals were French, and Folger could have preferred them for Scottish Rite Blue Lodges as more exotic than the work seen in L'Union Française or La Sincérité. In any event, Folger still had the Rituals of John the Forerunner in 1874, just nine years before he spoke at Elmira Consistory.

Even though the *Macoy Book* does not have "the consecration, the installation, and the table Rituals and ceremonials, with abundant and minute direction," it is quite probable that it or the *Supreme Council Book* must be the "beautiful and minute translation" to which Folger alluded. Indeed, if it is not, we must conclude that Folger possessed yet another Ritual, likewise translated from the French and appropriate for use in a Scottish Rite Blue Lodge, which has vanished without trace. This, surely, is asking too much of coincidence.

## REVOCATION OF THE PREFACE

One tantalizing clue remains unexplained: the revocation of the preface to Folger's manuscript. In the swirl of apparently clandestine activity by his Supreme Council, Folger managed to get himself expelled from the Grand Lodge of New York, but not for chartering a Scottish Rite Symbolic Lodge! (Which supports Atwood's contention that his Lodges only exemplified the work to Master Masons.) Folger took violent exception to the election of Reuben H. Walworth as Grand Master in 1853 and argued for the

---

[29] James Foulhouze, *Memoire à Consulter sur l'Origine du Rite Ecossais Ancien Accepté*, New Orleans: L. Marchand & Co., 1858.

reactivation of St. John's Grand Lodge, which had been formed by a schism in 1837 and had just reunited with the regular Grand Lodge in 1850.

The charges brought before the Grand Stewards' Lodge and his response, however, ignored his activity with John the Forerunner Lodge. On September 27, 1853, he was expelled by the Grand Stewards' Lodge, and a year later on September 25, 1854, he revoked the preface to his manuscript, taking great pains to obliterate almost completely the name of Ferdinand L. Wilsey, who was to receive the cipher Ritual after Folger died if Hans Gram were not available. Gram's name is untouched in the preface, he having died in 1840. We can only speculate about whether Wilsey was involved with Folger's expulsion from Grand Lodge or with the failure of his Supreme Council's foray into Symbolic Masonry or with some other activity.

## REVIEWING THE SOLUTION

Shortly after receiving his M.D. and starting his medical practice, Robert Benjamin Folger was Raised a Master Mason on February 10, 1826, in Fireman's Lodge No. 368 in New York City; he then began a most remarkable Masonic career. On May 25, 1826, he became a Royal Arch Mason in Jerusalem Chapter No. 8, with Hans B. Gram presiding. Gram had recently returned to America after a successful medical career in Copenhagen and while there had joined Zerubbabel of the North Star Lodge [*Zorobabel til Nordstjernen*].

Gram and Folger soon became fast friends, with Gram advising Folger on several patients and eventually converting him to Samuel Hahnemann's then new theory of homeopathy. During their growing professional and Masonic friendship, Gram taught Folger the Rectified Scottish Rite Rituals of his Lodge in Copenhagen and Initiated him at least through the fourth Degree of Scottish Master. In September 1826, four months after their first meeting, Folger introduced Gram to Ferdinand L. Wilsey, a merchant and Master of Minerva Lodge No. 371. Gram in turn introduced Wilsey to the "French" work of the R.E.R.

The three friends made plans to establish a Lodge in New York City working the Rectified Scottish Rite, and on June 8, 1827, Zorobabel Lodge No. 498, named after Gram's mother Lodge, was chartered with Gram as Master, Folger as Senior Warden, and Lewis Saynisch as Junior Warden. Folger enciphered the R.E.R. Rituals for Zorobabel Lodge into the *Supreme Council Book*. On July 12 he started but didn't finish another copy (owned today by Macoy Masonic Publishing and Supply Co). Included in the *Macoy Book* is a bizarre history of Masonry, attributing much of Masonic philosophy to Oliver Cromwell. This portion of the history is taken from Abbé Larudan's 1747 *Les Franc-Maçons Ecrasés* through some intermediate text. Folger's cipher is similar to other Masonic ciphers of the period but unique in the nonlinear way the characters were "stacked." Zorobabel Lodge closed shortly after it opened due to the the antimasonic movement in New York.

Some thirty years later, Folger planned to use his R.E.R. Rituals to exemplify French work in John the Forerunner Lodge, chartered March 8, 1853, by the Scottish Rite, but it was dissolved before holding any meetings. On September 25, 1854, Folger revoked the preface to his Ritual book and almost completely obliterated the name of Ferdinand L. Wilsey. On February 26, 1881, at the Reunion of Elmira Consistory in Elmira, New York, Folger proposed a toast using a portion of the Disciple's Catechism from his manuscript. From 1881 to his death in 1892, Folger served as Grand Secretary General of the Cerneau Supreme Council. His offices were at the same address as the Masonic Publishing Co., 63 Bleeker St., one of the predecessor firms of Macoy Co. On his death, at least one of the R.E.R. Ritual books came to the Masonic Publishing Co. and eventually to Macoy where it is still today.

Most of the major questions about the *Folger Manuscript* are now answered, though a few small issues remain. Did Hans Gram reproduce the R.E.R. Rituals from memory, or was there a book or manuscript, perhaps in French? Were the Rituals ever actually used in a Lodge? Where did Folger get his cipher? What is the origin of the odd history of Masonry? Why are portions of the *Macoy Book* unfinished? Why didn't he include more of the secret work for the Degrees? What happened to make Folger revoke his preface and nearly obliterate the name of Ferdinand L. Wilsey?

Much of the satisfaction in studying the *Folger Manuscript* has come from the digging required to locate answers rather than from the answers themselves. These open questions are left for better investigators with greater patience so that they too can gain satisfaction in studying the *Folger Manuscript*.

# THE CRYPTANALYSIS OF THE FOLGER CIPHER

ON A CHILLY DAY IN 1955, Wil Baden returned to his New York house and fixed some hot lemonade. He then sat down and opened an envelope from Harold Voorhis, Master of the American Lodge of Research, containing about ten pages copied from Robert Folger's cipher writing. Baden earlier had deciphered *Mnemonics,* the ritual book of Rob Morris's Conservators of Symbolic Masonry, and Voorhis had found out about his cryptanalytic abilities. Macoy Publishing and Masonic Supply Co., Inc. owned a copy of the *Folger Manuscript,* and Voorhis wanted to see the cipher broken, both as a Vice-President of Macoy and as a student of Masonry. He had, in fact, already published a paper in the 1952 *Proceedings of the Ohio Chapter of Research,* entitled "Masonic Alphabets," illustrated with two pages from the *Macoy Book.*

As Baden studied the pages, his initial enthusiasm turned to dismay. The cipher had no readily identifiable characters and appeared impregnable. Two of the pages were laid out similarly, with some of the same text written in plain English on each. However, one had portions encrypted where the other had text. Hoping for the best, he carefully compared the phrase *contains great treasures* on one page with the matching cipher on the other and discovered he could read the manuscript! In less than thirty minutes Folger's cipher had fallen to the cryptanalytic technique of "matched plain and cipher." Baden then translated the entire manuscript but never published his solution. The enciphered phrase essential to his solution was from page 84 of the *Macoy Book* (see Figure 1), and the page with the key phrase written in plain English came from the *Supreme Council Book,* now lost.

# The Cryptanalysis

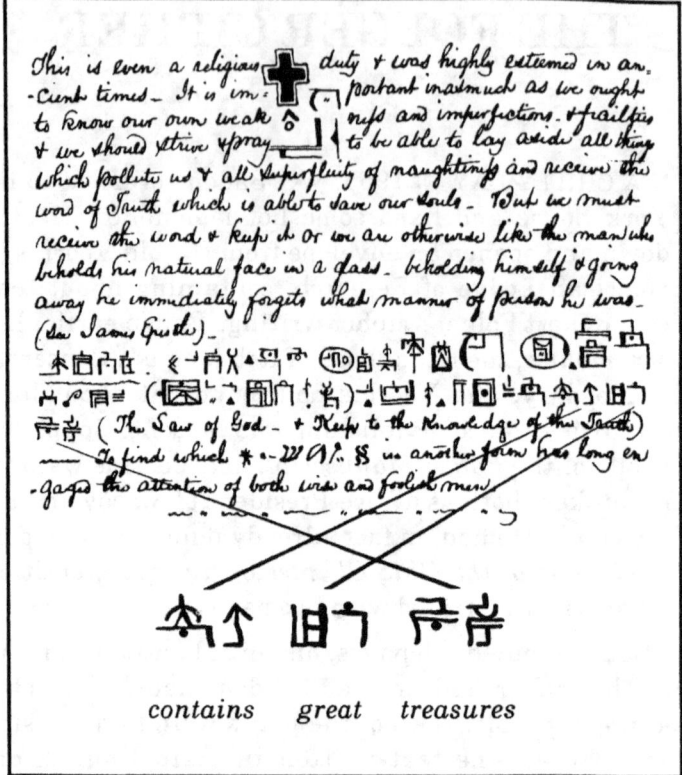

FIGURE 1. Page 84 from the Macoy Book

In 1982, Donald H. Bennett sat down at his computer and started a lengthy program. While it was running he read Brent Morris's article, "Fraternal Cryptography," which showed page 21 of the *Macoy Book* as an example of an exotic, unbroken, possibly Masonic cipher (Baden's solution was unknown then to Morris or Bennett). The unsolved puzzle challenged Mr. Bennett, and he set about applying classical cryptanalytic techniques. In a few hours he had independently broken the cipher as it yielded to his "cipher text only" attack. Bennett published his results as "An Unsolved Puzzle Solved" in *Cryptologia* magazine, and his work forms the basis for the discussion which follows.

## ASSUMPTIONS

Before beginning the cryptanalysis of an unknown message like page 21 (see Figure 2), certain fundamental assumptions must be made. Little was known to Mr. Bennett, except that the document was composed by Robert B. Folger, M.D. in 1827. Because of his Masonic membership, the cipher was assumed to conceal some message relating to Masonry. A number of words commonly used by Masons, such as *grand, lodge, council, brother, companion, freemason*, etc. had been suggested in Morris's article. Each group or cluster of cipher symbols was suspected to represent a syllable or word. There were other theories and speculations advanced regarding the Folger cipher, but, after more than 150 years, its solution was unknown to the public.

Some of the assumptions, explicit and implicit, are given below with their reasons.

- *The underlying language is English.* This follows from the author living in New York and having an English sounding surname.

- *The orientation of the page is correct as shown, with the cipher reading from left to right and top to bottom.* A paragraph seems to end in the middle of the second line, and a new paragraph, indicated by the illumination of its first few characters, starts on the next line. This one ends on line 8, and another paragraph starts on the next line, indicated by a slight indentation.

- *The cipher is homogeneous throughout.* Cipher symbols are repeated throughout the text and are not limited to one part of the page.

- *Clusters of symbols represent, in general, words rather than individual letters or syllables.* If clusters represent only letters, then each cluster must contain many meaningless strokes, because hundreds of discrete clusters can be identified. These clusters are referred to as cipher words.

The Cryptanalysis

FIGURE 2. Page 21 from the Macoy Book

- *There is no transposition of the order of letters within a cipher word.* If rearranging the order of symbols were part of the enciphering process, then repeats of longer words would be rare, but in fact, exact repeats of many words do occur.

- *The order of the symbols within a cipher word is from top to bottom and/or from left to right.* This corresponds to the order of normal English writing.

- *A discrete set of approximately 26 cipher symbols represent English letters.*

- *The size of and minor artistic variations in individual cipher symbols is immaterial, but dark shading of certain strokes may have special meaning.*

## ANALYSIS

Folger disguised his cipher symbols well; little can be gained from examining the individual characters. The symbols are angular, a characteristic of most Masonic ciphers, and only a few curved strokes can be found, each of which might be an elemental symbol (see Figure 3). Nine other symbols which showed up repeatedly in

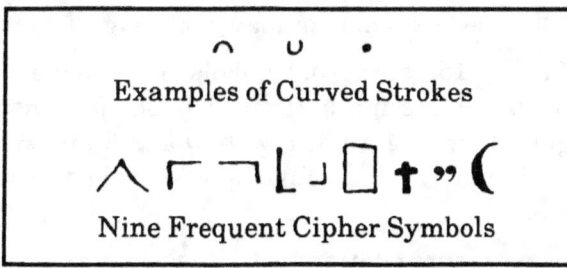

**FIGURE 3. Possible Elemental Cipher Symbols**

the text are also shown. The last three symbols, which occurred less frequently than the first six, are assumed to be infrequent letters, the first six to be frequent ones.

The Cryptanalysis

**BOXED-IN SYMBOLS**

The only other useful information gained from individual characters is the observation that many words are surrounded by boxes (see Figure 4). The box-like character is probably the first

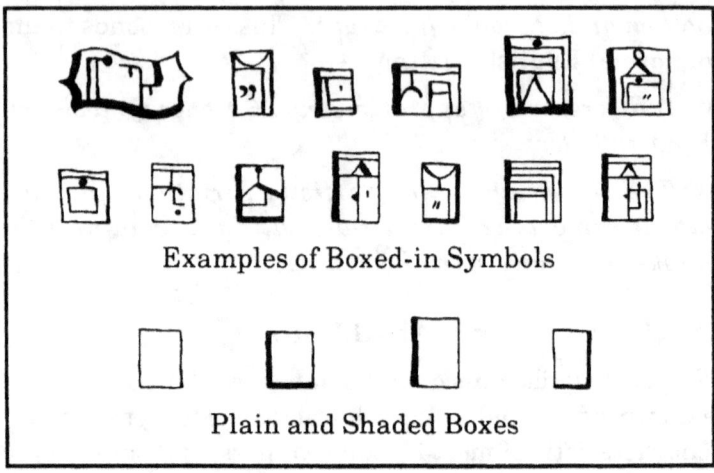

FIGURE 4. Boxes in Cipher Text

letter, with the rest of the word inside the box. The dark shading on the sides of some boxes may or may not be significant.

Out of about 150 boxed-in symbols on the page, no less than forty two, or 28%, contain a horizontal stroke just inside the box, near the top (e.g., in Figure 4, row 1, words 3 and 4, and row 2, words 1, 2, 4, 6, and 7). The stroke appears to be the second letter in these words.

The most frequent letter in English is *e* and it most often occurs as the second letter of a word; the horizontal stroke could be the symbol for the letter *e*! This symbol occurs throughout the text but is relatively inconspicuous, a desirable feature for a cipher character representing a high frequency letter. However, it is too soon to firmly identify cipher symbols.

## THE MYSTERY DIGRAPH

The analysis continues by searching for digraphs or pairs of symbols with noticeable positional limitations. In English the most striking example of a positional limitation is *qu*: the letter *q* is always followed by the letter *u*. A pronounced limitation is found with the *crescent moon*, (, and *backward gamma*, ⏌: the crescent moon is always followed by the *backward gamma*, ⏍, without exception! The *backward gamma*, however, is preceded only occasionally by the *crescent moon*. Next, all cipher words containing this "mystery digraph" are listed (see Figure 5). It appears twenty-three times in thirteen different words. The first word on the list occurs seven times, the second and third three times each, and all others only once. The first three words should be fairly common, consisting of perhaps three to five letters each.

The Mystery Digraph

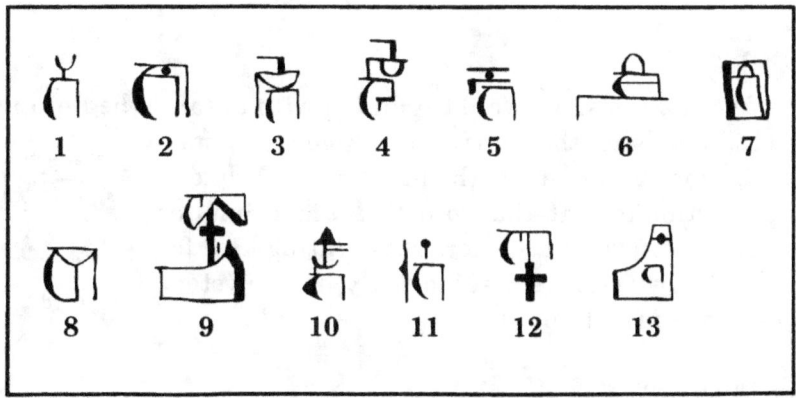

**FIGURE 5.** The 13 Words with the "Mystery Digraph"

The most distinctive feature of the digraph is that it occurs as the last two letters in fifteen times out of twenty-three, and as the first two letters six times. Only twice (in words 4 and 6) does it occur within a word, and word 4 appears to be the same as word 3 with a suffix added. The *crescent moon* is probably an infrequent

# The Cryptanalysis

letter and the *backward gamma* a common one, and, if so, then what is the mystery digraph? Certainly not *qu*, because *qu* cannot occur at the end of words. It is most likely the letters *th*, with the *backward gamma* as *t* and the *crescent moon* as *h*.

## WORD 1

Testing this hypothesis proves interesting and fruitful. Word 1 has *th* or *ht* as its last two letters, with either one or two letters preceding. Since no three-letter English word fits this format, it must be a four-letter word, such as *both*, *with*, *hath*, or *doth* (taking into consideration that verb forms such as *hath*, *doth*, *goeth*, *doeth*, etc., might occur more often in English written in 1827). There's no use guessing which four-letter word this might be, but if the other cipher symbols represent two letters of plain text, then the most logical way to split this combination is into a *cup*, ∪, and a short, vertical line, ˡ.

## WORD 2

Word 2 is a short word beginning with *th* (an *ht* beginning is impossible). Since the *backward gamma* is assumed to be *t*, Word 2 must have the form *th - t*. Only one word fits this format—the word *that*—which implies the dot, •, stands for *a*. Before substituting an *a* for every dot, however, it's wiser to analyze the mystery digraph words further.

## WORDS 3 AND 4

The third word seems to begin with *t* and to end in either *th* or *ht*. Since the *cup*, ∪, was assumed to be a single letter, all that remains to decide is whether the *gamma*, Γ, represents one letter or two. Word 3 could be of the form *t - - th*, *t - - ht*, *t - - - th*, or *t - - - ht*, with ∪ representing the third from the last letter. Some possibilities are *tenth*, *troth*, *taketh*, or *taught*, but *truth* is just the sort of word a Mason might use three times on one page. If *truth* is assumed to be correct, then ⌈ and ∪ equate to r and u in some order. These assumptions however, present problems with Word 4, which appears to be *truths*, but this leads to the unlikely situation where ⌈ represents both *r* and *s*. Rather than reject earlier, seemingly sound assumptions, Word 4 is put aside for the moment and the analysis continues.

Word 4

## WORD 5

Word 5 has five letters, four of which have been tentatively identified. Its form is - *arth* or - *auth*, depending on whether ⌈ is *r* or *u*. the only candidate is *earth*, which confirms the earlier idea of the horizontal stroke as *e* and clearly indicates that ⌈ stands for r. At this point, the following cipher letters have been tentatively identified: *a*, *e*, *h*, *r*, *t*, and *u* (see Figure 6).

Word 5

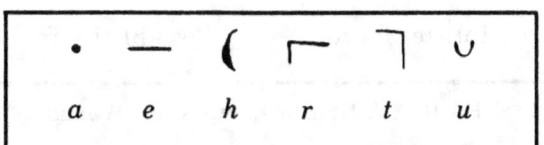

**FIGURE 6. Tentative Cipher Characters**

## WORDS 6 AND 7

An upper semicircle, ∩ , begins Word 6 followed by *ther*. This suggests *other*; the only alternative, *ether*, begins with *e*, a horizontal stroke . Thus ∩ is identified as *o*. The seventh word contains ∩ followed by *th*. It seems to be a short word of the form - *oth*, like *doth*, or *both*, but there is not enough information to decide. Word 7 *does* neither proves nor disproves ∩ as *o*.

Word 7

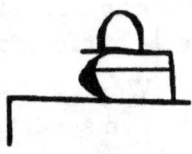
Word 6

*Page 41*

## SYNTHESIS

The ∩ symbol does not occur again in the word list, so a different approach is needed to continue its analysis. The answer is to synthesize a short, common word containing *o* and then to look for it in the cipher text. The symbols for *a, e, h, o, r, t,* and *u* have been identified, which allows (among other possibilities) the construction of the words *to* and *or* (see Figure 7). The first possibility for *to* occurs seventeen times in the message and the first possibility for *or* three times, which pretty well confirms ∩ as *o*. As the text is searched for *or*, a similar cipher word, *our*, can be found, and this leads to an interesting discovery: a circle can be split into two parts: the top half, ∩, representing *o* and the bottom half, ∪, representing *u*.

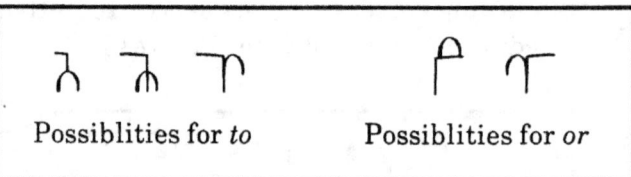

Possiblities for *to*     Possiblities for *or*

FIGURE 7. Synthesizing Short Words

## WORDS 8–13

Returning to the list brings up Word 8, which is of the form *thu -* or *thu - -*. The word must be *thus*, but the last cipher symbol is difficult to distinguish because it seems to merge with the bottom of the crescent moon. Thus, the symbol for *s* could be either Ⅰ or ⌐, but further analysis is required.

Word 8

Words 9 through 12 are either too long or have too many unknown symbols for good assumptions. Word 13, however, lends itself to partial analysis. It is one of the "boxed-in" words and, if the box is the first letter, it has the form *- eath* or *- - eath*. This could be a five-letter word such as *death* or a six-letter word like *breath* if the box is a combination of two symbols. A final decision must wait. It is important to note a missing "bite" from the upper left corner of the box. Is this just an artistic variation of a plain box, or is it significant?

Word 13

**OTHER INTERESTING WORDS**

Word 13 exhausts the list, but analysis can continue by looking for "interesting" words in which most of the symbols have been tentatively identified. Such a word ends line 25. It begins with *ru*, followed by three to five additional letters, one of which is *e*. The last character may be *s*, if the analysis of Word 8 was correct. The word is of the form *ru - es* or *ru - ees*, depending on whether the symbol L represents one letter or two. Some possiblities are *rules*, *runes*, *ruses*, or *rupees*. The most likely word is *rules*, which goes nicely with the earlier recovery of *truths*. This means the symbol for *l* is, of all things, an *l*!

*Rules*

Another interesting word occurs in the middle of line 17. It starts with *e*, followed by a repeated letter, and then ends with *orts*: *e - - orts*. The obvious choice is *efforts*, which provides additional confirmation of the *backward l*, ⌐, as *s* and establishes the *half mast flag*, ⊣, as *f*.

*Efforts*

**THE SOLUTION**

From this point on, the rest of the alphabet can be recovered using the ten known letters: *a, e, f, h, l, o, r, s, t,* and *u*. Only *z* cannot be recovered from page 21, because it was not used. Folger seemed to have used page 11 for practice and to have copied the alphabet there (see Figure 8).

Note that the cipher symbol ∪ is used for the letters *u, v,* and *w*. Thus Word 1 from the list is *with*, even though the symbol ∪

FIGURE 8. Folger's Cipher Alphabet from Page 11

was originally recovered as *u*. The letter *h* is represented by either of two symbols: the standard symbol is ⊓ or ⊓, but a variant symbol, (, is used sometimes after *t*. When Folger began writing his manuscript he used the standard *h* exclusively. About page 15, however, he started using the variant more and more often after *t*. This variant could have been for ease of writing, but the *th* digraph ⊓ looks like the Hebrew letter *tauv*, ת, and Folger may have tried to introduce Hebrew into his cipher.

## SUMMARY

Folger's alphabet is unlike any other Masonic cipher, even though several of his symbols can be found in some *hauts grades* ciphers. This, however, is not surprising because of the small possible number of simple geometric shapes. It is most likely that he invented his system on his own, with inspiration from some other Masonic book or manuscript. However, his technique of "stacking" his symbols is unique to him and greatly increases the cryptographic security of the system. Based on the mixture of good and bad cryptographic practices and on the evolving nature of the cipher through the manuscript, it can be concluded that Folger was a self-taught amateur who invented a rather good cipher.

Breaking this cipher and reading the text solves only part of the puzzle. Some important questions are still unanswered: who was Robert Folger and what kind of a person was he? Several interesting conclusions can be reached from studying the *Macoy Book*, many of which are confirmed in Chapter 6.

- *Robert Folger was a well-educated man.* His grammar, syntax, and spelling are quite good. He was a meticulous draftsman; his characters are well-defined and precise so that little ambiguity is encountered in the deciphering process. There are virtually no errors on page 21; the few misspelled words, such as *hapy* and *intereresting*, could be clerical errors in encryption, while words like *beautifull* probably reflect the spelling of the day. Using one cipher character for $u$, $v$, and $w$ and interchanging the symbols for $i$ and $j$ in the text hint at a knowledge of Latin. The use of Hebrew letters elsewhere shows a crude knowledge of that alphabet.

- *Robet Folger was an experienced speaker.* The homily on the Bible on page 21 shows careful, simple wording of complex ideas, suitable for a general audience.

- *Robert Folger was an enthusiastic Mason.* Many, many hours were devoted to writing and decorating the manuscript, showing an intense interest in Masonry.

- *Robert Folger was a man of strong passions.* The almost complete obliteration of Ferdinand L. Wilsey's name in the preface goes well beyond a simple revocation.

# THE COADJUTORS OF ROBERT B. FOLGER

ROBERT FOLGER did not work in a vacuum while preparing and using his cipher manuscripts. He was helped and influenced by several people, including Hans Burch Gram, Ferdinand Little Wilsey, and Henry Clinton Atwood. Gram was the source of the rituals and a major influence on Folger's medical career. Wilsey was involved in some way with the manuscripts, was a fellow pioneer of homeopathy with Folger, and served with Folger as a Knights Templar Officer. Atwood had a profound effect on Folger's Masonic career and led him to use the rituals in a clandestine Scottish Rite Lodge. While there were others who influenced Folger's Masonic and medical careers, these three had the most direct effect on the *Folger Manuscript*. Their biographies are included to give further insight into Folger and his curious books.

## HANS BURCH GRAM

Dr. Hans Burch Gram was the pioneer of homeopathic medicine in America. Homeopathy is a medical theory, developed in the early nineteenth century by Dr. Samuel Hahnemann in Germany, that treats a disease by administering minute doses of a substance which in a healthy person would produce symptoms of the disease. Thus a patient suffering from a fever is given a fever-inducing medicine. Homeopathy has been largely discarded by medical schools, but it was a radical advance in its day, largely because of the gentle, holistic methods it encouraged. In contrast, standard medical practice of the early 1800s relied heavily on purgatives, bleedings, and other harsh and largely ineffective techniques.

The Coadjutors

## FROM BOSTON TO COPENHAGEN

Hans Burch Gram was born in Boston on July 13, 1786 or 1787. After the death of his grandfather in Denmark in 1802, Hans Burch's father prepared to sail for Copenhagen the next year to take care of the estate but died just before setting sail. Hans Burch's mother died two years later when he was barely eighteen, and he soon thereafter sailed for Copenhagen to claim his father's inheritance. His father, Mr. Hans Gram, had been secretary to the Governor of Santa Cruz Island in the Danish West Indies before settling in Boston after marrying a Miss Burdick.[1]

Arriving in Copenhagen in 1806 or 1807, Hans Burch Gram was admitted to the Royal Academy of Surgery with the help of his uncle, Dr. Fenger, physician in ordinary to the King. Within a year Gram was appointed Assistant Surgeon in a large military hospital, where he remained during the last seven years of the Napoleonic Wars. In 1814 he resigned his post in the military hospital, having attained the rank of Surgeon. He graduated from the Academy with the degree of C.M.L. and began a private practice in Copenhagen. For several years he was secretary to his uncle, Dr. Fenger, then the State Medical Counselor. During the years 1823 and 1824, Gram studied and applied the principles of homeopathy in his medical practice.[2]

## ZERUBBABEL LODGE

While in Copenhagen Gram became a Freemason, which later provided him important contacts in New York City. The 1871 register of the Copenhagen Lodge Zerubbabel and Frederick of the Crowned Hope [*Zorobabel og Frederik tel det kronede Håb*] has the

[1] Henry M. Smith, "Homeopathic Directory: New York Historical Sketch," *The New England Medical Gazette*, Vol. VI, No. 2, Feb. 1871, pp. 91-94; Jørgen Vagn Jørgensen, Præses, Den Danske Frimurerorden Informationsdirektoriet, Copenhagen, To S. Brent Morris, Columbia, Md., Nov. 8, 1990, Typescript, In the possession of the author.

[2] Thomas Bradford, *The Pioneers of Homeopathy* (Philadelphia: Boericke & Tafel, 1897), p. 289; "The Late Dr. Gram," *The Homeopathic Examiner*, Vol. I, No. 2, Feb. 1840, p. 101; "An Historical Note of Dr. Gram," *The Hahnemannian Monthly*, Vol. VII, No. 1, 1871, p. 84.

**FIGURE 1. Hans Burch Gram, M.D.**
From *United States Medical and Surgical Journal*,
Vol. II, July 1867, facing p. 449.

following entry: Hans Benjamin Gram, practicing doctor of medicine, born in Boston July 13th, 1787, entered the Lodge November 3rd, 1819. Zerubbabel and Frederick Lodge was formed in 1855 by the merger of two Lodges, Zerubbabel of the North Star [*Zorobabel tel Nordstjernen*] and Frederick of the Crowned Hope [*Frederik tel det kronede Håb*], both working the Rectified Scottish Rite or R.E.R.

The Coadjutors

Circumstantial evidence indicates that Gram joined Zerubbabel of the North Star Lodge (see Chapter 1) and was initiated through at least the R.E.R. Fourth Degree, Scottish Master.[3]

## FROM COPENHAGEN TO NEW YORK CITY

In 1824, after a financially successful medical career in Copenhagen, Gram decided to return to his homeland and to enjoy his retirement. He sailed from Stockholm on the ship *William Penn* and landed at Mount Desert, Maine, where he stayed for some time. He finally arrived in New York City in 1825 and lived with his brother, Neils B. Gram, at 431 Broome St. Hans Gram soon lost his fortune by cosigning loans for his brother and was compelled to enter again the practice of medicine.[4]

By 1826 Gram had proved himself well enough in the Masonic establishment of New York City to be officiating at the conferral of Degrees. On May 25 of that year he presided at the Exaltation of a young Mason and physician, Robert B. Folger, to the Degree of Royal Arch in Jerusalem Chapter No. 8, R.A.M. Folger had been Raised a Master Mason only three months before and recently had established a medical practice. Common Masonic and medical interests fueled a lasting friendship between Gram and Folger after their initial meeting in Jerusalem Chapter, and "the acquaintance there formed soon ripened into very close intimacy...."[5]

## FOLGER AND WILSEY

Four months after Gram met Folger, Folger introduced him to Ferdinand Wilsey, a successful merchant and Master of Minerva Lodge No. 371. "Dr. Folger having received from Dr. Gram some important information in Masonry, desired that [Wilsey] should

---

[3] Vagn Jørgensen to Morris.

[4] William H. King, *History of Homeopathy* (New York: Lewis Publishing Co., 1905), Vol. I, pp. 60-61; Bradford, *The Pioneers of Homeopathy*.

[5] Robert B. Folger, "Recollections of a Masonic Veteran," Part 11, *New York Dispatch*, Sept. 28, 1873; King, *History of Homeopathy*, p. 61.

also receive the benefit of it." This "important information in Masonry" was Initiation into the Rectified Scottish Rite through at least the Fourth Degree, Scottish Master. The meeting had significant Masonic and professional implications for Gram. He translated the Rituals into English (whether from memory or a manuscript is not known), and Folger enciphered them into two (or more) small books. One of the volumes, the *Macoy Book*, dated July 12, 1827, has instructions that Gram or Wilsey were to receive the book upon Folger's death. On June 8, 1827, one month before the *Macoy Book* was dated, a charter was granted to Zorobabel Lodge No. 498 of New York City with Hans B. Gram, Master; Robert B. Folger, Senior Warden; and Lewis Saynisch, Junior Warden. The Rituals may have been used by the Lodge, but it had a brief existence and then closed during the antimasonic excitement.[6]

## PROFESSIONAL ACTIVITIES

Gram later used homeopathic methods to successfully treat Wilsey for dyspepsia, and Wilsey's enthusiastic endorsements helped him establish a thriving medical practice. From 1826 to 1828 Folger studied homeopathy with Gram as his only student and assistant. Gram attempted to bring the tenets of homeopathy to the attention of the medical profession by publishing a translation of Hahnemann's *Spirit of Homeopathic Healing Laws [Geist der Homöopathischen Heillehre]*. The booklet was addressed to Dr. Hosack, President of the College of Physicians and Surgeons in New York City, but was not well received among the medical profession because of its radical departure from accepted theory. Two years after receiving his copy Dr. Hosack had yet to read it. "Unhappily for [Gram], the medical doctrines which he taught and practiced were so lightly esteemed, that his acquaintance was rather shunned than sought," and he published nothing more on homeopathy. Gram was elected to the New York Medical and Philosophical Society in February, 1828, and was elected its President in July,

---

[6] *Transactions of the Grand Lodge of Free and Accepted Masons of New York, 1816–1827* (New York: Masonic Publishing and Furnishing Co., 1880), p. 477.

1829. In January, 1828, Folger traveled to Charlotte, North Carolina, for his health, and Gram made plans to join him there in the fall of 1828 to open a joint practice. However, business problems forced Folger to move from Charlotte, and Gram abandoned his medical plans with Folger.[7]

The last few years of Gram's life must have been disappointing. While his medical practice flourished, he was largely unsuccessful in getting the theories of homeopathy accepted; many in the New York medical establishment considered him a quack. His brother Neil went insane and eventually died, and, just as homeopathy began to be accepted among medical practitioners, he suffered a paralyzing stroke in May, 1839, and died on February 26, 1840. Gram was a member of the Church of the New Jerusalem (Swedenborgians) and was buried in St. Mark's Burial Ground on Second St. in New York City. A plate on his coffin read: HANS B. GRAM, M.D., a Knight of the Order of St. John, died Feb. 18, 1840, aged 53. On September 4, 1862, his remains were removed to Greenwood Cemetery where they rest today. His marble tombstone still stands in Greenwood Cemetery.[8]

---

**H. B. GRAM, C.M.L.**

**HAFNIAE · PIONEER
OF HOMEOPATHY,
IN AMERICA.
DIED 1840,
AET. 54.**

---

[7] Smith, "New York Historical Sketch"; S. B. Barlow, "Miscellaneous: Dr. Gram," *The American Homeopathic Review*, Vol. III, No. 4, Oct. 1862, p. 185; Bradford, *The Pioneers of Homeopathy*; Folger, "Recollections" Part 11; King, *History of Homeopathy*, p. 61.

[8] Barlow, "Dr. Gram"; "Obituary: Hans B. Gram," *The United States Medical and Surgical Journal*, Vol. II, July 1867, pp. 449-452; "The Late Dr. Gram."

## FERDINAND LITTLE WILSEY

Ferdinand Little Wilsey was born in New York City, on June 23, 1797. In February, 1822, he was "Admitted" to Hiram Lodge No. 10 after paying an initiation fee of $1.25. Fifteen months later on May 6, 1823, he withdrew from Hiram Lodge to become the charter Senior Warden of Silentia Lodge No. 360. Then ten months later on March 16, 1824, he withdrew from Silentia Lodge and on March 25 became the first Master of Minerva Lodge No. 371. In 1825 he was Captain General of Morton Commandery, No. 4, Knights Templar. A year later, in 1826, he was again Master of Minerva Lodge, served as Generalissimo of Morton Commandery, and was listed in Longworth's *New York City Directory* as a comb manufacturer at 33 Fulton St.[9]

**FOLGER AND GRAM**

In September, 1826, while serving his second term as Master of Minerva Lodge, Wilsey was introduced to Hans Gram by Robert Folger, whom he had met the year before. "Dr. Folger having received from Dr. Gram some important information in Masonry, desired that [Wilsey] should also receive the benefit of it."[10] This "important information in Masonry" was Initiation into the Rectified Scottish Rite through at least the Fourth Degree, Scottish Master. Folger enciphered the rituals in at least two small books with instructions dated July 12, 1827, in the *Macoy Book* that Gram or Wilsey were to receive the book upon Folger's death.

Another motive may have led Folger to introduce Gram and Wilsey: medical care. Dr. John F. Gray had been treating Wilsey unsuccessfully for dyspepsia, and after meeting Gram Wilsey turned to him for care. Wilsey thus became the first patient in America to be treated by homeopathy when Gram used these tech-

---

[9] Allan Boudreau, [Librarian, Grand Lodge of New York, F.&A.M.], N.Y., to S. Brent Morris, [Columbia, Md.], June 7, 1990, Typescript, In the possession of the author.
[10] Smith, "New York Historical Sketch."

niques to cure him. Wilsey was so enthusiastic about homeopathy that he convinced Dr. Gray to study the subject and induced his friends to turn to Dr. Gram for medical treatment. Wilsey's enthusiasm for Gram and homeopathy was responsible for much of the early spread of this medical theory throughout the United States.[11]

In September, 1826, when Wilsey met Gram, William Morgan was removed by Masons from the jail in Canandaigua, New York, and disappeared, supposedly murdered because he planned to publish secret Masonic rituals. The antimasonic frenzy produced by these lurid allegations produced the first major third political party in the United States, the Antimasonic Party, and caused a social upheaval of amazing intensity. Antimasonic excitement gripped New York and the country from about 1826–1840 and resulted in the closing of eighty percent of the Lodges in New York. Throughout this difficult period Wilsey remained a staunch Mason. He maintained his membership in Minerva Lodge until it surrendered its charter in 1836, and he served as an officer of Morton Commandery for eight of the years from 1827-1841. His acquaintance with Robert Folger must have continued, as Folger was an Officer of Morton Commandery for three of those years, and in 1845 Wilsey was Generalissimo while Folger was Captain General.[12]

**FROM MANUFACTURING TO MEDICINE**

Sometime after his favorable introduction to homeopathy, Wilsey began studying medicine under Gram until he acquired the title of "Doctor." Wilsey established a medical practice but only treated friends gratis. He remained in the comb-manufacturing business until 1837, when financial reverses nearly ruined him. In 1841 he took a position with the Custom House, and in 1844 he was graduated with an M.D. from the College of Physicians and Surgeons (later with Columbia University). About 1845 or 1846 he

---

[11] "Obituary, Ferdinand L. Wilsey," *The American Homeopathic Review*, Vol. II, No. 9, June and July 1860, pp. 431-432.

[12] Boudreau to Morris; William L. Gardner, *Historical Reminiscences of Morton Commandery, No. 4, Knights Templar* (New York: John W. Keeler, 1891), p. 24.

joined a copper mining company in Cuba and moved there to superintend the operations. This venture proved disastrous because in less than a year his health failed and he was forced to return to New York City where he commenced the public practice of medicine. In 1850 he was listed in Longworth's *New York City Directory* as a physician at 588 Houston St.[13]

On September 25, 1854, Folger revoked the preface to the *Macoy Book*, almost completely obliterating Wilsey's name. It is not clear what Wilsey did, if anything, to cause Folger's reaction; as recently as 1845 they had served together as officers in Morton Commandery. Folger had had troubles with the Grand Lodge of New York, which had led to his suspension on September 27, 1853, and his Supreme Council was getting more deeply embroiled in controversies at this time. It is most likely that Wilsey spoke out against one of Folger's Scottish Rite schemes, but no evidence of any specific action by Wilsey can be found.

In 1856 or 1857 Wilsey had a severe, protracted illness, which left him weakened and often confined to bed. He would resume his activities when his strength returned, but finally about 1858 he turned over his practice to his successor, Dr. Forbes, and moved with his family to Bergen, New Jersey, where he died May 11, 1860.[14]

## HENRY CLINTON ATWOOD

Henry Clinton Atwood was a Mason who had a great impact on the Craft in New York State and on the Masonic career of Robert Folger. Atwood was born on March 13, 1801, in Woodbury, Connecticut, to Elijah and Abigail Atwood. He started his Masonic activities on March 25, 1823, when he was initiated an Entered Apprentice in Morning Star Lodge No. 47 in Oxford, Connecticut; on April 22 he received the Second and Third Degrees. He then took the Capitular Degrees in Solomon Chapter No. 3, Royal Arch Masons, in Denby, Connecticut: Mark Master, Past Master, and

---

[13] Boudreau to Morris; "Obituary, Ferdinand L. Wilsey."
[14] "Obituary: Ferdinand L. Wilsey."

Most Excellent Master on October 9, and Royal Arch on December 17. His first year in Masonry was completed with his appointment as Senior Deacon of Morning Star for 1824. In 1825 Morning Star Lodge elected Atwood Junior Warden , and on March 25 he was Received and Greeted in Harmony Council No. 8, Royal and Select Masters. Then on November 22 he moved to New York City and was "declared off" (withdrawn) by Morning Star Lodge.[15]

## MYSTIC LODGE AND THE CROSS WORK

Atwood began working in New York City as a journeyman hatter and wasted no time in getting involved in Masonry. On March 10, 1826, he was the charter Master of Mystic Lodge No. 389, and on May 25 he joined Rising Sun Chapter No. 16, R.A.M. Mystic Lodge met in St. John's Hall on Frankfort St. and caused quite a stir within the Fraternity with its rituals. In Connecticut Atwood had studied under Jeremy L. Cross, the Masonic Ritualist. As Master of Mystic Lodge, Atwood introduced the "Cross work" (Masonic Ritual as organized and taught by Cross) into New York Lodges, whose Grand Lodge had earlier rejected it. This introduction was different, though, because from 1823–1827 New York suffered from a schism between the "City Grand Lodge" and the "Country Grand Lodge." While both bodies undoubtedly were opposed to Cross's innovations, their dispute kept them from taking much notice of Atwood and Mystic Lodge. However, the Masons of New York City noticed, "and hundreds flocked to the place every meeting night to see the spectacle." Cross himself visited the Lodge on September 18 and exemplified the first two Degrees.[16]

There was such interest in the Cross work that Atwood established classes of twenty Masons each to learn the new style of Ritual. Robert Folger was in the first class, all of whom were young and eager to excel, and which met from 2:00 to 6:00 P.M. twice a

---

[15] Harold V. B. Voorhis, "Henry Clinton Atwood–A Connecticut Yankee in New York," *Transactions of the American Lodge of Research* [New York], Vol. III, No. 1, 1960, pp. 89-96.

[16] Folger, "Recollections," part 4.

FIGURE 2. Henry Clinton Atwood
From Henry C. Atwood, *The Master Workman*
(New York: Simons and Macoy, 1850), frontispiece.

week. Atwood converted many individual Masons to this style of working as well as a few Lodges; "the few Lodges which [espoused] Bro. Atwood's [style] were overrun with candidates and members, drawn there by a love of decoration, finery and new things." During a meeting of Atwood's first class the Ineffable or Scottish Rite Degrees came up. The information was scant, as the bodies were quite secretive and selective; the Gourgas or regular Supreme Council was unknown to the class and the fees of the Cerneau Supreme Council were prohibitive. However, Atwood found in one Abraham Jacobs a cut-rate source of the Ineffable Degrees.[17]

**ABRAHAM JACOBS AND THE 32°**

Abraham Jacobs was a one of a small number of itinerant "degree peddlers" who helped spread Masonry in North America. He taught Hebrew for a living and supplemented his income by conferring various Masonic degrees on interested Brethren. While today such entrepreneurs are viewed with disdain, they were considered a legal if not honorable source of "advanced Degrees" in the late 1700s and early 1800s, and Jacobs seemed scrupulous in requiring his clients to obtain charters for their subsequent activities.

On November 9, 1790, Jacobs had been advanced by Moses Cohen to Knight of the Sun, 23° in Morin's twenty-five Degree "Rite of Perfection." Then on November 24, 1809, Jacobs was promoted to 32° by John Gabriel Tardy, Deputy Inspector General of the Scottish Rite of thirty-three degrees, the successor to Morin's Rite. This final promotion presumably was made in return for Jacobs' submission to the authority of the Scottish Rite. After falling on hard times, however, Jacobs began again to confer degrees to supplement his income. Oliver Lowndes, 33°, Sheriff of New York County, and member of the Cerneau Supreme Council, offered Jacobs a clerkship in the Sheriff's Office in return for his agreement to not confer any Scottish Rite Degrees within forty miles of New York State. It was after this point that Henry Atwood met with Jacobs to negotiate the site, time, and fees for conferring the Degrees on his class.[18]

[17] Folger, "Recollections," part 4, and part 5, June 29, 1873.

[18] Abraham Jacobs, "Register, Rules & Status. of the Sublime Degrees of Masonry [ca. 1809]," Archives, Supreme Council, 33°, N.M.J., U.S.A., Lexington, Mass.; Folger, "Recollections," part 6, June 29, 1873.

Trenton, New Jersey, was selected as the site, and in late winter 1826 Jacobs Initiated the class, including Atwood and Folger, through the 32° of the Scottish Rite for an unreported fee. "The members of the class were well-satisfied,"[19] but they had been misled – Jacobs' patent from Tardy gave no authority to confer degrees. This type of situation was not uncommon in the early, chaotic days of the Scottish Rite, and most of the class members were probably legitimized by joining some regularly chartered Scottish Rite Body.

**JAMES CUSHMAN AND THE 33°**

In 1827 Atwood traveled again to Trenton to meet with James Cushman, his friend and a fellow student of Cross. Cushman had an honorary 33° from the Southern Supreme Council with no authority to confer any degrees, especially in the jurisdiction of the Northern Supreme Council. Undeterred, Cushman conferred the 33° on Atwood in the fall of 1827. In 1828 Atwood was High Priest of Rising Sun Chapter and represented it at the meeting of the Grand Chapter of Royal Arch Masons in Albany on February 5-7. While there, he called on Governor De Witt Clinton, 33°, Sovereign Grand Commander of the Cerneau Supreme Council, who "approved" his patent on February 7, 1828, four days before he died. Atwood must have considered the legitimacy of his Scottish Rite Degrees adequately certified, regardless of their origin.[20]

On November 17, 1828, Atwood withdrew from Mystic Lodge and returned to Oxford, Connecticut. He was restored to membership in Morning Star Lodge No. 47 in late 1829 or early 1830, and on December 27, 1830, was elected and installed Master of the Lodge. He was reelected in 1831 when he also served Eureka Chapter No. 22, R.A.M., in Oxford as High Priest. Atwood was

---

[19] Folger, "Recollections," part 6, June 29, 1873.

[20] Folger, "Recollections," part 5; Jacobs, "Register"; Edmund B. Hays, "Hays Register," Archives, Supreme Council, 33°, N.M.J., U.S.A., Lexington, Mass.; Henry W. Coil, et al., eds. *Coil's Masonic Encyclopedia* (New York: Macoy Masonic Publishing and Supply Co., Inc., 1961), s.v. "Henry Clinton Atwood," by Edward R. Cusick.

clearly a staunch supporter of Freemasonry, because in 1832 he signed the "Declaration of Principles" which had been prepared by Massachusetts Masons in response to the antimasonic fervor. Defiance in the face of overwhelming opposition was a characteristic Atwood would demonstrate over and over in his Masonic activities. He was again High Priest of Eureka Chapter in 1832 and Master of Morningstar Lodge in 1833. In 1835 he returned to New York City and was admitted a member of York Lodge No. 367 (now No. 197).[21]

## THE ST. JOHN'S DAY PARADE

When the rumors of William Morgan's abduction and murder were first heard in 1826, the Grand Lodge of New York had 480 Lodges on its rolls; by 1835 only 75 remained. The Grand Lodge took a very conservative approach towards bringing attention to Masonry in those days and issued an edict "forbidding all public processions and public displays." In 1836 Atwood's Lodge Lodge, York No. 367, tried to get Grand Lodge permission to openly celebrate St. John's Day, but failed to get an exception to the edict. The next year York Lodge pressed the issue again by calling a meeting of Masons to discuss the propriety of a public celebration of St. John's Day. James Herring, Grand Secretary, cautioned the meeting that the edict was still in full effect, but he was reminded that he himself had violated the edict by having a Masonic banner flown outside the offices of the Grand Lodge. After a raucous debate, York Lodge succeeded in convincing Benevolent, Silentia, and Hibernia Lodges to join in their plans for the celebration.[22]

On June 24, 1837, St. John's Day, several hundred Masons assembled at Warren Hall to celebrate the feast day of one of their patron Saints. Just before the festivities began, James Van Benschoten, Deputy Grand Master, and James Herring appeared and once again warned the participants against defying a Grand Lodge edict. The warnings were ignored, and the Masons showed

---

[21] Voorhis, "Henry Clinton Atwood"; Cusick, "Henry Clinton Atwood."

[22] *Coil's Masonic Encyclopedia*, s.v. "Anti-Masonry"; Folger, "Recollections," part 14, November 9, 1873.

their firm attachment to their ancient, honorable Fraternity. Their brave public display in the face of recent vicious attacks attracted positive interest in the Craft and, many believed, helped restore the health of the Grand Lodge.

> They marched several hours up one street and down another, through the length and breadth of the metropolis, reaching the City Hall Park late in the afternoon, where they marched and countermarched, the music playing sweetly to the amusement and satisfaction of the throng of spectators.... The church where the exercises were held was completely thronged, everything passed off remarkably well, and all were well pleased with the demonstration. The brethren were dismissed, and retired to finish up the whole with a sumptuous dinner, which proved a very pleasant affair.[23]

Even though the parade seemed to leave a positive impression on citizens of New York, the Grand Lodge was unwilling to let such open flaunting of its authority go unpunished. A special meeting of the Grand Lodge was called on July 12 for the purpose of preferring charges against Atwood and his fellow conspirators. Some of the enthusiasm for pursuing this case seems to have stemmed from the longstanding dislike of James Herring for Atwood. Herring strongly objected to Atwood's promotion of the Cross work, referring derisively to its changes as "wooden nutmegs and horn gunflints, imported fresh from Connecticut." Atwood's defiance of the Grand Lodge edict gave Herring an opportunity to discipline someone who had dared question the Masonic status quo.[24]

Atwood and William F. Piatt were charged at the special meeting, but the members would not agree with the Grand Officers on how to prosecute the charges. After a great deal of parliamentary maneuvering and after losing two votes, the Deputy Grand Master declared a resolution against Atwood adopted over strenuous protestations, and the meeting was adjourned. The Grand Steward's Lodge (dominated by Herring and other Grand Officers) expelled Atwood and Piatt on August 26, 1837, and the Grand

---

[23] Folger, "Recollections," part 14 and part 17, December 14, 1873.
[24] Folger, "Recollections," part 4 and part 15, Nov. 23, 1873.

Lodge confirmed their punishment at its quarterly meeting on September 11, 1837. Further, all who marched in the parade were expelled and the charters of the participating Lodges were annulled. It is ironic that, as an economic depression spread through New York State and as antimasons continued their fierce opposition, the Grand Lodge was most concerned with internal conformity.[25]

**ST. JOHN'S GRAND LODGE**

The expulsions of Atwood and the others did nothing to solve the problems of the Grand Lodge of New York but rather exacerbated them. The immediate result was a schism and the establishment of St. John's Grand Lodge. Atwood was not the founder or a Grand Officer, but he became the major force driving the institution–a charismatic opponent to reckon with. Folger described Atwood as "one of the most noisy and disputatious men which that Grand Lodge contained, and withal, when excited, very abusive. He was a man ... obstinate in his prejudices and preconceived opinions, very easily excited, and slowly appeased." Atwood was

> never content unless engaged in some way in the promotion [of Masonry].... Contention and argument were his 'forte,' accompanied with loud and boisterous declamations. On this account he always managed to draw after him the crowd, while his nature was so genial that his followers became strongly bound to him.[26]

York Lodge changed its allegiance to St. John's Grand Lodge, and Atwood served as its Master in 1838 and 1840. Atwood devoted his considerable energy on the new Grand Lodge and vigorously promoted the cause of Masonry as he saw it. From 1841 to 1847 he was Master of Independent Lodge No. 7 (now No. 185), in 1847 and 1848 he was High Priest of Orient Chapter No. 1 (now No. 128), R.A.M., and about this time he was Commander of Palestine Commandery No. 1 (now No. 18), K.T. For ten years, 1838-1848, Atwood served as Deputy Grand Master, and for 1849 and 1850 he was Grand Master. In this capacity he presided at the "Great Union"

[25] Folger, "Recollections," part 15.
[26] Folger, "Recollections," parts 17 & 4.

on December 27, 1850, when St. John's Grand Lodge reunited with the Grand Lodge of the State of New York. This union was eas̪d by the fact that there had been yet another schism in 1849, and James Herring, Atwood's nemesis, had abandoned the Grand Lodge to become Grand Secretary of the new breakaway group. When Atwood returned to the Grand Lodge, he brought with him twenty-five Lodges and 3,000 members, and he was recognized with the full honors of a Past Grand Master.[27]

## THE CERNEAU SUPREME COUNCIL REVIVED

Atwood's triumphant return was not without its dark side. The opponents of St. John's Grand Lodge persecuted its members, with Atwood at the center of their efforts; "he was literally 'hounded down' in his business affairs, until he was reduced to abject poverty, and was, at one time without a place which he could call a home for his family." By 1841 many of the members of St. John's Grand Lodge despaired of their isolation from all other Masonic contact and were ready to return to the regular Grand Lodge on whatever terms might be offered. Atwood would hear nothing of this and kept St. John's going by force of his personality. He started Independent Lodge No. 7 and oversaw ritual instruction for his Grand Lodge, demanding strict uniformity and perfection. In 1842 St. John's reduced the fees for its Degrees to attract candidates.[28]

On October 27, 1846, the Cerneau Supreme Council had divided its funds among its four remaining members and disbanded. Atwood and others from St. John's Grand Lodge stepped into this breach and revived the Supreme Council on May 15, 1849, on the theory that Scottish Rite authority reverted to the 33° Inspectors General with the dissolution of the Supreme Council.

[27] Voorhis, "Henry Clinton Atwood" p. 92.

[28] Supreme Council for the United States, their Territories and Dependencies [Thompson-Folger Cerneau Supreme Council revived], *Official Manifesto*, (New York: Isley & Marx, 1881), p. 15; Samuel H. Baynard, Jr., *History of the Supreme Council, 33°*, (Boston: Supreme Council, 33°, N.M.J., 1938), vol 1, pp. 244-246, 251; Josiah H. Drummond, "Ancient and Accepted Scottish Rite of Freemasonry," in *History of Freemasonry and Concordant Orders*, H. L. Stillson et al., eds., (Boston: Fraternity Publishing Co., 1912), p. 819.

Atwood was elected Grand Commander. Folger later claimed the revival was in 1846, but this could hardly be so as all except Atwood received their 33° *after* the summer of 1848.[29]

The revolt of St. John's Grand Lodge had resulted in its members being shut out of most of the Masonic activities in New York State. Atwood tried to address this by using his position in the revived Cerneau Supreme Council to reward St. John's members with the 33°. He also had the Warrant of the suspended and dissolved Lafayette Chapter of Rose Croix, a Cerneau body. Later comments by Atwood indicate that he apparently believed that any use of the Warrant was justified if it promoted his Grand Lodge.

> The warrant of that body has done us good service, inasmuch as it served its purpose for the document founding and establishing Orient Chapter of Royal Arch Masons and Palestine Encampment of Knights Templar. It was shifted over from one body to the other at every meeting, as occasion required, and was never called in question. It had plenty of large seals in silver cases, it passed off admirably, and no one knew the difference. If any brother made any objections after receiving the degrees of the chapter or encampment, I always threw myself upon my patent as a Sov. Grand Inspector-General, 33°, and last degree, which gave me full power to establish lodges, chapters, councils, and other bodies, at my pleasure.[30]

When the Great Union occurred, Orient Chapter and Palestine Encampment, both created by the "full power" of Atwood's 33° patent, were welcomed into their respective Grand Bodies. Atwood's bitter treatment must have led him to these desperate, autocratic actions which, however, established a later pattern of authoritarian rule.

### THE SUPREME COUNCIL FOR THE NORTHERN HEMISPHERE

After seeing his Grand Lodge restored to legitimacy and himself increased in prestige, Atwood seemed to have set his sights on

---

[29] Folger, "Recollections," part 16, Dec. 7, 1873, part 18, Jan. 4, 1874, and part 30, May 24, 1874.

[30] Folger, "Recollections," part 30.

building up "his" Supreme Council. If he had had as much success with the Scottish Rite as with St. John's Grand Lodge, his influence would have been magnified even more. Further, he would have had the control of honors with which to reward his friends and the power to punish his enemies–especially J. J. J. Gourgas, Grand Commander of the Northern Supreme Council, who had vigorously and regularly denounced the Cerneau Supreme Council for years. Comments by Atwood indicate that this rivalry provided some of the motive for the revival of the Cerneau Supreme Council.

> By all means [the Supreme Council] will be continued, but must undergo a complete and full reorganization. This is rendered the more imperative by a movement which has been set on foot by a few members of our jurisdiction who have called in question my authority, and have gone to Bro. J. J. J. Gourgas.... We cannot stand idly by, and see this intrusion succeed without making some effort to stop it.

Atwood "was really a very difficult man to get along with. Sensitive in the highest degree from the slightest provocation, he would go off like a rocket...." He was "never content unless engaged in some way in the promotion of the cause [of Masonry]...," and the Scottish Rite was now his cause.[31]

In early January 1851, a few weeks after the Great Union, Folger called on Atwood to find out about the Masonic papers of Abraham Jacobs, which had been given to Atwood just before Jacobs' death in 1834. Atwood asked Folger to join him in reviving the Supreme Council, and Folger agreed, taking on the task of locating a new Grand Commander. He wanted to find someone "who had not been mixed up with past troubles, and who would carry a strong influence as a Mason." Jeremy Cross the Masonic lecturer, then a merchant in New York City, was just that person.[32]

Cross received his 33° and joined the Southern Supreme Council on June 24, 1824, but never exercised his authorities nor

---

[31] Folger, "Recollections," part 29, May 10, 1874, and part 4.

[32] Folger, "Recollections," part 30; Samuel Oppenheim, *The Jews and Masonry in the United States* (Bronx, N.Y.: S. Oppenheim, 1910), p. 36.

participated in its activities. Folger convinced him to serve as Grand Commander, but not without some conditions from Cross. Cross had spent his life promoting and propagating the York or American Rite, which consisted of the Symbolic Lodge, Royal Arch Chapter, Royal and Select Council, and Knights Templar Commandery. He insisted on these conditions: 1) the Supreme Council would not charter Symbolic Lodges; 2) only Royal Arch Masons could join the Scottish Rite; and 3) only Knights Templar could advance beyond the 14°. In essence the Scottish Rite would be subservient to the York Rite. Atwood and Folger were willing to agree to anything, at least for a time, to bring to their Supreme Council the respectability of Cross and the authority of his patent. Their blatent cynicism was made clear in later comments by Folger.

> While the propositions made by Bro. Cross seemed to be fatal to the interests of the Sup. Council, on the other hand it was deemed necessary to secure an establishment of the body, knowing well that Bro Cross would not long remain the Commander on account of the infirmities of age.[33]

"... [I]t became the duty of the members [of the Supreme Council] to select from personal friends such persons as ... [probably] would accede to the proposals of forming a new Council in the place of the then local body." To be blunt, Atwood "stacked the deck" to insure approval of the changes demanded by Cross. In April, 1851, a meeting was held of this expanded Supreme Council, consisting of Atwood, Folger, and three others, and they agreed to Cross's conditions. On May 29, 1851, the "Supreme Council for the Northern Hemisphere" was organized with Cross as Grand Commander, Atwood as Grand Master of Ceremonies, and Folger as Grand Treasurer General.[34]

The organizers appointed prominent Masons from around the country as Officers. Their zeal to select influential Masons led them to make at least one appointment without regard for the

---

[33] Baynard, *History*, pp. 253-254; Folger, "Recollections," part 31, May 31, 1874.

[34] Folger, "Recollections," part 31; Enoch T. Carson, "History of Ancient and Accepted Scottish Rite Masonry in the United States," *The History of Freemasonry*, R. F. Gould et al., eds., (New York: John C. Yorston, 1889), Vol. IV, p. 674.

Officer's interest or membership in the Scottish Rite. Nathan B. Haswell, Grand High Priest of Vermont, was listed in their proclamation in the June 20, 1851, *New York Herald* as Grand Keeper of the Forest of Lebanon. On July 14, 1851, Haswell responded to his appointment as follows (emphasis added).

> I received a letter from J. L. Cross, of New York, under date of the 18th of June, last, saying that he has ventured to put my name on the list of officers of a General Consistory of the Gen∴ Grand Council of the 33d Degree of Masonry in New York, without consulting me, and requesting my acceptance of the appointment. At the time of my receiving this letter, which was on the 21st or 22d of June, I deemed it Masonic and proper, *having, myself, never taken those degrees*, to make the necessary inquiries respecting the organization of a body of whose correct and regular standing I had doubts.[35]

On August 16, 1851, Atwood began publishing the *Masonic Sentinel*, a weekly journal with the purpose of advancing the position of the Cross Supreme Council; the belligerent tone of the *Sentinel* reflected the style of its editor. Atwood tried to present the history of the Cerneau Supreme Councils in the most favorable possible light, but his writing demonstrates either his ignorance, his lack of access to records, or his willingness to rewrite history to suit his ends. The *Masonic Sentinel's* life was brief; it ceased publication on February 7, 1852, after only twenty-six issues. Cross's tenure as Grand Commander was also brief, as well as inconsequential. After a serious illness, he resigned on April 29, 1852, and retired to Haverhill, New Hampshire, where he passed away in 1861. Atwood resumed the helm as Acting Grand Commander.[36]

**THE SUPREME COUNCIL FOR THE STATE OF NEW YORK**

Atwood's resumption of control of the Supreme Council was over two more senior officers, William H. Ellis, Minister of State, and Rev. Salem Town, Grand Keeper of Seals, contrary to the

---

[35] William Sewall Gardiner, *A History of the Spurious Supreme Councils in the Northern Jurisdiction of the United States* (Washington: Pearson's Steam Press, 1884), p. 52.

[36] Carson, "History of Ancient and Accepted Scottish Rite Masonry," p. 675.

## The Coadjutors

regulations of the Supreme Council. Ostensibly this was done because both Ellis and Town were from Connecticut and could not tend to the business of the Supreme Council in New York. More likely this was done because Atwood remained the power behind the throne during Cross's short term in office.[37]

On October 28, 1852, six months after Cross's resignation, Atwood reorganized again and created the "Supreme Council for the Sovereign, Free, and Independent State of New York," appointing Robert Folger as Grand Secretary General. He was influenced in this change of territorial control by James Foulhouze, Grand Commander of the "Louisiana State Supreme Council, Scottish Rite." It was Foulhouze's goal to have a Supreme Council in every state in control of both the Higher Degrees and the Scottish Rite Symbolic Degrees, and New York was the first state to sign on to this program.[38]

Radically reorganizing the Supreme Council and ignoring its regulations disturbed some of the members. In fact John Simons, Grand Secretary General of the Cross Supreme Council and later Grand Master of the Grand Lodge of New York, apparently was not consulted at all about either the reorganization or his replacement by Folger. Simons was so outraged that he issued an edict in 1853 as "Acting Grand Commander," condemning Atwood's autocratic actions (emphasis in original).

> Now, therefore, be it known that ... inasmuch as the various other subordinate officers, myself excepted, have *strayed* from the TRUE FOLD to parts unknown, therefore, by virtue of the constitution and regulations of the Order, as herein before set forth, the power and authority devolve on me, and I hereby accept them, and duly notify all Chapters and Councils ... that all bodies of Scottish Masons held in contravention of this, *my edict*, and the authority of the Supreme Grand Council, of which I am the *sole representative*, are irregular, clandestine, and spurious....[39]

---

[37] Gardiner, *A History of the Spurious Supreme Councils*, p. 54.

[38] Carson, "History of Ancient and Accepted Scottish Rite Masonry," p. 675.

[39] "The Spurious Council 33d, New York," *The Freemason's Monthly Magazine*, Vol. XII, No. 8, June 1, 1853, p. 240.

Simons was mollified somehow and withdrew his objections, giving further testimony to Atwood's strength of personality. Later events, though, hint that Simons did not forget his summary replacement.

## SCOTTISH RITE SYMBOLIC LODGES

On December 23, 1852, James Foulhouze was received by the Supreme Council for the State of New York, and he installed Atwood and the other Officers. Under the influence of Foulhouze's theories of Masonic authority, Atwood's activities took a fateful turn. Foulhouze convinced Atwood that the Scottish Rite had the inherent authority to control Symbolic Lodges, and Atwood decided to exert this prerogative for his Supreme Council. This radical change in jurisdiction was surprising, not only because Atwood was a Past Grand Master, but also because it flew in the face of earlier pronouncements by his Supreme Council.[40]

In 1851 the Grand Master of the Grand Lodge of Louisiana was faced with the problem of the Supreme Council of that state chartering Symbolic Lodges. He addressed a circular letter to the other Grand Lodges seeking their advice. His letter produced a presumably authoritative edict from the first Atwood Supreme Council on April 14, 1851, signed by John W. Simons, Lieutenant Grand Commander, Daniel Sickels, Grand Secretary General, and George E. Marshall, Grand Treasurer General. After a lengthy discussion of the facts, the edict reached three conclusions.

> *First.*-That the creation of symbolic Lodges by the Grand Council of La∴ in that State, is unjust and an unwarrantable assumption of power, and a direct interference with the established usages of the Order, and the recognized authority of the regular Grand Lodge.
>
> *Secondly.*-That being constituted under the Scottish Rite, they are not "York or Ancient Craft Masons."
>
> *Thirdly.*-That being constituted in open defiance of the lawful authority of the State, they are illegal and unconstitutional, and

---

[40] Carson, "History of Ancient and Accepted Scottish Rite Masonry," p. 675.

of course cannot be recognized as regular, nor be permitted to communicate with or visit the Grand Lodge or its constituents.[41]

In 1852, when the Supreme Council reorganized according to Cross's dictates, it reaffirmed its earlier position in a public notice in the *New York Herald* on June 20, 1852, (emphasis added).

> This body is formed for the purpose of conferring the ineffable degrees, ... and for that purpose branch councils will be established in the various States comprising the jurisdiction, as fast as applications are made, all of which will be governed in their work by an order issued from this Grand East, *forbidding the initiatory degrees to be conferred at all* .... This Supreme Council and Branches will acknowledge, and, to the extent of their jurisdiction, cause to be respected, the rights of all regularly established organizations in the several branches of the order, as Grand Lodges, G∴ Chapters, and Grand Encampments, with their general heads in this country .... By Order,
>
> JOHN W. SIMONS, G∴ Secretary

In spite of these solemn pronouncements, Atwood reversed the position of his Supreme Council. His motivation was probably power–to have complete control over all of Masonry from 1° to 33°, but he genuinely may have been convinced by Foulhouze that the Scottish Rite had abdicated its responsibility to govern the Craft. In any event Atwood persuaded the Supreme Council to change its position, and on March 8, 1853, the minutes clearly record the chartering of two Symbolic Lodges (underlining in original).

> The Ill∴ Bro∴ Folger then proceeded to lay before the Council the following Petitions for the constituting and establishing Symbolic Lodges of the Ancient Free and Accepted Scottish Rite.
>
> From Bro Robert B. Folger and others for a Lodge of St∴ John by the distinctive title of "<u>John the Fore-runner</u>" and by Number 1 (see document on file) which petition was granted and the Patent ordered to be made out and executed bearing date March 8$^{th}$ 1853 of the Christian Era.
>
> From Bro Deszelus, Roullier, Vatet, Ploquin & others, in all 14, for a Lodge of St. John, the ritual etc. in the French Language,

---

[41] [Henry C. Atwood], "The Supreme Grand Council of the Northern Masonic Jurisdiction," No. 9, *The Masonic Sentinel*, Oct. 11, 1851, pp. 34-36.

by the distinctive title of "La Sincerite" and by number 2 (see documents in French and English on file) which petition was granted and the Patent ordered to be made out and executed, bearing date March 8th 1853 of the Christian Era....
Attest,
Robt. B. Folger, G∴C∴G∴ Secy of the H∴E∴[42]

Twenty-one years later Folger tried to temper the appearance of the actions of his Supreme Council with a revisionist interpretation of the events. "Although the powers [then] assumed, not only over the Ancient Accepted Rite, but over all other Rites, were unlimited, there was a conservative stand taken by the minority [of the Supreme Council], which would always prevent any overt act on the part of the majority...."[43] It is hard to imagine a more overt act than the chartering of Symbolic Lodges, and Masonic authorities of the day seemed to agree.

The response to this usurpation of power from the Grand Lodge was swift. On June 7, 1853, Grand Master Nelson Randall reported in his address to the Grand Lodge of New York that he was "informed that one or more [Lodges], in the Scotch Rite, have been established within the last few months in the city of New York, under the patronage and countenance, or assumed authority of a distinguished Past Grand Master in this Grand [Lodge]...." A special committee was appointed, considered the evidence, and reported back on June 10. They deemed "the fact of the establishment of such Lodges an invasion of the jurisdictional rights of [the Grand Lodge of New York]." The committee concluded that "[a] Grand Lodge has, of undoubted right, supreme control over the Symbolic degrees within its temporal jurisdiction.... This body, therefore, cannot, in self-respect, or in the protection of her undoubted rights of supremacy do less than to resist this invasion of its authority."[44]

---

[42] Minutes of the Cerneau Supreme Council (Second Atwood Council), Mar. 8, 1853, Transcript in the hand of Robert B. Folger, Collection Number SC012, Archives, Supreme Council, A.A.S.R., N.M.J., U.S.A., Lexington, Mass.

[43] "Recollections," Part 34, July 19, 1874.

[44] *Transaction of the Grand Lodge of New York, F.&A.M., from July 8th, A.L. 5852 to June 11th, A.L. 5853* (New York: Robert Macoy, Printer, 1853), pp. 65-66, 237.

## ST. JOHN'S GRAND LODGE REVIVED

While the controversy over Atwood's Scottish Rite Symbolic Lodges was growing, yet another crisis in New York Masonry developed with Atwood and Folger in the lead. On June 9, 1853, Reuben H. Walworth, Chancellor (now Governor) of New York, was elected Grand Master of the Grand Lodge. His election caused an uproar because Atwood and others alleged that during the antimasonic period (ca. 1826–1840) Chancellor Walworth had publicly denounced Masonry; Atwood stated he would not sit in Grand Lodge with Walworth. On June 13 a meeting of Masons opposed to Walworth was held in Tollerton Hall where Robert Folger and others spoke against the election. A committee of three, including Folger, was appointed to consider grievances against the Grand Lodge and reported back on June 20, urging the reestablishment of St. John's Grand Lodge until Chancellor Walworth's term as Grand Master expired. "Whereupon, all present came forward, and pledged themselves to the firm support of the same." St. John's Grand Lodge was revived formally on June 24 when Henry Atwood installed the new Grand Officers.[45]

On August 12, 1853, Deputy Grand Master Joseph D. Evans issued an edict to all New York Lodges. In it he declared St. John's Grand Lodge clandestine and further noted "that the Lodges instituted by Henry C. Atwood, to work in the Scottish Rite, have conferred those degrees upon persons who are not Masons . . . ." Evans forbade all Masonic communication with St. John's Grand Lodge and with Atwood's Scottish Rite Lodges. In Grand Lodge on September 6, 1853, charges of unmasonic conduct were preferred against Folger and others for reactivating St. John's Grand Lodge. Atwood was summoned to appear before the Grand Lodge Officers to explain his actions, but he refused "in very abusive and unbe-

---

[45] Peter Ross, *A Standard History of Freemasonry in the State of New York* (New York: The Lewis Publishing Co., 1899), p. 445; *Statement of Proceedings Relative to Grievances Existing in the Grand Lodge of the State of New York, and the Reasons for Reviving St. John's Grand Lodge* (New York: Charles Shields, 1853), p. 28.

coming language." He was expelled from Masonry on September 27, 1853.[46]

Responding to the charges brought against him, Folger wrote to James M. Austin, Grand Secretary, on September 26, 1853. While Atwood's reply with its "abusive and unbecoming language" has been lost, Folger's reply has not. It indicates the level of the passion these issues generated.

> I assure you Sir that my expulsion from that body will prove ... but very little mortification to me, but rather an honour .... It strikes me that it would have been more proper on the part of the body to which you belong to have selected some member from my own Lodge to have preferred these charges ... but like all other filthy proceedings of that Grand Body, I suppose they were unable to find a man who was acquainted with me, who would so far debase himself, as to brings these charges, based upon falsehood, against me ....[47]

Folger was expelled from Masonry by the Grand Steward's Lodge on September 27, 1853.

**THE GRAND PLAN**

The rebirth of St. John's Grand Lodge seemed to play right into Atwood's grand plan. "It was supposed that on the withdrawal of the Lodges from the Grand Lodge, they would seek the protection of the Supreme Council, and work under its jurisdiction." If this indeed had happened, Atwood would have quickly had an organized power base from which to carry forward his design of building up his Supreme Council. Such a plan of expansion easily fit Atwood's demonstrated character, but it seemed to be too much for some members of his Supreme Council, even though they had just chartered two Symbolic Lodges.

---

[46] Joseph D. Evans, Deputy Grand Master, Edict, Aug. 12, 1853, Archives, Grand Lodge of New York, F.&A.M.; *Transactions of the Grand Lodge of New York, F.&A.M., from August 16th A.L. 5853 to June 10th A.L. 5854* (New York: Robert Macoy, Printer, 1854), pp.10, 18.

[47] Robert B. Folger, New York, to James M. Austin, [Grand Secretary], Sept. 26, 1853, Typescript, Archives, Grand Lodge of New York, F.&A.M.; *Transactions of the Grand Lodge of New York, A.L. 5854*, p.14.

> "The conservative feelings of the Council, however, [were] sufficiently strong to prevent any such step, and the whole matter was referred back to the Lodges, with the expressed wish that they would conclude to remain as individual Lodges, and proceed with Masonic work, or revive for the time being the old St. John's Grand Lodge...."[48]

Atwood's decision to brazenly challenge the authority of the Grand Lodge of New York proved ruinous for him and ultimately led to disaster for his Supreme Council, as the stigma of chartering Symbolic Lodges plagued it for another fifty years until its final demise. Atwood tried to gain power for his Supreme Council by trying to play the various Grand Lodge factions in the state against themselves. He laid out this bold strategy to his mentor and fellow agitator, James Foulhouze of the Supreme Council of Louisiana, in a letter written sometime shortly after St. John's Grand Lodge had been revived. Atwood explained that the "Phillips Grand Lodge," the Past Masters' faction, was trying to split New York State into eastern and western Grand Lodges, and

> [f]ailing in this, they will continue their present organization, charter all the Lodges they can of the York Rite–cheap–offer to us a "Chamber" in their Grand Lodge, giving us the exclusive control of the Scottish Rite & any union after that is done will never be brought about.[49]

Atwood was confident his Supreme Council would survive because both the Phillips Grand Lodge and the Grand Lodge of New York, or Willard Grand Lodge, were courting him, or so he wrote to Foulhouze. Having sustained one grand body, St. John's Grand Lodge, in the face of fierce opposition, Atwood believed he could do it again with his Supreme Council–at least until his goals were achieved. He wanted a Grand Lodge organized along the lines of the Grand Orient of France: his Supreme Council would have official recognition, a legislative chamber, and exclusive control of the Scottish Rite from 1° to 33°. These grandiose plans

---

[48] Folger, "Recollections," part 34.

[49] [Henry C. Atwood] to [James Foulhouze], New Orleans, [ca. July, 1853], Transcript in the hand of Robert B. Folger, Archives, Supreme Council, 33°, N.M.J., U.S.A., Lexington, Mass.

apparently grew from a desire for power or revenge and Atwood's new beliefs of the inherent authority of Supreme Councils (emphasis in the original).

> [W]e are a Supreme Council yet & must either have a chamber in the <u>Grand Lodge proper</u> & be acknowledged or we hold the balance of power now & will shiver them into fragments & ride over the ruins. We do not want a Chamber now, until the <u>Union</u> takes place or else a <u>Break up</u>. If the former, we shall have the Chamber, that is understood, & being still in full communion with the Willard party we labour diligently to bring about the same, but if the latter, viz. a break up, then we have a Chamber, & thus control both Rites and draw with us a large body of the Lodges of their side....
>
> ...But one of two things will take place, 1st there will be a grand Union in which the Scottish Rite will participate, maintaining at the same time all its powers & its prerogatives & thus killing the Gourgas, Moore & Mackey imposition effectually in this country by giving us the acknowledgement & power, or 2d there will be 5 distinct powers in the State of New York, viz. the Willard Power, the Phillips Power, the St. Johns Grand Lodge renewed power, the Pythagoras or Hamburg power, & ourselves as the Scottish Rite. We are prepared for either event, & shall so endeavour to conduct ourselves as to get the best part of the victory if we can.[50]

The idea of establishing Scottish Rite Lodges and extending the authority of the Supreme Council seemed to have been plotted for some time by Folger and Atwood. Folger hinted at some of their plans in a letter to Dr. Barthe of Foulhouze's Louisiana Supreme Council, dated May 26, 1852, nine months before the chartering of John the Forerunner and La Sincérité Lodges.

> All Lodges having intercourse with each other in this country must be York. It is easy to have our Lodges nominally York-secretly Scottish. This gives us the advantage over them. We can

---

[50] [Atwood] to [Foulhouze]. The "Gourgas, Moore & Mackey imposition" refers to the Northern Supreme Council started by J.J.J. Gourgas, Charles W. Moore was its Grand Secretary General from 1844-1862, and Albert G. Mackey was the Grand Secretary General of the Southern Supreme Council which supported Gourgas and Moore. The "Willard Power" is the Grand Lodge of New York, the "Phillips Power" is the Past Masters' Grand Lodge, and the "Pythagoras or Hamburg power" is the German-speaking Pythagoras Lodge illegally chartered by the Grand Lodge of Hamburg.

visit them as York Masonry, while they will be entirely ignorant of our Scottish Rite. This we can easily arrange.[51]

## THE CRUMBLING EMPIRE

If Atwood's separation from the Grand Lodge had been based solely on his complaint against Reuben Walworth, he may have once more emerged from the battle a hero. However the notion of Supreme Council autonomy, if not superiority, was simply too much to be accepted by American Masons. Atwood's empire began crumbling almost as soon as he decreed it.

The Grand Lodge of New York, the "Willard Faction," sent letters to its sister Grand Lodges explaining the situation in New York. The response was almost immediate condemnation of Atwood's Supreme Council. For example in December, 1853, only six months after the chartering of John the Forerunner and La Sincérité Lodges, the Grand Master of Alabama denounced Atwood and his Supreme Council.

> Disobeying and setting at naught the mandates of the Grand Lodge of [New York], Henry C. Atwood has claimed and exercised the same right and power to grant charters to subordinate Lodges in New York to work the Scotch Rite, which the Supreme Council of the 33d degree for the valley of New Orleans does in Louisiana.[52]

Atwood was St. John's Grand Master from June 1854 to June 1855, during which time defections from his cause, both big and small, began to mount. On June 10, 1854, Atwood Lodge No. 208 of the Grand Lodge of New York changed its name to Cyrus Lodge. Five months later on November 30, 1854, Atwood changed the name of his Supreme Council back to "The Supreme Council for the United States of America, their Territories and Dependencies" and resumed its "ancient jurisdiction."[53]

---

[51] [Albert Pike], *Beauties of Cerneauism. No. 1*, [ Washington, D.C.: Supreme Council, 33°, S.J., 188–], p. 4.

[52] *Proceedings of the Grand Lodge of Alabama* (Montgomery, Ala.: Masonic Signet Office, 1853) p. 19.

[53] *Transaction of the Grand Lodge of New York, A.L. 5854*, p. 200; Carson, "History of Ancient and Accepted Scottish Rite Masonry," p. 675.

General Tomás Cipriano de Mosquera, Past Grand Commander of the Supreme Council for and former president of New Grenada (now Colombia), made a grand visit the Supreme Council on April 4, 1853; some time after this Andres Cassard, his private secretary was proposed for the 33°. This met with great opposition from the French members of the Supreme Council, and after two or three hours of debate the proposal was tabled. "... [S]ome months after the proposition had been disposed of by the Supreme Council, a peremptory official order came to [Folger] requiring ... [him] to confer the 33° upon [Cassard] forthwith." Folger tried to dissuade Atwood from thwarting the will of the Supreme Council, but Atwood was adamant. Ever the faithful servant, Folger eventually communicated the 33° to General de Mosquera's private secretary, but this action alienated La Sincérité Lodge which had stopped meeting in early 1854.[54]

The Members of La Sincérité Lodge seemed to have had enough of Atwood's autocratic rule and on February 20, 1855, petitioned the Grand Lodge of New York for a charter. Their letter to the Grand Master says much about their frustrations and Atwood's apparent promises of eventual recognition by regular Masonry.

> When we made an application to the Supreme Council whose rite is so congenial with our manners and habits, it was with the hope that within a short time a fraternal fusion of the two rites would take place, and allow us to become members of the great Masonical [sic] order of the United States.
>
> Without expanding upon the motives which incite us to place ourselves under your authority, we will only mention that long since our expectations such as we cherished them, have never been realised, and after being constituted two whole years, we still remain at the same point from which we started.[55]

No meetings of the Supreme Council are recorded from April 4, 1853 until March 1, 1855, when the members of La Sincérité

---

[54] Folger, "Recollections," part 35., Folger, *A History of the Ancient & Accepted Scottish Rite in the U.S.*, 1877, Typescript, Collection No. SC087, Archives, Supreme Council, 33°, N.M.J., Lexington, Mass, p. 221

[55] La Sincérité No. 2, New York City, to the Grand Master of the Grand Lodge of New York, February 20, 1855, Transcript, Archives, Grand Lodge of New York.

Lodge resigned their positions in the Supreme Council. These were Eugene Vatet, Deputy Grand Commander, and Deszelus, Lt. Grand Commander. Also resigning that day was Edward Unkart, Grand Treasurer and a member of the illegally chartered Pythagoras Lodge, who had resigned under pressure from the Grand Lodge of Hamburg. Unkart seemed to tire of controversy and turned to the Grand Lodge of New York to reestablish Pythagoras Lodge with a legitimate charter. Despite alienating firm supporters, losing La Sincérité Lodge, and having four of his principal Officers resign, Atwood kept stubbornly on his course.[56]

> A complete line of demarcation had been formed between the supporters of Ill. Bro. Atwood, and his opponents, in this controversy, and so far did this feeling extend, that it was not thought proper to continue the meetings of the body until a better feeling on both sides was manifest.... [A]t the next meeting after the resignations were received and acted upon, Ill. Bro. Atwood, as Sov. Grand Commander–filled all the offices of the Supreme Council by appointment, and determined to go forward, notwithstanding the existing bad feeling....
>
> ...[A]mong those who remained [in the Supreme Council] there were not such hearty good feelings manifested toward the interests of the Council as there might have been. The prospect was discouraging, and Bro. Atwood not at all inclined to pacify the discontented by the offer of concessions of any kind. As a natural consequence there was but little interest felt in the meetings and business of the Council was transacted by Bro. Atwood himself.[57]

By 1856 Atwood's health began to fail, "on account of repeated attacks of neuralgic disease, attended with many complications," and he began to look for some place to retire where he could end his days in peace. Still a believer in his absolute power as Sovereign Grand Commander, Atwood appointed Edmund Hays Deputy Grand Commander on November 19, 1857, and on May 14, 1858, named Hays to succeed him upon his death.[58]

---

[56] Drummond, "Ancient and Accepted Scottish Rite," p. 820; Folger, "Recollections," part 35, July 26, 1874; Minutes of the Cerneau Supreme Council, Apr. 4, 1853, and Mar. 1, 1854.

[57] Folger, "Recollections," part 35.

[58] Folger, "Recollections," part 36, Aug. 2, 1874; Drummond, "Ancient and Accepted Scottish Rite," p. 820.

Atwood's preference of Hays and eventual appointment of him as Deputy Grand Commander, was too much for even the faithful Folger, who resigned as Grand Secretary General. Atwood had succeeded in driving away another of his supporters. Folger's great dislike of Hays and his reasons for leaving the Supreme Council were made clear in a letter to Enoch Terry Carson in 1881.

> Hays was an infidel in opinion, but exceedingly ignorant and uncultured, & being the pet of Henry C. Atwood, was named by him as his successor.... Like all uncultured men he was a worshiper of Albert Pike, & never rested until he had completely transferred the Rituals & Degrees into the blasphemous languages & doctrines of that plausible deceiver.
>
> In consequence of their perversion of the Truth I have never been at one of their meetings, or associated with them in their bodies, although I loved the order, & wished it well....[59]

Even though Folger was expelled from the Grand Lodge of New York for "aiding and assisting in the formation and organization of a Body, claiming to be a Grand Lodge...,"[60] it's not entirely clear that he ever joined one of St. John's Lodges. On the heels of his fiery response on September 26, 1853, to the charges of unmasonic conduct, Folger meekly requested restoration of membership on June 2, 1857, which was granted June 6. Unlike the month of March, Folger went out like a lion and came back in like a lamb.

> To the Most Worshipful Grand Lodge
> State of New York
>
> The undersigned would respectfully present the following request.
>
> At a Communication of the Grand Stewards Lodge in 1853 he was expelled by that body for Contempt. The expulsion was confirmed by the Grand Lodge. He asks that the said expulsion may be rescinded and he be restored.

---

[59] Robert B. Folger, New York, to Enoch. T. Carson, [Past Lt. Grand Commander], [Ohio], Nov. 9, 1881, Typescript, Archives, Supreme Council, 33°, N.M.J., U.S.A., Lexington, Mass.

[60] F. G. Tisdall, Charges of unmasonic conduct against Robert B. Folger, [ca. June 1853], Typescript, Archives, Grand Lodge of New York.

The Coadjutors

Being one of the oldest living members of Independent Royal Arch Lodge No. 2 and having served her faithfully for a long series of years, he desires to be placed in a position by which he can constitutionally commute and pay his dues to his Lodge.

He is not now, nor has he been, a member in any other Lodge nor is he in any manner connected with any other subordinate Lodge of any kind.

A warm attachment to the Masonic Institution and the principles which it inculcates has prompted this request.

Respectfully submitted,
Robert B. Folger[61]

## THE FINAL YEARS

Atwood doggedly pressed ahead with Foulhouze's notion of a Supreme Council in every state, even though on November 30, 1854, he had readopted the name "Supreme Council for the United States, their Territories and Dependencies." On March 8, 1858, he conferred the 33° on his nephew, Edward Washington Atwood of Bridgeport, Connecticut, who went on to become Grand Commander of a short-lived and ineffectual Supreme Council for that state. Henry Atwood bought property in Seymour, Connecticut, for his final years and, after selling his business on October 21, 1858, moved back to his home state. He had worked in the New York Custom House under Presidents Jackson and Van Buren. Afterwards he ran for Sheriff of New York County and lost and then served as Surveyor of the Port of New York under President Tyler. In late 1845 he became proprietor of a hotel, the Hermitage Hall on the corner of Allen and Houston streets. In 1855 he is listed in Trow's *New York City Directory* as proprietor of the Keystone Hotel at Division and Christie streets. The scant evidence indicates it was this business he sold before moving to Connecticut.[62]

[61] Robert B. Folger, [New York City], to the Grand Lodge of New York, June 2, 1857, Typescript, Archives, Grand Lodge of New York.

[62] Carson, "History of Ancient and Accepted Scottish Rite Masonry," p. 674; Folger, "Recollections," parts 26 & 37; Voorhis, "Henry Clinton Atwood," p. 95.

On November 1, 1858, the Phillips Grand Lodge and the Grand Lodge of New York rejoined on terms honorable to both parties, but they now had no interest in dealing with either St. John's Grand Lodge or Atwood's Supreme Council. Atwood still sounded optimistic on September 14, 1858, just before he left New York.

> We have not yet made much progress as far as regards the first three degrees of the Scottish Rite, but our preparations are good. We have fourteen Lodges in New York which are under the jurisdiction of the Grand Lodge of St. John, and each of these numbers about a hundred members, of which the greater number wish to receive the first three degrees of Scotticism [sic].[63]

John Simons was Grand Master of New York at this time; when Grand Secretary General of the Cross Supreme Council in 1852 he had been summarily replaced by Atwood. It was now Simons' turn to issue decrees: no treaty of any sort would be made with St. John's Grand Lodge; its members would be subject to balloting, fees, and initiation like any other non-mason; and its Lodges, if they chose to continue, would have to pay the Grand Lodge of New York the normal fees to receive new charters. There was a lining of generosity in these harsh terms–the St. John's Lodges that joined the Grand Lodge of New York had their fees and their members' fees returned to their treasuries. By 1859 St. John's Grand Lodge had been reabsorbed with barely a whimper.[64]

The last hurrah of Atwood as a schismatic Scottish Rite Mason seems to have occurred on April 11, 1859, when he, Hays, and the other officers of his Supreme Council issued a manifesto. He railed against the Grand Lodge of New York and tried to justify the positions taken by his Supreme Council (emphasis in original): "The Grand Lodge of the State of New York Commits a *monstrous error*, and endeavors to USURP POWER, in arrogating to herself the exclusive administration of the *first three degrees*."[65] Compromise or conciliation were foreign to Atwood's personality.

---

[63] Folger, Recollections, Part 39, September 6, 1874; Peter Ross, *A Standard History of Freemasonry in the State of New York* (New York: Lewis Publishing Co., 1899), p. 463.

[64] Ross, *A Standard History*, p. 463.

[65] Gardiner, *A History of the Spurious Supreme Councils*, p. 56.

On Thursday, September 20, 1860, Henry Clinton Atwood was called from labor. His body was returned to New York City where he lay in state in his son Charles' home. On Saturday evening, a meeting was held at the Masonic Temple to pay tribute to Atwood's memory. A committee chaired by John Simons prepared resolutions of respect which were presented to Atwood's family. On Sunday an "immense concourse" attended the religious services and accompanied the body to Greenwood cemetery. Because he was still an expelled Mason, Atwood did not receive a Masonic burial service, but members of his Supreme Council acted as pallbearers and provided a Scottish Rite service.[66]

A memorial published in *The Masonic Messenger* nicely summarized Atwood's turbulent relationship with Masonry.

> "... [H]is whole life has been enthusiastically devoted, right or wrong, to the Institution [of Masonry].... [W]hatever of difficulties may have arisen between our lamented friend and the Craft at large, have been solely on matters of governmental policy; we do assert the esoteric duties of a craftsman were always conscientiously performed, that the call of duty or the cry of distress were ever promptly responded to, and that the arcana of the institution were never committed to more trustworthy hands....
>
> Though of an impulsive nature, and firm in what he deemed to be right, no warmer or more generous friend ever existed.[67]

Nine months later his friends in the Grand Lodge of New York, with whom he had feuded for so many years, set about to ensure that history knew they forgave their errant Brother. On June 6, 1861, the Grand Lodge paid its final tribute to Atwood.

> *Resolved*, that, as far as within the power of this Grand Lodge so to do, the memory of HENRY C. ATWOOD be, and is hereby relieved from censure, and his name be restored to our roll as one of the Past Grand Masters of this Grand Lodge.[68]

---

[66] "The Late Henry C. Atwood," *The Masonic Messenger*, Vol. V, No. 12, Sept. 15, 1860, pp. 110-111; Voorhis, "Henry Clinton Atwood," p. 94.

[67] "The Late Henry C. Atwood."

[68] *Transactions of the Grand Lodge of New York, F. & A.M., at its Annual Communication Commencing June 4, A.L. 5861* (New York: T. Holman, Printer, 1861), p. 171

# THE BIOGRAPHY
# OF A REMARKABLE MASON

*May you live in interesting times.*

Ancient Chinese Curse

IT IS INTERESTING TO SEE WHO IS REMEMBERED BY HISTORY, who is forgotten, and who is vilified. Among those who have figured prominently in American Masonry, George Washington has been remembered (and deified), Joseph Cerneau has been vilified, and Robert Folger has been forgotten. Anything Washington did has taken on mythical proportions, and his every involvement with the Craft has been carefully preserved. Cerneau unwittingly lent his name to a movement that almost fractured the harmony of American Freemasonry, and he is now an exemplar of unmasonic cupidity and ambition. Folger's effect on American Masonry was negative. He has earned well-deserved condemnation for reestablishing the Cerneau Supreme Council in 1881 and for the years of turmoil that action produced, but to be completely forgotten seems too harsh a punishment. He was a complex man and dedicated Mason; his life is an interesting study in the sometimes consuming passions of Freemasonry.

Folger lived during times that can be best described as very "interesting." He experienced the antimasonic movement first hand, witnessed at least six different Grand Lodges for the state of New York, lived through the Civil War, and saw more than a dozen Supreme Councils of the Scottish Rite. Through all of this he was seldom an idle bystander, but was actively involved in many of the controversies. He is today viewed as a schismatic, a troublemaker, and one of the most ardent proponents of Cerneauism ever seen. While his Masonic career is perhaps as checkered as the ground floor of King Solomon's Temple, one cannot study his life without feeling that he was indeed a remarkable Freemason.

The Biography

## EARLY LIFE

Robert Benjamin Folger was born on December 16, 1803, in Hudson, New York, a city in Columbia County that had been settled earlier by Quakers. His education began in the Quaker schools and then was continued at a boarding school in Lenox, Massachusetts, some thirty-five miles from Hudson. He returned to Hudson with the intention of completing his preparatory education, but was unable to enter college and moved to New York City in 1817.[1]

After a year in New York, he decided to become a physician and was apprenticed in a wholesale drug store. His apprenticeship lasted a year, following which he took the position of a druggist in an apothecary and entered the College of Physicians and Surgeons (later with Columbia University) in 1821. He graduated from medical school, probably in 1824, with the M.D. degree and is listed in the 1825 *New York Directory* as a physician living at 39 Harrison Street.[2]

**LIGHT IN MASONRY**

In 1824 he was initiated in Fireman's Lodge No. 368 (which later became New York Lodge) at the Old City Hotel in Broadway; this Lodge was a daughter of Independent Royal Arch Lodge No. 2. On February 10, 1826, he was raised to the Sublime Degree of Master Mason, and then began a period of extensive Masonic labors. According to Folger, the Lodges meeting in the Old City Hotel had a "rule in those days for every member to come 'in full dress,' ... the ordinary gentleman's dress for dinner, or an evening party. (Black was the rule, with white vests and gloves, etc.)" Refreshments were just as important then as any Lodge ceremony, and members were assessed from $8 to $10 per year for the food. After the first hour or so of a typical meeting, a Lodge would "call off" from about 9:00 to 9:30 to enjoy a half hour of light refreshments: "cold boiled ham, tongue, bread,

---

[1] *Proceedings of the Supreme Council, 33°, for the U.S.A., their Territories and Dependencies* [Thompson-Folger revived Cerneau Supreme Council] (New York: Masonic Publishing Co., 1892), p. 65.

[2] *Proceedings*, p. 65; *Columbia University Alumni Register: 1754–1931* (New York: Columbia University Press, 1932), p. 285.

cheese, wines, liquors, etc." After another hour or so of work, Lodges would close and prepare for supper, which was provided by the hotel for $14 per night, with "the Lodge furnishing its own liquors, cigars, etc." "The supper was always plain and substantial, but varied according to the season," and would be completed by midnight.[3]

New York was quite a cosmopolitan town and offered a great variety of Masonic experiences; Folger indulged in many of these. Though not speaking French, he visited L'Union Français Lodge, which also met in the Old City Hotel, and there witnessed their lengthy initiations in which "[t]he nature of Fire, Air, Earth, and Water were fully demonstrated and developed." (This would imply by today's ritual practices that L'Union Français worked French Modern or Scottish Rite rituals.) Folger also attended their elaborate, quarterly Table Lodges. He did speak German and regularly visited German Union Lodge, especially during the antimasonic period, as it seemed unaffected by the excitement.[4]

**MORE LIGHT IN MASONRY**

Folger's thirst for more Masonic activity seemed unquenchable. On May 25, 1826, three months after becoming a Master Mason, he became a Royal Arch Mason in Jerusalem Chapter No. 8, R.A.M. Dr. Hans B. Gram presided at his exaltation, and "the acquaintance there formed soon ripened into very close intimacy. . . ." Later he joined Columbia Council No. 1, R.&S.M., with the noted Masonic lecturers James Cushman and John Barker officiating. On June 23, he was made a Red Cross Knight at a joint ceremony of Columbian Encampment No. 1 and Morton No. 4, and on June 30 he was created a Knight Templar by James Herring and joined Morton No. 4. Folger joined the first class organized by Henry C. Atwood to teach the "Cross work" (Masonic Ritual as organized and taught by Jeremy L. Cross). There were twenty Masons in this class, which met from 2:00 to 6:00 P.M.

[3] "Return of New York Lodge No. 368, from December 27, 1825, to December 27, 1826," Manuscript, Archives, Grand Lodge Of New York, F.&A.M.; Robert Folger, "Recollections of a Masonic Veteran," *New York Dispatch*, Part 1, Apr. 20, 1873.

[4] Folger, "Recollections," Part 3, May 18, 1873, and Part 8, Aug. 17, 1873.

twice a week. On August 23, three months after becoming a Royal Arch Mason, Folger resigned from Jerusalem Chapter to help form Temple Chapter, which later closed during the antimasonic period. Its members (including Folger, presumably) consolidated with Ancient Chapter No. 1, which also closed for the same reason.[5]

**FURTHER LIGHT IN MASONRY**

The event to have the most lasting impact on Folger's Masonic career came in the winter of 1826, at the end of a busy Masonic year for him. Folger, Atwood, and the Cross class were initiated through the 32° of the Scottish Rite by Abraham Jacobs for an unreported fee. Trenton, New Jersey, was the site because Jacobs had agreed to stop selling the degrees within forty miles of New York City. "The members of the class were well-satisfied," but they had been misled—Jacobs' patent gave him no authority to confer the degrees! Nonetheless, Folger and Atwood returned to New York content that they were 32° Scottish Rite Masons and joined Lafayette Chapter of Rose Croix, operating under the Cerneau Sovereign Grand Consistory.[6]

Abraham Jacobs moved from New York to Georgia to New York and supplemented his income selling Masonic degrees. While he was willing to stretch his Masonic prerogatives, he did appear scrupulous in requiring his newly elevated Brothers to obtain charters from proper Masonic authorities. Though Folger and Atwood received their degrees in all good faith, their honorable intentions did not save them or the Craft from later controversy and dissension.

It is ironic that some sixty years after receiving the Scottish Rite degrees Folger, at the cost of questioning the regularity of his Scottish Rite Degrees, expressed the utmost contempt for Jacobs and his activities. Jacobs had thrown in his lot with the Bideaud Supreme Council,

[5] Folger, "Recollections," Part 11, Sept. 28, 1873; Robert B. Folger, *A History of the Ancient and Accepted Scottish Rite in the United States*, 1877, Typescript, Collection No. SC087, Archives, Supreme Council, 33°, N.M.J., Lexington, Mass.; Peter Ross, *A Standard History of Freemasonry in the State of New York* (New York: Lewis Publishing Co., 1899), p. 805; "Recollections," Part 4, June 1, 1873; *Proceedings*, p. 65.

[6] Folger, "Recollections," part 6, June 29, 1873; *Proceedings*, p. 65; Robert B. Folger, *The Ancient and Accepted Scottish Rite*, 2nd ed. (New York: by the Author, 1881), Appendix, p. 69.

and Folger, ever the faithful defender of Cerneauism, could not allow even a shadow of respectability for anyone who had opposed his beloved movement.

> Jacobs was a Jew peddler of the degrees of the Ancient Accepted Rite, up to the year of his death, 1840. He was not connected with any legitimate body of that Rite, but was arrayed against them all, by being a peddler and selling the degrees for what he could get from any one who would take them. He had no Masonic standing here whatever, and the introduction of his name in connection with the Ancient Accepted Rite in a favorable manner displays . . . ignorance and folly.[7]

In 1824 James Cushman, a well-known American Masonic itinerant lecturer, was made a 33° Inspector General Honorary. From this distance in time it cannot be known if he fully understood the limitations of being an *honorary* member of the Supreme Council. In any event, whether through ignorance or opportunism, Cushman assumed the prerogatives of an active Inspector General and on November 9, 1827, elevated Henry C. Atwood, his friend and a fellow student of Jeremy L. Cross, to the 33°. Atwood in turn conferred the 33° upon Folger sometime later that year. Folger's reception of all the Scottish Rite degrees, from 4° to 33°, was irregular and illegitimate. When he was eighty-one, it was claimed he was a member of the Supreme Council for the Western Hemisphere during Elias Hicks's term as Grand Commander (ca. 1832–1846). Baynard found no connection of Folger with any Supreme Council prior to 1851, and Folger, in testimony in 1889, only claimed active membership from 1850.[8]

## MEDICINE AND MASONRY FROM DENMARK

Folger's friendship with Hans B. Gram had a great effect on his medical and Masonic career. Gram is known as the Father of Ameri-

---

[7] Robert B. Folger, "Reply to John D. Caldwell," in *Rites and Supreme Councils* (Cincinnati: Masonic Review, Oct. 1885), p. 68

[8] Edmund B. Hays, "Hays Register," Archives, Supreme Council, 33°, N.M.J., Lexington, Mass., Folger, "Recollections," part 7, July 20, 1873; "Pen Pictures of the Active Members of the Ancient Council, A∴ & A∴S∴Rite," *Masonic Chronicle*, Vol. VI, No. 10, Sept. 1884, p. 147; Samuel H. Baynard, Jr., *History of the Supreme Council, 33°*, 2 vols. (Boston: Supreme Council, 33°, N.M.J., 1938), p. 103; "Scottish Rite Testimony," *Masonic Chronicle*, Vol. XV, No. 7, June 1893, p. 199.

can homeopathy, and shortly after exalting Folger in Jerusalem Chapter, Gram introduced this then new theory of medicine to him. Folger originally dismissed homeopathy, but in August 1826, Gram successfully treated several patients that Folger had deemed incurable. At this point Folger became Gram's student and assistant in order to learn homeopathy.[9]

While living in Copenhagen, Gram had joined Zerubbabel of the North Star Lodge, which worked the rituals of the Rectified Scottish Rite or R.E.R. In addition to teaching Folger the theories of Homeopathy, Gram must have taught him the workings of the R.E.R. through at least the Fourth Degree, Scottish Master. In September, 1826, Folger introduced Dr. Gram to his friend Ferdinand L. Wilsey, Master of Minerva Lodge. "Dr. Folger having received from Dr. Gram some important information in Masonry, desired that his friend should also receive the benefit of it." This "important information in Masonry" was initiation through at least the Fourth Degree of the Rectified Scottish Rite. Gram, Folger, and Wilsey then made plans to start a Lodge in New York working the R.E.R. rituals.[10]

**THE CIPHER MANUSCRIPTS**

Folger took on the task of preserving the R.E.R. ceremonies. He created a remarkably secure cipher in which he wrote the rituals in at least two blank books. The *Macoy Book*, owned today by the Macoy Publishing and Masonic Supply Co., Inc., of Richmond, Virginia, was dated July 12, 1827, and copied from the *Supreme Council Book*, formerly in the possession of the Supreme Council, 33°, S.J. but now lost. The close involvement of Folger, Gram, and Wilsey in the project is shown on the dedication or bequest page. (Underlining in original.)

> It is my earnest prayer that this book, if it be found among my earthly remains after my decease may be handed over to my

---

[9] William Harvey King, *History of Homeopathy*, 2 Vols. (New York: Lewis Publishing Co., 1905), Vol I, p. 62.

[10] Jørgen Vagn Jørgensen, Præses, Den Danske Frimurerorden Informationsdirektoriet, Copenhagen, To S. Brent Morris, Columbia, Md., Nov. 8, 1990, Typescript, In the possession of the Author; Henry M. Smith, "Homeopathic Directory: New York Historical Sketch," *The New England Medical Gazette*, Vol. VI, No. 2, Feb. 1871, pp. 91–94.

dearly beloved Friend and Brother Dr. Hans B. Gram to whom I bequeath it with my thanks for the constant and untired kindness which he has shewed me from the first hour of my acquaintance with him to the present.... If he is not in America at the time of my dissolution—it may be given to Mr. Ferdinand L. Wilsey who will know what it contains and also how to preserve the substance in his mind while he commits the manuscript to the <u>flames</u>.[11]

On June 8, 1827, nine months after Wilsey received the benefit of Gram's important information in Masonry and a month before the *Macoy Book* was dated, a charter was granted to Zorobabel Lodge No. 498 in New York City. Hans B. Gram was the Master; Robert B. Folger, Senior Warden; and Lewis Saynisch, Junior Warden. The Lodge most likely was named to honor Gram's mother Lodge in Copenhagen and must have worked the Rectified Scottish rituals transcribed by Folger. Zorobabel Lodge closed shortly after opening, probably due to the antimasonic fever sweeping New York.

In January 1828, Folger moved to North Carolina for his health, and made plans for Gram to join him in the fall in Charlotte to establish a joint practice. Business reverses prevented Gram from coming south and starting a partnership with Folger. Folger became involved in mining and seemed to abandon the practice of medicine. He did not return to New York City until 1835.[12]

## RETURN TO NEW YORK

A brief biography of Folger was published during his lifetime in the article, "Homeopathic Directory: New York Historical Sketch," by Henry M. Smith, M.D., in *The New England Medical Gazette*, Vol. VI, No. 2, February 1871. Smith stated that "[f]rom conversations with Drs. Wilsey, . . . , Folger, . . . and others, I have obtained many of the facts herein mentioned." According to Smith, Folger "returned to this city in 1835, was for some time connected with a patent medicine, subsequently retired from the practice of his profession, and gave his

---

[11] Robert B. Folger, "Cipher Manuscript [*The Macoy Book*]," July 12, 1827, Transcript in the hand of R. B. Folger, Archives, Macoy Publishing and Masonic Supply Co., Richmond, Va.

[12] Smith, "New York Historical Sketch."

The Biography

attention to mercantile pursuits." William Gardner's *Historical Reminiscences of Morton Commandery No. 4*, however, indicates that Folger returned earlier, as it showed he served as Captain General in 1833. There were no entries for Folger in any New York City directories from 1830–1838. Apparently in 1871, at sixty-eight, Folger's memory had him returning to New York two years before he actually moved.

It is not known if Folger joined or visited any Masonic Lodges while in North Carolina, but he wasted no time in becoming active upon his return to New York City. He was Captain General of Morton No. 4 in 1833. In 1835, New York Lodge No. 368 surrendered its charter, and Folger affiliated with Independent Royal Arch Lodge No. 2 on November 9, 1835, where his advancement was rather rapid. He was Junior Warden in 1836, Senior Warden in 1837, and Master in 1838, 1839, and 1840. In 1838 while serving his first term as Master of I.R.A. No. 2 he was Commander of Morton No. 4. In 1840 he is recorded as attending Grand Lodge twice: on September 2 when he served as Junior Grand Warden and on December 2 when he served as Grand Standard Bearer, both times with William Willis, Deputy Grand Master, sitting as Grand Master.[13]

**THE DUTCHER AFFAIR**

On February 3, 1841, Folger assumed the East at the Shakespeare Hotel for Benjamin C. Dutcher, Master of I.R.A. No. 2, and held an extra meeting under a dispensation from Deputy Grand Master William Willis, also a member of No. 2. A Mr. Page was initiated that evening. During the course of the meeting Folger permitted some "informality" in the proceedings.

Willis visited I.R.A. No. 2 on February 8, 1841, discovered there was no record of the extra meeting, and pointed out Folger's errors. Folger stated that he had the minutes of the meeting, attempted to justify his actions (whatever they were), and held that he would repeat the act under similar circumstances. Willis then apparently

---

[13] Gardner, *Historical Reminiscences of Morton Commandery No. 4*, p. 24; William J. Duncan, *History of Independent Royal Arch Lodge No. 2, F. & A.M.* (New York: Charles S. Bloom, 1904), p.268.

## The Biography

bullied the Lodge into unanimously disapproving the proceedings of the earlier meting. We may infer Folger's actions from the resolution offered by Richard Pennell:

> Resolved, That this Lodge consider it improper to bring any Candidate to light until he has taken the usual obligations, and invoked the penalties attached thereto.[14]

### SUSPENDED FROM MASONRY

Folger later made a statement to the Grand Lodge, and the affair was referred to a special committee. He asked to speak before the committee with counsel and was denied. The committee then summoned him to appear before them. Folger responded with a letter which was deemed improper to be read, and it was destroyed by the Grand Secretary. On June 4 Folger was suspended until he acknowledged his error. He answered that afternoon with a letter that was held unsatisfactory as it did "not contain an acknowledgment of his error in unequivocal language, nor a satisfactory apology for the indignity offered the Grand Lodge...."[15]

Folger withdrew from Masonry on June 28, 1841, apparently in response to his suspension, though on September 6 and 8 he presided at extra meetings of No. 2. Three weeks later, on September 27, he applied as an adjoining member, and on November 8 his application was rejected by the Lodge. The episode ended on December 13 for Folger when the Master, by authority of Deputy Grand Master Willis, declared Folger a member and ruled his withdrawal invalid because of some technicality. (It is worth adding that during the course of this dispute, Dutcher withdrew from the Lodge, took the Charter to his house, and made arrangements for it to be buried with him!)[16]

---

[14] Duncan, p. 126.

[15] Charles T. McClenachan, *History of Free and Accepted Masons in New York*, 4 vols. (New York: Masonic Publishing Co., 1892), Vol. III, pp. 58–60, *Transactions of the Grand Lodge of New York, F. & A.M.*, 1841, pp. 44–45.

[16] [Wendall K. Walker, Librarian, Grand Lodge of New York, F. & A.M.], to the Grand Secretary, [Charles H. Johnson], Sept. 1, 1937, Typescript, "Memorandum, Subject: Robert B. Folger," Archives, Grand Lodge of New York, F. & A.M.

Folger had the last word thirty-three years later when he alluded to his case before the Grand lodge and and had the opportunity to describe Willis for his readers:

> All [of Willis's] education was of a business kind. Being of limited intellect, as a natural consequence, he was a very superficial man. All that he knew about Masonry was what he had heard and witnessed; research and study were matters that never entered his mind.... He never felt his own incompetence more than when, in the absence of the M.W. Grand Master, he occupied his chair, and he verily believed his decisions, while there, partook more of the fiat of a monarch than the expression of the opinion of a simple member of the fraternity.
>
> We cite only one instance among many equally striking. A brother who was under accusation, and who demanded an open trial by his peers, with counsel to conduct his case, in preference to going before the Grand Stewards' Lodge, made a motion to that effect before the Grand Lodge. At first, his application was bluntly rejected by him as being out of order and unmasonic, but finding that a majority of the body were largely in its favor, he stated, 'that he was entirely and utterly opposed to the proposed course, because he believed it not only contrary to the constitution by which we were governed, but also contrary to the whole spirit of Masonry—still, as he had a great respect for his constituents, he would in the face of his own convictions, put the motion.' Strange to say, the vote appeared as unanimous in favor of an open trial, which to him was more than a common disappointment.[17]

## MASONIC, MEDICAL, AND MERCANTILE PURSUITS

A circular in 1843 listed Folger as a member of a committee to form a Freemasons' Hall and Asylum Fund. In 1844 he was again Master of No. 2. He served briefly as Secretary of No. 2 and Trustee of the Asylum Fund in 1845, resigning from each on April 28, 1845. He and Ferdinand Wilsey served together as officers of Morton No. 4 in 1845, Wilsey as Generalissimo and Folger as Captain General; Folger repeated this office in 1846. He tried to start another Lodge in 1847, but for reasons unknown it never was instituted, as the *Proceedings* for 1847 indicate. "The Warrant granted to W. Brother Folger and others,

[17] Folger, "Recollections," part 20, Jan. 25, 1874.

under the name of 'Andrew in the East,' has not been taken up; it is now for the Grand Lodge to say if it should be given, if applied for; no fee has been paid." At a special meeting of Grand Lodge on April 28, 1851, to dedicate the Masonic hall at the corner of Broome and Crosby Streets, Folger participated as Grand Marshal.[18]

Dr. Smith's biography of Folger said he "returned to [New York] city in 1835, was for some time connected with a patent medicine, subsequently retired from the practice of his profession, and gave his attention to mercantile pursuits." Folger's later mercantile pursuits are unknown, but an advertising booklet was published in 1845 entitled *Folger's Hygeiangelos*, which described "Dr. Folger's Olosaonian or All-Healing Balsam." The medicine was claimed to be an effective remedy for consumption, dyspeptic consumption, and asthma, with as little as half a bottle effecting a cure; the testimonials were effusive in their praise. Folger's advertising did not claim any homeopathic origin for his miraculous elixir, but his training with Dr. Gram must have influenced the recipe.[19]

Though Smith's biography said Folger retired from medicine after returning to New York, various city directories showed otherwise. New York City directories from 1839–1860 and Brooklyn directories from 1860–1867 have Folger listed as a physician, usually with separate addresses for his home and for his practice. It is hard to reconcile Dr. Smith's biography, written in consultation with Folger, with the record of the city directories. Perhaps Folger continued to call himself a "physician" for either professional or social prestige but pursued some medically related business? He did serve in the New York Assembly in 1849, representing the thirteenth ward of the eleventh district of New York County, so any professional or social prestige could have had political value.[20]

[18] [Walker] to [Johnson].

[19] Smith, "New York Historical Sketch"; Robert B. Folger, *Folger's Hygeiangelos* [Advertising Booklet] (New York: N.p., 1845), passim.

[20] *The New York Red Book* (Albany: J. B. Lyon, Publisher,1895), p. 408.

The Biography

**THE REVIVAL OF THE SUPREME COUNCIL**

Up to 1850 Folger's Masonic activities had been entirely local. His only involvement with the Grand Lodge of New York had been to challenge its authority, though he was unwilling to go so far as to join with the schismatic St. John's Grand Lodge (1837–1850). After the "Great Union" of the two Grand Lodges in December 1850, Folger sought out his old Masonic friend, Henry C. Atwood.

> We had commenced, in a measure, our Masonic life under his tuition, we had worked together for years, the separation which took place in 1837 had estranged us from each other as Masons for thirteen years, and we now felt a strong desire to have a familiar interview with him, in order to talk over the past.[21]

At their reunion in January 1851, Atwood and Folger discussed their Supreme Council and its future. For largely personal reasons Atwood was insistent the Supreme Council be restored to health with him again in power. (See Chapter 3.) Atwood was hampered by being widely recognized as the force behind the schismatic St. John's Grand Lodge, recently reunited with the regular Grand Lodge. He had served as St. John's Grand Master during its last two years. Folger agreed to help locate a new Grand Commander "who had not been mixed up with past troubles, and who would carry a strong influence as a Mason." Jeremy Cross, the Masonic lecturer, then a merchant in New York City, was just that person.[22]

Cross agreed to help revive the Supreme Council, but insisted on these conditions: 1) the Supreme Council would not charter Symbolic Lodges; 2) only Royal Arch Masons could join the Scottish Rite; and 3) only Knights Templar could advance beyond the 14°. Atwood and Folger agreed to this subservience of the Scottish Rite to the York Rite, in order to use the reputation of Cross to revive their Supreme Council. Their ready agreement, however, was carefully calculated to advance their cause and was not intended to be permanent, as revealed by later comments of Folger:

[21] Folger, "Recollections," part 30, May 24, 1874.
[22] Folger, "Recollections," part 30.

While the propositions made by Bro. Cross seemed to be fatal to the interests of the Sup. Council, on the other hand it was deemed necessary to secure an establishment of the body, knowing well that Bro. Cross would not long remain the Commander on account of the infirmities of age.[23]

The Supreme Council for the Northern Hemisphere was organized on May 29, 1851, with Cross as Grand Commander, Atwood as Grand Master of Ceremonies, and Folger as Grand Treasurer General. Cross served briefly and resigned in April 1852 because of his health. In October 1852 Atwood resumed the Grand Commandership and reorganized the Supreme Council again, now restricting its jurisdiction to the State of New York. He appointed Folger as Grand Secretary General.

**SCOTTISH RITE SYMBOLIC LODGES**

In 1853 Atwood made the fateful decision to have his Supreme Council charter Symbolic Lodges, which is the exclusive right of Grand Lodges, and Folger agreed to serve as Master of one of them. The Cerneau Supreme Council's decision plagued it for another fifty years until its final demise. Atwood's motivation was probably power—to have complete control over all of Masonry from 1° to 33°. Folger's motivation is more difficult to understand. He could have been a faithful officer doing everything to support the Grand Commander, regardless of whether he agreed with him. He may have wanted to finally use Gram's R.E.R. rituals, believing them to be for the *Ancient and Accepted* Scottish Rite, not the *Rectified* Scottish Rite. The minutes for March 8, 1853, confirm the deed:

> From Bro. Robert B. Folger and others for a Lodge of St∴ John by the Distinctive title of 'John the Fore-runner' and by Number 1 (See document on file) which petition was granted and the Patent ordered to be made and executed bearing date March 8$^{th}$ 1853 of the Christian Era.

The other officers were Charles W. Willets, Senior Warden, and George L. Osborne, Junior Warden.[24]

[23] Folger, "Recollections," part 31, May 31, 1874.

In 1874, over twenty years after the event, Folger revealed his thoughts on the Lodge and gave a clue that it intended to use Gram's R.E.R. rituals (emphasis added):

> The petition [to charter John the Fore-runner Lodge] is believed to have been the first effort made in this country to establish the French system in the English language. *And for this purpose a very beautiful and minute translation of the French ritual into the English, together with the consecration, the installation, and the table rituals and ceremonials, with abundant and minute directions, had been procured,* and everything was in readiness to go forward. But at this juncture there was some misgivings on the part of the founders—although the ritual was entirely and essentially different from the York Rite—so much so that it could not be taken for Masonry, as practiced at the present day; yet there were certain things about it which led to the determination, on the part of the founders, to abandon the project altogether—and it proved to be a wise course. The lodge was never constituted, and *the rituals, etc., are now in our possession.*[25]

Whatever Folger's motivation, the Grand Lodge of New York reacted forcefully. A committee was appointed on June 7, 1853, to investigate the matter; it reported back on June 10. They deemed "the fact of the establishment of such Lodges an invasion of the jurisdictional rights of [the Grand Lodge of New York]." Folger, Atwood, and their Supreme Council were on a collision course with the Grand Lodge of New York.[26]

**FURTHER CONTROVERSY**

While the controversy over the Scottish Rite Symbolic Lodges was growing, yet another crisis in New York Masonry developed with Atwood and Folger in the lead. On June 9, 1853, Reuben H. Walworth, Chancellor (Governor) of New York, was elected Grand Mas-

---

[24] Minutes, Supreme Council in and for the Sovereign and Independent State of New York [Second Atwood Supreme Council, Cerneau], Mar. 8, 1853, Transcript in the hand of R. B. Folger, Collection No. SC012, Archives, Supreme Council, 33°, N.M.J., Lexington, Mass.;Folger, *A History*, 1877, p. 219.

[25] Folger, "Recollections," Part 34, July 19,1874.

[26] *Transactions of the Grand Lodge of New York, F. & A. M., from July 8$^{th}$, A.L.5852 to June 11$^{th}$, A.L. 5853* (New York: Robert Macoy, Printer, 1853), pp. 65-66.

ter of the Grand Lodge. His election caused an uproar because Atwood and others alleged that during the antimasonic period (ca. 1826–1840) Chancellor Walworth had publicly denounced Masonry. Atwood stated he would not sit in Grand Lodge with Walworth. On June 13 a meeting of Masons opposed to Walworth was held in Tollerton Hall where Robert Folger and others spoke against the election. A committee of three, including Folger, was appointed to consider grievances against the Grand Lodge and reported back on June 20, urging the reestablishment of St. John's Grand Lodge until Chancellor Walworth's term as Grand Master expired. "Whereupon, all present came forward, and pledged themselves to the firm support of the same." St. John's Grand Lodge was revived formally on June 24, 1853, when Henry Atwood installed the new Grand Officers.[27]

**SUSPENDED AGAIN FROM MASONRY**

Fitz Gerald Tisdall, a Past Master of St. John's Lodge No. 1, preferred charges against Folger for his activity with the revived St. John's Grand Lodge. The Scottish Rite Symbolic Lodges must have become a non-issue, as they were not mentioned in the charges against Folger.

> **Charge 1st.** Unmasonic Conduct . . . For aiding and assisting in the formation and organization of a Body, claiming to be a Grand Lodge . . . .
>
> **Charge 2nd.** For exciting by inflammatory appeals a spirit of revolt against the Grand Lodge and its Officers, amongst a portion of the fraternity of the City and State.[28]

Folger answered these charges with a strongly worded letter, no doubt similar to his 1841 letter to the Grand Lodge, which had been deemed "improper to be read" (underlining in original):

---

[27] Peter Ross, *A Standard History of Freemasonry in the State of New York* (New York: The Lewis Publishing Co., 1899), p. 445; *Statement of Proceedings Relative to Grievances Existing in the Grand Lodge of the State of New York, and the Reasons for Reviving St. John's Grand Lodge* (New York: Charles Shields, 1853), p. 28.

[28] F. G. Tisdall, New York, to the Grand Lodge of New York, F. & A. M., [1853], Typescript, Archives, Grand Lodge of New York, F.&A. M.

> It strikes me that it would have been more proper on the part of the body to which you belong to have selected some member of my own Lodge to have preferred these charges, or any others, against me.... But like all other filthy proceedings of that Grand Body, I suppose they were unable to find a man who was acquainted with me, who would so far debase himself, as to bring these charges, based upon falsehood, against me, & so they used the most fitting tool they had at hand—I will not sully this paper by mentioning his name....
>
> The 'aiding & assisting in the formation & organization of a Grand Lodge' in accordance with the spirit of the institution, was not an invasion of the rights of the body now styled by yourself & others 'The Most Worshipful Grand Lodge'—For if the malappropriation of the monies in its treasury was not sufficient cause to deprive it of its name & power, the election of Reuben H. Walworth to the office of Grand Master was so humiliating to the friends & advocated of the true principles of Masonry, that it gave rise to a feeling of utter contempt toward those who participated in the deed....
>
> I demand of you & the body which you represent, that if my Expulsion is published this answer (of which I have an attested copy) together with the whole proceedings, be published—in full—
>
> And further—hereby notify you & through you, the body which you represent, that any publication of my name with a view to injure my character or reputation
>
> Or in any way so that the full proceedings are not published & made known—Will be met on my part with all the redress which the Law gives me—
>
> Besides which, if you do not publish the full proceedings I will publish them for you & take excellent care that they have an honest circulation.
>
> Respectfully,
> Robt. B. Folger[29]

He was suspended on September 27, 1853, by the Grand Lodge of New York for refusing to appear at Grand Lodge and for an unmasonic communication. It is not known if the root cause was organizing a schismatic Grand Lodge, chairing a clandestine Lodge, or perhaps

---

[29] Robert B. Folger, 27 Suffolk St., to James M. Austin, [Grand Secretary], Sept. 26, 1853, Typescript, Archives, Grand Lodge of New York, F. & A. M.

some other offense. On December 9, 1853, he was suspended by Morton Encampment.

**REVOCATION OF THE PREFACE**

Folger revoked the preface and bequest contained in the *Macoy Book* on September 25, 1854. An X was drawn through the page, and the name of Ferdinand L. Wilsey was almost totally obliterated. Hans Gram's name was untouched, but he had died in 1840. No reason for the revocation was given, but tenuous circumstantial evidence points to events surrounding Folger's recent expulsion from Grand Lodge.

It is clear from his blistering letter of September 26, 1853, to Grand Lodge that Folger did not like Fitz Gerald Tisdall. Tisdall was a member of Morton Encampment No. 4, Folger's Encampment, and had served as Generalissimo in 1852. After preferring charges against Folger in September 1853, Tisdall had charges of unmasonic conduct brought against him on December 6, 1853, and was expelled from his Lodge on March 9, 1854. Tisdall also was expelled from Morton No. 4, and tried to fight that by claiming "the alleged offense was committed before he (Tisdall) became attached to this branch of the Order; therefore, Morton Encampment [should have] no jurisdiction." On June 8 Tisdall's expulsion from Grand Lodge was rescinded, and his case referred back to his Lodge, St. John's No. 1. During all this legal maneuvering, Morton No. 4 held a meeting on September 23, 1854, the day before Folger revoked the preface of the *Macoy Book*.[30]

Neither Folger, Wilsey, nor Tisdall is shown as members of Morton No. 4 in 1854. The minutes do not show any of them attending the meeting on September 23 nor do they record any discussion relating to any of them. But the issue of Tisdall and Folger could have been discussed after the meeting. What if Wilsey had spoken favorably of Tisdall's appeal, either as an unrecorded attendee or shortly after the meeting? What if Folger heard of Wilsey's support of Tisdall's position? Perhaps this would have been enough to set off the

---

[30] Gardner, *Historical Reminiscences of Morton Commandery No. 4*, p. 24; *Proceedings and Constitution of the Grand Encampment of Knights Templar of the State of New York*, Feb. 10, 1854 (New York: McSpedon & Baker, Printer, 1854), pp. 23–24.

fiery-tempered Folger and to cause him to obliterate Wilsey's name from the preface? In the absence of more evidence, this flimsy but possible explanation is all that is available.

### RETURN TO THE FOLD

St. John's Grand Lodge eventually was abandoned about 1859. Folger clearly states that he never participated in its activities, even though he was expelled for advocating its reestablishment.

> We were not one of their number, nor did we ever visit one of their lodges. We were intimately connected with Ill. Bro. Atwood, in the Supreme Grand Council, and from him received all the leading matters which have been published concerning St. John's Grand Lodge of 1853.[31]

Shortly before June 2, 1857, Folger petitioned for restoration of membership in the Grand Lodge of New York. His mildly worded request is an ironic contrast to his earlier answer to the charges of unmasonic conduct; Folger left like a lion and returned like a lamb.

> To the Most Worshipful Grand Lodge of the State of New York
>
> The undersigned would respectfully present the following request.
>
> At a Communication of the Grand Stewards Lodge in 1853 he was expelled by that body for Contempt. The expulsion was confirmed by the Grand lodge. He asks that the said expulsion may be rescinded and he be restored.
>
> Being one of the oldest living members of Independent Royal Arch Lodge No. 2 and having served her faithfully for a long series of years, he desires to be placed in a position by which he can constitutionally commute and pay his dues to his Lodge.
>
> He is not now, nor has he been, a member in any other Lodge nor is he in any manner connected with any other subordinate Lodge of any kind.

[31] Folger, "Recollections," part 39, Sept. 6, 1874

A warm attachment to the Masonic Institution and the principles which it inculcates has prompted this request.

> Respectfully submitted,
> *Robert B. Folger*[32]

He was restored to membership on June 6, 1857, with the Committee on Grievances noting that "... he was expelled for words used in the heat of debate, and not for 'any violation of the moral law or the fundamental principles of Masonry' as required by ... the present Constitution...." There is no record that he actually rejoined Independent Royal Arch Lodge No. 2 or any of the other bodies in which he had been active.[33]

With his 1841 suspension overturned on a technicality and his 1853 expulsion rescinded because he had not violated any "fundamental principle of Masonry," Folger was able to say in 1884 with a clear conscience (and perhaps a selective memory):

> No charges have ever been preferred against me by the Fraternity, nor have I ever been expelled (except by the *'Highest Prerogatives of the Northern Jurisdiction,'* without charges or specifications, without a Summons to answer, without a Trial or Conviction) and this I consider an HONOR rather than a DISGRACE.[34]

## RESIGNATION AS GRAND SECRETARY GENERAL

In 1856 Henry Atwood's health began to fail "on account of repeated attacks of neuralgic disease, attended with many complications," and he made plans for a transfer of power in his Supreme Council. He appointed Edmun Hays Deputy Grand Commander on November 19, 1857, and on May 14, 1858, named Hays to succeed him upon his death. Atwood's appointment of Hays as Deputy Grand Commander was too much for even the faithful Folger, who resigned as Grand Secretary General at the same meeting.[35]

---

[32] Robert B. Folger, New York, to the M. W. Grand Lodge, State of New York, June 2, 1857, Typescript, Archives, Grand Lodge of New York, F. & A. M.

[33] Committee on Grievances, "Report," *Proceedings*, Grand Lodge of New York, F.&A.M., 1857, p. 168.

[34] Robert B. Folger, *Information for Members of the Ancient Accepted Scottish Rite* (New York: Edward O. Jenkins' Sons, [1884]), p. 38.

The Biography

Folger's published reasons for his resignation reflect only credit upon his beloved Supreme Council:

> In consequence of the removal of Bro. Atwood from New York City, the Grand Secretary General thought proper to tender his resignation. he had served four years under the direction of Ill. Bro. Atwood, during which he had labored hard, and 'had done what he could' to promote the interests of the body. The calls of business had very much increased upon him during the then recent panic, beside which he was engaged in collecting documents and collating a history of the Rite.

Further, he expected to be absent from the city for several months for unspecified reasons, though there is no evidence he ever left.[36]

In a letter to Enoch Terry Carson in 1881, Folger revealed his great dislike for Hays, which doubtless was the real reason for his resignation.

> Hays was an infidel in opinion, but exceedingly ignorant and uncultured, & being the pet of Henry C. Atwood, was named by him as his successor .... Like all uncultured men he was a worshiper of Albert Pike, & never rested until he had completely transferred the Rituals & Degrees into the blasphemous languages and & doctrines of that plausible deceiver.
>
> In consequence of their perversion of the Truth I have never been at one of their meetings, or associated with them in their bodies, although I loved the order, & wished it well ....[37]

## LATER YEARS

With his resignation as Grand Secretary General, Folger changed the nature of his involvement with Masonry. He became a historian and writer of the gentle craft, even as he continued his strong opinions and sharp words. In 1862 he published his notorious book, *The Ancient and Accepted Scottish Rite in Thirty-Three Degrees*,

---

[35] Folger, "Recollections," part 36, Aug. 2, 1874; Josiah H. Drummond, "Ancient and Accepted Scottish Rite of Freemasonry," in *History of Freemasonry and Concordant Orders*, H. L. Stillson et al., eds. (Boston: Fraternity Publishing Co., 1912), p. 820; Folger, *A History*, 1877, p. 233.

[36] Folger, "Recollections," part 36.

[37] Robert B. Folger, New York, to Enoch T. Carson, [Past Lt. Grand Commander], [Ohio], Nov. 9, 1881, Typescript, Archives, Supreme Council, 33°, N.M.J., Lexington, Mass.

which was the most rigorous defense of Cerneauism ever seen. It formed the foundation for all later claims of legitimacy for Cerneauism. While he claimed no partiality in his history, a casual reading contradicts this.

**DEFENDING THE CERNEAU SUPREME COUNCIL**

Enoch T. Carson summarized the strengths and weaknesses of Folger's book:

> Mr. Folger belonged to what was known as the 'Cerneau Supreme Council,' and his history throughout reveals a strong bias towards his party.
>
> The history proper, in that work, [is] the first part of the volume, . . . and in view of the author's well developed prejudice, this part of the work may be taken *cum grano salis*.
>
> The 'Documents' . . . form the second and by far the more valuable portion of the work, for they are authentic, and many of them are printed for the first time from the original manuscripts, or reprinted in many cases from the excessively rare original pamphlets.[38]

Among other things, Folger claimed "the whole proceedings of Stephen Morin and his successors, from the beginning, have been illegal and unmasonic . . . ." Folger attacked the Mother Supreme Council for admitting Jews to the 17° through the 32°, claiming these teach Christian doctrines and should be reserved for Christians:

> These degrees, or at least some of them, are founded upon, and promulgate the peculiar doctrines of Christianity, more especially, the Divinity, Death, Resurrection and Ascension of the Messiah, our common Lord. The right of possession to all the degrees of Masonry, up to the Sixteenth of the Ancient and Accepted Rite, is claimed by all sects of people alike, because they are not based upon, and have no direct allusion to these doctrines. But the Statutes of the Order, as well as the moral sense of the members of the institution require that a Jew should go no further in these mysteries, because he is not a believer in the doctrines which they assume to teach.[39]

---

[38] Folger, *A History*, 1877, p. i.

[39] Folger, *The Ancient and Accepted Scottish Rite*, pp. 332–333, 19.

Finally he claimed the Scottish Rite did not originate in Charleston in 1801, but had begun earlier in France where it eventually was taken over by the Grand Orient of France. Thus all authority for the Scottish Rite emanated from the Grand Orient. His theory was that

> [t]he Count de Grasse ... established a Sup. Gr. Council in Paris in 1804. That Council was in existence just 44 days, when ... it merged into, or united with, the Gr. Orient of France. Thus the Grand Orient came into possession of all that Sup. Gr. Council had in the way of degrees, although that was not much of an acquisition, as the Grand Orient had possessed all the degrees for Forty years before the Union [of the Cerneau and Norther Supreme Councils] took place.[40]

He went on to explain that the Grand Orient of France "regularized" Cerneau's Sovereign Grand Consistory in New York in 1813. In short, Folger's history at times confuses the Scottish Rite and the Rite of Perfection and is at odds with what can be accepted and verified today. Whether he willfully invented some of his "history" or was misled by others is not known. He seems to have interpreted the evidence to suit his prejudices.

### THE UNION OF 1867 AND TEMPORARY PEACE

The Cerneau and regular Supreme Councils united in 1867 to form the current Supreme Council, 33°, for the Northern Masonic Jurisdiction. Folger seemed happy to see the union, which ended the bitter factionalism tearing at the Scottish Rite:

> We now behold the fruits of these negotiations in the forming of one, united, and undivided Supreme Council, under the old banner of 'Union Toleration Power,' and we believe it to be the sincere desire of every brother of our beautiful Rite, that this union may continue for all time 'one and indivisible.'[41]

These words would become sadly ironic in 1881 when he and others withdrew from the united Supreme Council to reestablish the

---

[40] Robert B. Folger, New York, to Enoch T. Carson, [Past Lt. Grand Commander], Nov. 17, 1881, Transcript in the hand of R. B. Folger, Archives, Supreme Council 33°, N.M.J., Lexington, Mass.

[41] Folger, "Recollections," Part 38, Aug 16, 1874.

Cerneau Supreme Council. Folger signed an Oath of Fealty to the new Supreme Council and then seemed to have slowed his Masonic labors even more. His son, Robert Benjamin Folger, Jr., was born in 1868 when Folger was 68.

In 1872 he wrote to Josiah H. Drummond, Sovereign Grand Commander, N.M.J., and proposed rewriting and republishing his history, with the hope that the proceeds might benefit his family. This may have been an indication of financial difficulties for Folger. Drummond did not accept his offer. Still hoping to have the Supreme Council republish his book, Folger wrote to Enoch T. Carson, Lieutenant Grand Commander, in 1873. Folger explained about his book

> ... that it was written at a time when party spirit in Masonic matters ran high, & being an old member of the Cerneau body, devotedly attached to that section & all its interests, indulged largely in sharp words & many expressions which would now be deemed objectionable in the highest degree. But the true history of the Rite is not marred.

This is perhaps an indirect confession to some historical inaccuracies in the book. The Supreme Council finally purchased the manuscript for $500, though the book was never published. Its full title is "A History of the Ancient Accepted Scottish Rite in the United States: More Especially as Connected with the Operations of the So-Called Cerneau Supreme Council from its Organization in New York in 1807, to its Final Absorption into the Supreme Council of the Northern Jurisdiction of the U.S. in 1867."[42]

Much of the material is taken from a series of forty-three "Recollections of a Masonic Veteran," published by Folger from April 20, 1873, to September 20, 1874, in the *New York Dispatch*. These articles provide a fascinating glimpse into early New York Masonry and the many controversies that swirled around the fraternity. Folger's writing is peaceful and polite, even about those with whom he clashed. It is easy to conclude he thought this would be one of the last things he wrote, so he reviewed his career in Masonry through rose-colored

---

[42] Robert B. Folger, New York, to Enoch T. Carson, Lt. Grand Commander, July 18, 1873, Typescript, Archives, Supreme Council, 33°, N.M.J., Lexington, Mass.

glasses. He still maintained his partisanship for the Cerneau Supreme Councils but managed a few kind words for their opponents.

**THE REPRINTED HISTORY**

In 1876 Folger attended the only Supreme Council session after he signed the Oath of Fealty. By this time Harry Seymour's Ancient and Primitive Rite of about ninety degrees had condensed itself to a rite of thirty-three degrees and was claiming to be the only legitimate Supreme Council in the U.S. as the successor to Joseph Cerneau. In June 1880 Seymour resigned as Grand Commander in favor of William H. Peckham. (Peckham actually had bought the Grand Commandership from Seymour for several hundred dollars!) Peckham sought to put his Supreme Council on firmer footings and turned to Folger for help. Peckham contracted with Folger to reprint his history of 1862 with a supplement to bring it up to 1881. Five hundred copies were to be printed, and the Peckham Supreme Council paid $700 in advance for 175 copies. What happened next is confused.[43]

The second edition of Folger's history was printed in 1881 with the update, but pages 99–104 of the supplement emphatically argued that the Peckham Supreme Council was the only legitimate Scottish Rite body in the United States. Folger claimed his good name had been used dishonestly to advance the Peckham cause because these pages had been written by someone else and had been inserted without his knowledge. For a while Folger sold copies of the history with pages 99–104 cut out; later he kept the book intact but pasted in a note disclaiming authorship of the offending pages. His motives in disclaiming the pages were obscured when he soon thereafter revived yet another Cerneau Supreme Council, it too claiming to be the only legitimate source for the Scottish Rite. The pages in question were harmful to Folger's new cause as they argued against the legitimacy of any Supreme Council except Peckham's. Folger's detractors point to the deceptive reasoning of the supplement as an example of his unreliability as a historian and his willingness to prostitute himself.

[43] *The Masonic Chronicle*, Vol. VI, No. 9, August 1884, p. 137.

## THE FINAL CONTROVERSY

At its September 1881 session the Supreme Council, N.M.J., voted to publish a series of articles by Charles T. McClenachan. These were a condensed history of Scottish Rite Supreme Councils which contradicted much of Folger's writings. In particular McClenachan questioned Cerneau's possession of the 33°, the *sine qua non* of his authority to establish a Supreme Council. McClenachan said, "It has been asserted that prior to the year 1822, at least, Joseph Cerneau had not regularly received the 33d degree, and those whose greatest interest it was to prove the contrary have failed in response." On September 20 at the same session Albert Pike, Grand Commander, S.J., addressed the Supreme Council. In Folger's words, Pike, for the

> twenty-five years past, with all the polite bitterness he was capable of expressing, and all the malice he could politely bring to bear, Denounced, Defamed, & Spit at every man that loved the name of Joseph Cerneau, and every Masonic organization that manifested the least proclivity towards the doctrines taught by his bodies or himself.[44]

McClenachan's history was an assault, albeit in polite, scholarly terms, on Folger's crowning achievement as a historian. Albert Pike's mere presence was an assault on any Cerneau Mason, and it is not known what Pike may have said about Cerneau when he addressed the Supreme Council. On top of these indirect attacks on Folger, charges of unmasonic conduct had been preferred against him for the claims of legitimacy for the Peckham Supreme Council in the supplement of his recently reprinted history. Folger submitted his resignation from the Supreme Council, but it was refused on September 22 until the charges of unmasonic conduct could be resolved.[45]

On September 27, 1881, Folger began his last fight against the Masonic status quo. He, Hopkins Thompson, and several other old Cerneau men resigned their honorary memberships in the Supreme Council, withdrew their Oaths of Fealty, and revived the Cerneau

---

[44] Charles T. McClenachan, "A Synoptical History of all of the Supreme Councils that have Ever Existed, and the manner of their Formation in Chronological Order," *Proceedings of the Supreme Council, 33°, N.M.J.,* 1881, pp. 128, 4; Folger to Carson, Nov. 17, 1881.

[45] *Proceedings,* 1881, pp. 83–84.

The Biography

Supreme Council! All this came less than eight months after Folger had printed in his history that "... he [disclaimed] any partiality for either of the parties, having long since withdrawn his connection with the 'High Degrees.'" In the reborn Cerneau Supreme Council, Thompson became Sovereign Grand Commander and Folger resumed his old office of Grand Secretary General. This body had an uneven existence and died out about thirty years later. Charges were preferred against Folger and the other seceders on December 19, 1881, by the Supreme Council, N.M.J., and they were expelled at the September 1882 session.[46]

Folger tried to provide a rationale for his actions. He claimed the union of the Supreme Councils in 1867 was fatally flawed because of irregularities at the meeting of the Cerneau Supreme Council that planned it. Edward W. Atwood neatly captured the spirit of the union of 1867, "I got the impression that they thought that although they might not have done what was right in every respect, they had done what they thought was for the best." His arguments (and those of Cerneau supporters that followed him) are intricate and legalistic, as if they were arguing a point of constitutional law or religious doctrine. It was not enough that the Supreme Councils had put their differences behind them and joined to work for the common good. If the united Supreme Council would not acknowledge Joseph Cerneau as the only origin of authentic Scottish Rite Masonry in the United States, then Folger and his colleagues would not participate.[47]

Folger worked faithfully to establish the "Ancient Council" as a Masonic power. His efforts were remarkably successful and probably tell more about organizational weaknesses of the Supreme Council, N.M.J., than about Joseph Cerneau's authorities. Folger later took on the less strenuous job of Corresponding Grand Secretary in 1885 and on July 23, 1892, made a "... long journey of over six miles ..." from Brooklyn to New York City to attend an informal meeting of Sovereign Grand Inspectors General where he made a speech. This was his last recorded Masonic activity, for on September 13, 1892, at eighty-

[46] Folger, *The Ancient and Accepted Scottish Rite*, p.324.
[47] "Scottish Rite Testimony," *Masonic Chronicle*, Vol. XV, No. 5, April 1893, p. 137.

nine years of age, he was called from labor at his home. On September 16, 1892, Masonic services were conducted at his residence by Silentia Lodge No. 198, and he was buried the next day in the family plot in Oak Wood Cemetery at Nyack-on-the-Hudson. He left a wife, Anna C., and a son, Robert B., Jr. His wife survived him by only a few months, passing away on November 19, 1892.[48]

Thus ended the career of a zealous Craftsman. Folger's life and activities indicated a passion for the gentle Craft that was at times overwhelming in its intensity. He did not fear challenging established authority, whether the medical community, the Grand Lodge, or the Supreme Council. In almost all cases he acted in a manner that can be viewed as honorable and certainly in a manner that he felt was in the best interests of Freemasonry. Whether he is viewed as a rogue and a charlatan or a sincere Craftsman whose error was to choose the losing sides of several battles, it is easily agreed that he was indeed a remarkable Mason.

---

[48] *Proceedings of the Supreme Council, 33°, for the U.S.A., their Territories and Dependencies* [Thompson-Folger revived Cerneau Supreme Council] (New York: Masonic Publishing Co., 1892), pp. 12–14; "Anna C. Folger," *Masonic Chronicle*, Vol. XV, No. 1, Dec. 1892, p. 25.

# THE MANUSCRIPT
# AND ITS TRANSLATION

ROBERT B. FOLGER was a meticulous draftsman and a clever cryptanalyst; the penmanship in the *Macoy Book* is beautiful and its cryptography is ingenious. One of the more interesting aspects of studying the *Folger Manuscript* is to follow the evolution of Folger's penmanship and cryptography. A few issues remain about the text, which are noted below.

## THE MANUSCRIPT

**GENERAL COMMENTS**

On the inside front cover are instructions in cipher to "begin page three at top." The Grade of Disciple then starts on page 3 and is written on pages 2-10, with the text jumping from page to page, written in all directions. Most of the words are written without vowels; after four or five pages these abbreviations trail off until by page 10 nearly all words are spelled in full. These observations are confirmed on page 11: "The Grade of Disciple is written promiscuously on the first pages" (line 27); and "The Grade of Fellow is written regularly or from page to page and with many abbreviations" (lines 15-20). Presumably this technique was used to make the cipher more secure; it did make it more difficult to read and write. The text continues regularly for pages 12-23. Page 25 has a pencil sketch of a Lodge, and page 77 has a pencil sketch of a ship with broken masts. Finally, pages 81-88 are written with the book turned upside down and contain miscellaneous material: a history of Freemasonry; a rite of ablution; a mirror ceremony; prayers; questions for candidates; and a covenant for a Scotch Lodge.

The Manuscript and Translation

The text on pages 2-9 has no illustrations and almost no special symbols. By the tenth page, Folger seems to have become more comfortable with the cipher writing and began adding illustrations and inventing special symbols. Page 11 has a list of several of these symbols, as well as what seems to be a second, unused cipher alphabet. Page 15 starts the gradual introduction of the special *crescent moon–backwards gamma* digraph for *th*. As the text continues, Folger's drawings become more elaborate and artistic, usually illustrating material in the adjacent text, though there are a few unexplained drawings. The neat lettering and uniform-sized words suggest the manuscript was transcribed from a draft or from another copy; there are virtually no misspellings or mistakes.[1]

Folger's punctuation was, at best, erratic. He didn't seem to distinguish between periods and question marks, but occasionally used several end-of-sentence symbols. Sometimes he used short wavy lines, or wavy arrows, or three large commas with a line through them; the choice of symbol appears to be arbitrary. Punctuation was used much more at the beginning of the manuscript than at the end.

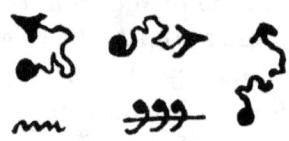

Typical Punctuation Marks

Plain numbers appear in the cipher on two pages. Their meaning on page 10, line 10 is clear, "toward low 12." However, the meanings of the numbers on page 28 is unknown: line 10, "willing to shew it to you. 5 & 17 ="; lines 15 and 16, "the important duties of a F[ellow] 23 via, that of checking"; and lines 16 and 17, "where he is a stranger 83." In all other instances in the cipher, Folger either spelled the numbers or used some special symbol.

**THE CIPHER**

Some of Folger's cipher symbols are similar to those found in other Masonic ciphers from the seventeenth and early eighteenth

---

[1] Alfred Engel, Lawrenceville, N.J., to S. Brent Morris, Columbia, Md., May 3, 1990, Typescript, In the possession of the author.

## The Manuscript and Translation

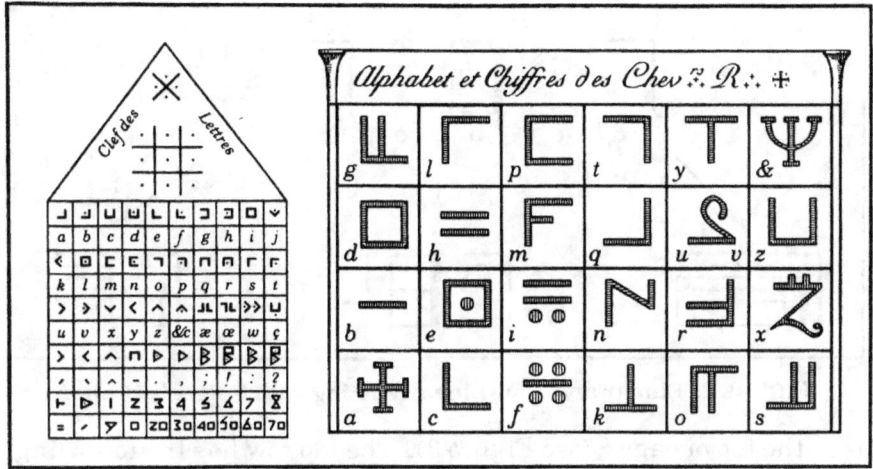

**FIGURE 1. Representative Masonic Ciphers**
Left from Antoine Guillaume Chéreau, *Explication de la Pierre Cubique*, ([Paris]: 1806), tipped in engraving, right from Chéreau, *Explication de la Croix Philosophique* ([Paris]: 1806), p. 22.

centuries. (This, however, is not surprising because of the small number of possible simple geometric shapes.) It seemed then as if each new degree (particularly the *hauts grades* from the continent) had its own cipher of 26 symbols. Figure 1 shows two representative ciphers from books that should have been available to Folger in New York in 1826.[2] However, he seems to have invented his own cipher, perhaps with inspiration from some other Masonic book or manuscript. The strength of his cipher comes not from its symbols, but from its non-linear method of writing, which makes distinguishing individual characters difficult (see Figure 2).

### HEBREW

Folger scattered Hebrew letters throughout the text in an odd fashion, as if he learned enough Hebrew to read a few words in the Bible and then tried to exceed his limitations. A curious chart of strange figures and ill-formed but still recognizable Hebrew letters

[2] For a more detailed discussion of Masonic ciphers, see Alfred Engel, *Die freimaurerischen Geheimschriften*, Bayreuth: Quatuor Coronati Lodge, 1972.

The Manuscript and Translation

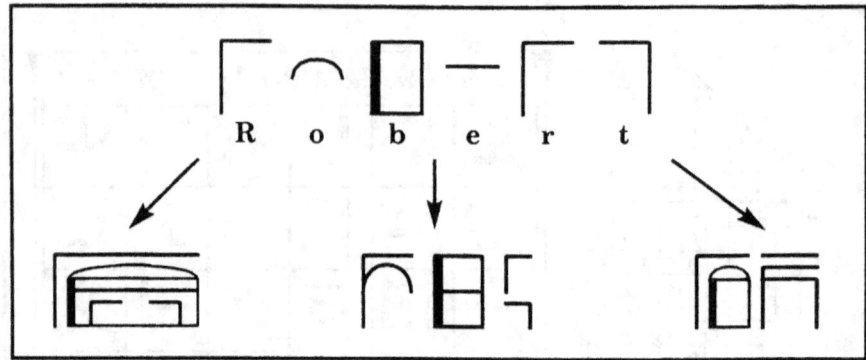

**FIGURE 2. Linear and Non-Linear Writing with Folger's Cipher**

is at the top of page 8 (see Figure 3). The top row has the following: *aleph*, א, left parenthesis, colon, right parenthesis, four unknown symbols, *daleth*, ד, *vauv* (?), ו, *gimel*, ג, *heth*, ח, *yod*, י, *qoph*, ק, *lamed*, ל, and five unknown symbols. (It could be the unknown symbols are just poorly formed Hebrew letters.)

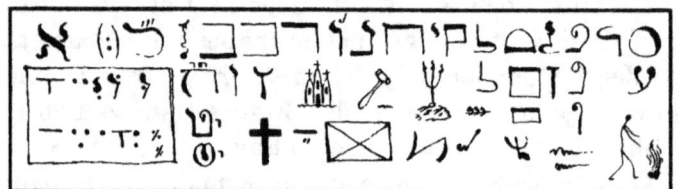

**FIGURE 3. The "Key" from Page 8**

In the lower left of the chart is a box with the Masoretic vowel points, long vowels on the top row and short vowels on the bottom. Immediately to the right of the box is a column of three characters. The top one is the *crescent moon–backwards gamma* "mystery digraph" (See Chapter 2), ⊓, but in this context it is recognizable as the letter *tauv*, ת, which equates to *th*. Immediately above it are small cipher symbols for *t*, ׀, and *h*, ⊓. Below it is a well formed *teth*, ט, equating to *t*, and below that is a poorly formed *teth*. Both versions of *teth* have to the right a small cipher symbol for *t*, ׀. To the right of these are the symbols †″, which spell *key*. Folger

Page 106

## The Manuscript and Translation

may have intended this chart to be the key to his manuscript, but its meaning is anything but clear.

To the right of *key* are four unknown symbols and a drawing of a figure facing a fire. The first of these symbols, a box with an *x* or two diagonals in it, appears again on page 11 below a drawing of a cubical stone and above a box with a single diagonal in it. On page 16, line 20 the box with an *x* and a cross on top seems to stand for *Grand Lodge*: "the permission of the G M of ⊠, so help me God."

Two further specific appearances of the *th/tauv* symbol are worth noting. On page 20 is a drawing of an open book that contains the "Lecture and Instruction" for the Grade of Fellow. At the bottom of the right hand page of the book is what appears to be an altar. Just above the altar, at the far right of the last line of text is the *th* symbol, and inside of it are the cipher symbols for *t* and *h*. A large list of abbreviations and special symbols is on page 23. The *crescent moon–backwards gamma* is the third one on line 3 and is equated with *th*.

Page 11, line 10 has several characters that might pass for Hebrew, including a reasonably formed *aleph* and *lamed*, but these letters are preceded by the note in cipher, "nothing." This line of text was probably designed to throw off cryptanalysts.

Page 13, line 1 has an *aleph* after a drawing of a figure standing in front of a fire and then on line 26 has what may be a backwards *aleph*: "sign and word. aleph(?) Boaz." The first character on page 16, line 1 looks to be a *gimel*. The last character on page 83, line 1 is another backwards *aleph*. In the middle of page 84, line 14 are several Hebrew letters and one unknown symbol: *shin* [?] *vauv aleph*. The history of Freemasonry on pages 81 and 82 abounds with Hebrew letters, some of which spell or transliterate words. For example, page 82, line 3, third word is a tortured transliteration of *Europe*, while page 81, line 9, last word is clearly *Jerusalem*. Other combinations of Hebrew letters in the history have an as yet undetermined meaning.

Hebrew, Page 84

## STICK FIGURES

Beginning on page 8, Folger started drawing stick figures in the text. They sometimes illustrate the accompanying action, and sometimes look like playful decorations. Several of the figures face or light candelabra or fires, e.g. page 11, line 9. Others face some further illustration, such as a Master's Carpet, page 12, line 17, or a cross and gavels, page 12, line 26. One completely unexplained drawing shows a figure throwing a spear over a fire towards a second figure falling backwards onto something, p. 13, line 26 (see Figure 4). No action in the ceremonies appears to match these latter figures.

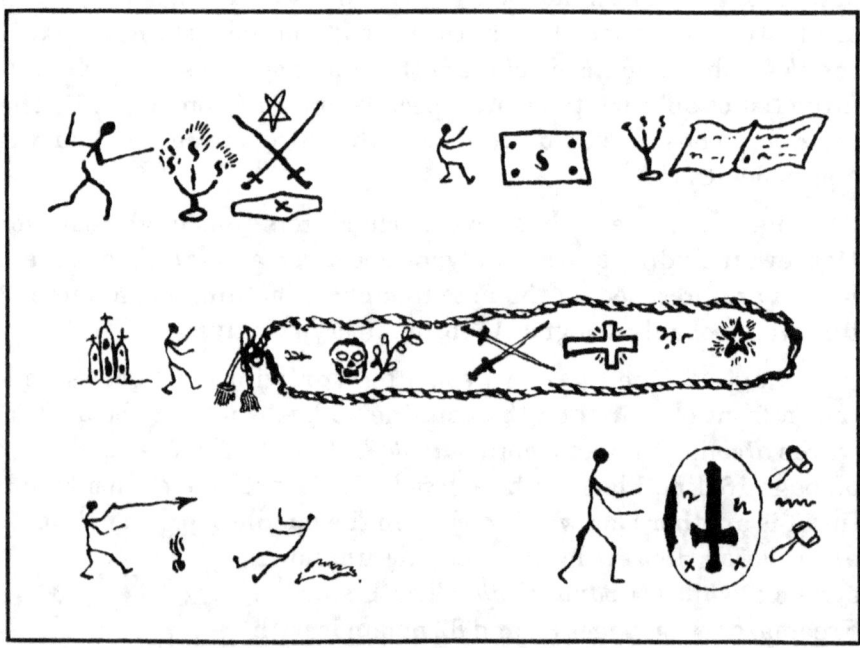

FIGURE 4. Representative Stick Figures

Upper left, from page 11; upper right, middle, and lower right, from page 12; lower left from page 13.

## UNKNOWN SYMBOLS

The *Folger Manuscript* has several symbols and drawings with no obvious meaning. For example, on the bottom row of the diagram of Hebrew letters, page 8, line 3, are three unknown symbols which curiously are repeated on page 13, line 26, followed by a gavel. Most symbols, even if used only once, are

Unknown Symbols, Pages 8 and 13

clear from context and some of the drawings are obviously decorative, like the scroll with stars and a skull with acacia sprig(?) on the bottom of page 21. Others have undiscovered meanings and seem to be unattached from the surrounding text.

The manuscript abounds with examples of these charming, unattached drawings. An altar and sideways cross are on page 13, line 23. On page 12, line 17, there is a rope containing a skull, acacia sprig(?), crossed swords, sideways cross, and blazing star (see middle drawing, Figure 3). Page 19 has a carpet with acacia sprigs(?), a cross, and a wreath; to its right are a crossed sword and gavel, and to its left are marks showing some sort of foot movements.

Altar and Cross, Page 13

Steps, Carpet, Sword, and Gavel, Page 19

The pyramid on page 21 is a complete mystery, particularly since the surrounding text is a homily on the Bible. The symbols for *ej* or *ei*, ⌐, are clearly contained in the pyramid, which itself might be interpreted as an *n*, ∧. Page 88 shows a cubical stone on which rests a cross surmounted by a star. This is vaguely reminiscent of symbolism found in the Rose Croix Degree.

# THE TRANSLATION

The *Macoy Book* and its translation appear on the following pages. A few conventions have been adopted in presenting the text.

    **Plain type**    is used for cipher letters.

    *Italics*    are used for plaintext letters.

    [Brackets]    are used for descriptions of drawings and for special symbols (except those for *and* and *the*).

    •    a heavy period indicates an end-of-line symbol.

Some large illustrations are outlined to help in locating text, and questionable translations are indicated by a question mark in parentheses. The pagination adopted here treats the first physical page, the dedication or bequest page, as *page 1* and continues the numbering through the entire book. Folger skipped the dedication or bequest page and started his pagination with the first page of cipher text. Thus his *page 1* is our *page 2*. However, Folger has so few references to page numbers that little confusion should result. Figure 5 gives the key to Folger's cipher and illustrates several of his special symbols. Lists or tables of special symbols are on pages 11 and 23, though some symbols seem to have been invented on the spot and used just once.

The Manuscript and Translation

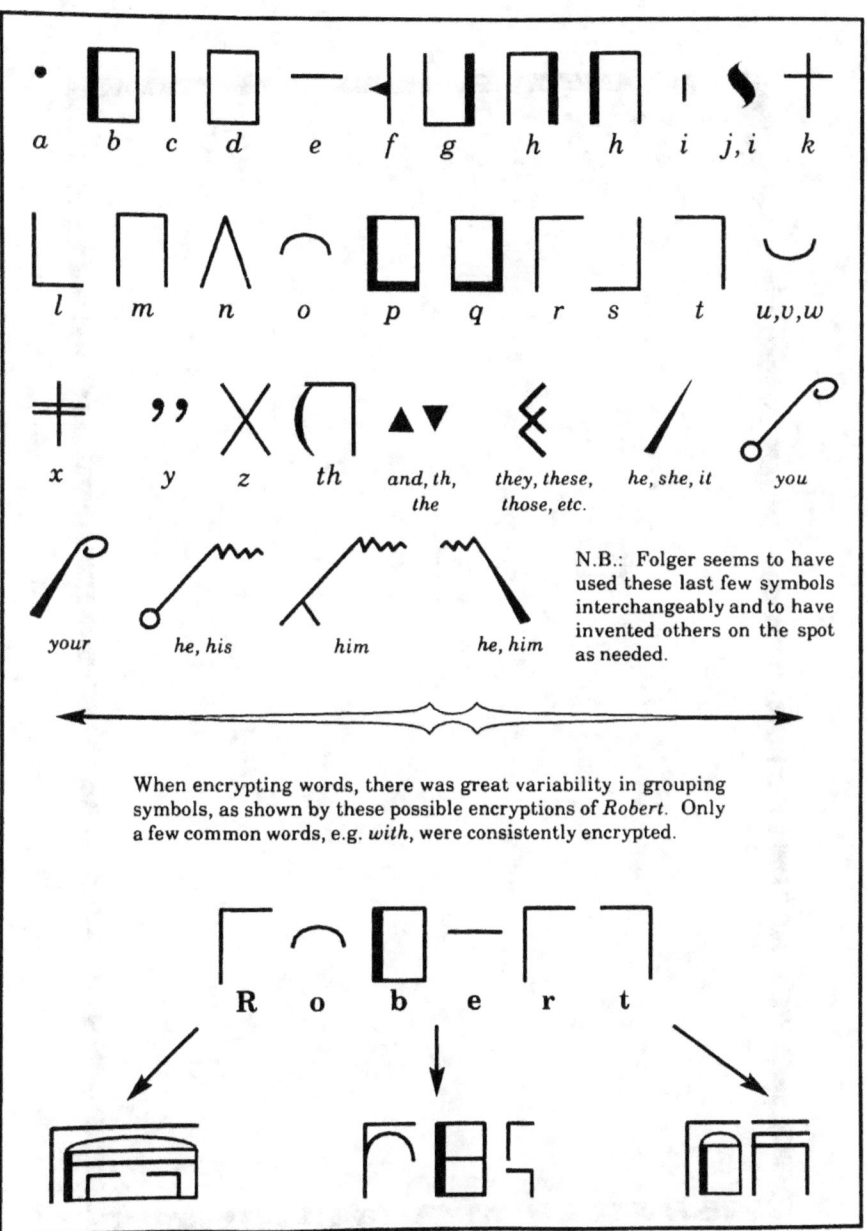

FIGURE 5. The Key to Folger's Cipher

## The Manuscript and Translation

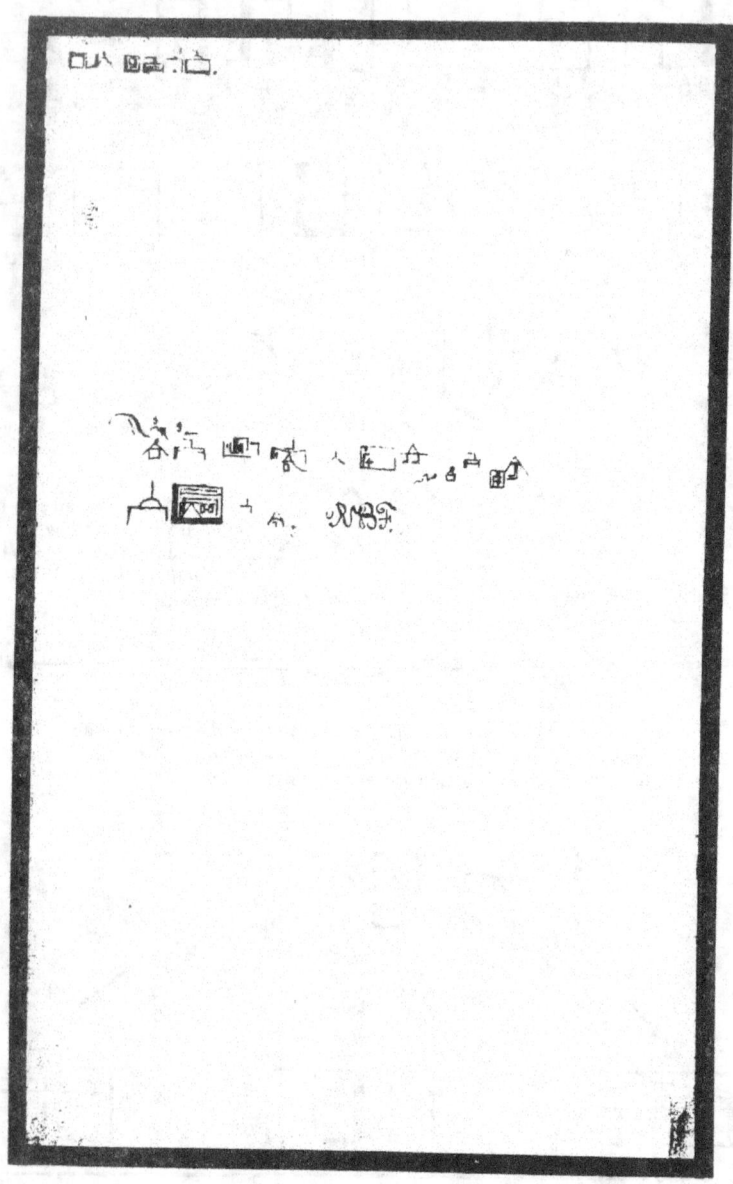

*Inside Front Cover of the Folger Manuscript*

# The Manuscript and Translation

## Inside Front Cover of the Folger Manuscript

1   Begin page three at the top●

2   (?) John
3   And the light shined in darkness and the darkness
4   comprehended it not   *RBF*

# The Manuscript and Translation

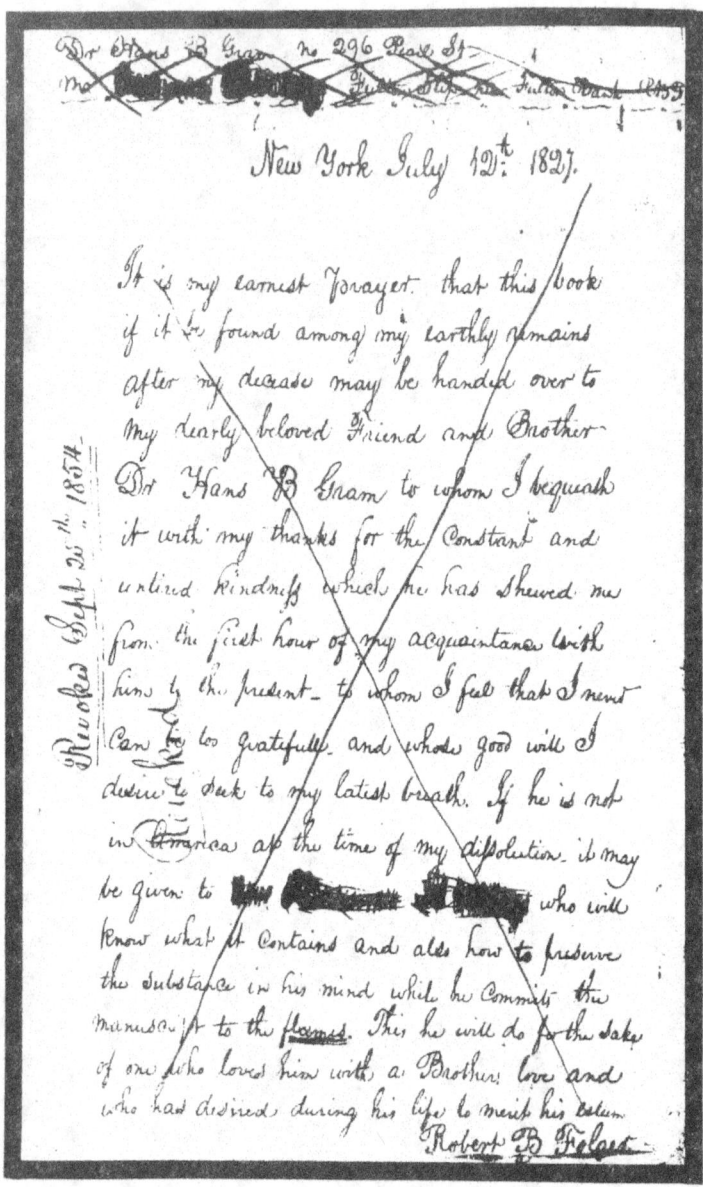

*Page 1 of the Folger Manuscript*

## Page 1 of the Folger Manuscript

*Revoked Sept. 25th 1854*

22

1  Dr Hans B Gram No 296 Pearl St
2  Mr Ferdinand L Wilsey Fulton Slip near, Fulton Bank RBF
3  New York July 12th 1827•
4  it is my earnest prayer that this book
5  if it be found among my earthly remains
6  after my decease may be handed over to
7  my dearly beloved Friend andBrother
8  Dr Hans B Gram to whom I bequeath
9  it with my thanks for the constant and
10 untired kindness which he has shewed me
11 from the first hour of my acquaintance with
12 him to the present – to whom I feel that I never
13 can be too gratefull and whose good will I
14 desire to seek to my latest breath. If he is not
15 in America at the time of my dissolution – it may
16 be given to Mr. Ferdinand L. Wilsey who will
17 know what it contains and also how to preserve
18 the substance in his mind while he commits the
19 manuscript to the <u>flames</u>. This he will do for the sake
20 of one who loves him with a Brothers love and
21 who has desired during his life to merit his esteem.

21  <u>Robert B. Folger</u>

The Manuscript and Translation

*Page 2 of the Folger Manuscript*

# The Manuscript and Translation

## Page 2 of the Folger Manuscript

1  Pag first• Tablet• Questn first• Do you beliv in th xstnce of a J perft and good the crt of all things•
2  scnd do you blve in the immortality of the soul• Thrd• F so what do you believ to b your Duty towrd J
3  yor neighbor and youself• Here it is proper fa depty to retrn to the Master the aspirants answer• Page two•

---

4  To be rcvd mng us• Ths your rqst we have srsly attndd to and fm the good opnn we hve cncvd of your character
5  and as one of our Brthrn has pledgd hmslf fr you in a solmn mannr and he who I snt to inqre as to your
6  motvs n jng us and your opnn of or nstutn has reportd so favrbly of you we hve thrfre snt you a G
7  who has opnd our door to you and now you are n the mdst of us in a stte ft fr trls whh you must endure and
8  whh evry one who wshs to be recvd amng us must endure rmbrng that the prsnt is a state of trial• But
9  sir before we can proceed frthr I have some qstns to ask to you whh I must reqre an audible and unequvocl an
10 swr but frst sir I must state to you that there is nothng n our rdr whh is ncmpatible with
11 reign or with cvl or morl duties. For the trth of this we pldge you our honour and I now sk you if you
12 are prmptd to join us by a dsre of bng charitble and usefll to you fllow mn.• Secnd re you prmptd to join
13 us by a desire of the knwldge oc trth and to be assciatd with those who profess to promulgate it and
14 ncrge virtue and laudable pursuits [Third] Wil you cnform to the regultns of the F and do you volntrly rqst to be made a
15 Masn.• Wll thn you rqst small be grantd you Gd gv at sme futre day it may serve to make you happy.• You are about
16 gong on a mystrious journy and although you cnnt see the way yet cnfdng n hm who lds you go forwd with
17 firmnss yet with cautn and rest assurd that your G will nt brng you in pths whre you shld not go [three gavels]
18 G sir the nkd swrd pondg to your hrt is but a weak symbl of the dngrs whh surrnd you one who wanders in drknss bt but
19 your trst in G and fear nt.• Fme wth me.• Pg three.• Sectn secnd.• First [round]

---

20 Da and then you receivd the tests f ths degree by whh you cn make yourslf known to Br Masons.• Do not my
21 Br be amng [those] who strive to publsh to the world that they are masons neither countenancle any thng tndng
22 to this end and for the honour and usflness f the ordr are much more xtnded by cnclmnt and by an in
23 tmate acquaintnce wth the xldt aim f our labours and the probable xtnt f their nfluence upn the
24 wlfre f the humn race you will be assured that silnce and crcmspectn tend to give our order
25 force. The carpet before you cntng the prncple smbls f our ordr dserves your attntion. The br
26 dr incldng the whole is a representatn f mason work and this is the covering to all the other smbles and shld remnd us f
27 that cnclmnt f whh we have already spok'n. The [rough stone] and [square stone] are smbls the one f the raw
28 and nclturated mn the other ffm whh hs subjctd hmslf to the dscplne f truth and virtue. The trstle board should admnsh us carefully to study and to follow the
29 blns f the Mstr.• You see the sn and mn.• They are here rprsntd to rmnd us f aplictn to our duties
30 bay and nght tr this is all a man cn do without errng. There are the dffrnt instrumnts usd by Masns as
31 plmb levl and sq and so trth.• They are adoptd as hieroglphs.• Pge three.• By us and therfre are

## The Manuscript and Translation

*Page 3 of the Folger Manuscript*

## The Manuscript and Translation

### Page 3 of the Folger Manuscript

1. Introductor the [Lodge] have commanded me to inform you respecting som of our customs and to prpare you in a proper manner to be ~~presnted~~
2. brought to the [Lodge] in ordr to be accptd a Discpl. Permit me to advise you. I wold ncourage you to xrcis fortu
3. de in the trls you are about to endure and to place cnfdnce in those who shall conduct you on the way in which you
4. have cnldd to ntr upon. The first sign of your ready determnton to jon us is(?) to delver me you had and sword
5. Br please dlver this to the [Lodge] and return hither to me again. Sir will you please to lay
6. from you all money jwls metall and other signs of disstinction uncover your lft breast and xpose
7. the knee tread down the left shoe. Now sir you are xtrnlly ppd to be psntd to the [Lodge] and it is pl
8. easing to me to belive that your hert and thoughts corspond with this xtrnl ppn and that you
9. hve tkn and will cntnue to take all possible pains to eradicate all prjdcs and emotns of the mind
10. whh militate agnst your prpr duties as a man. Bage four. But sir you must be convndc that a
11. Thn I ccpt you as a D in M to the hnour f lmght G. N the nme of F and by vrtue f the pwer vstd
12. n me amen. Rsponse. Arse. Ths last trial your bng wllng to snctn your vows wth your blood
13. is cnvncng of your sncrty and I now slte you by the nme f Br bt frgt not under what cndtns you obtnd ths nme
14. Br wrdns bear hm to the wst thre to cme to lght. SW. He is prd. [Gavel]. Hwevr wk the prsnt
15. lght that flms bfre you may be yet my Br it is sffcnt to show you our wpns turnd agnst you thrtng
16. you wth shme and dsdn if vr you shld nhpply btray the trust we hve rposd in you lt hm be veild agn
17. [Gavel]. Sic Transt Gloria Mundi. Fr a momnt snce you saw our wpns turnd gnst you aprntly hostle. Look at us
18. now armed fr your dfnce and wlfre. Yes my Br the ordr will nt and shll not frske you as lon as you are
19. fthflly dng your duty and keepng your cvnants. Br M f C lt our nw Br be clothd and return with hm to
20. the Lodge. Nd f the frst sctn f Discpulus. Pge six. Bgns the secnd sctn. WM. One Knocks

---

21. The veil f the tbrncle ws drwn side with and it is mblematicl f the tie whh unites all good men and
22. Masons and we should rmbr ever that since is the veil whh keeps our snctury in safety. Close before
23. you is the mosak pvemnt whh n Solmns Tmple covrd the courts and on whh the sanctuary stood. It
24. mblematcl
25. of the foundatn whh we seek in [those] we accpt amng us. They should be men of a firm and fair
26. character fit for surrounding and supporting a snctuary. On the lft you see a [pillar] with the intitl f the word
27. f your degree. Bear in mind the meaning f the word in hm is strength. You ascnded [those] three first stps
28. f the Tmple but as your tme was not yet come the door remnd shut and you was led back gan and it is
29. reccommnded to you to wait with patnce and to labour dilgntly yet with meekness that when the door
30. f the Tmple shall be opnd to you you may hope yes believe to ntr nto the inner aprtmnts
31. with great joy. End. Opning the Dscpiles D. Br wr are you a D. I am. Br's and what is the
32. frst duty f every good Mason and in the prticularly f the Br wardns. Page four. To see

*Page 119*

# The Manuscript and Translation

*Page 4 of the Folger Manuscript*

## The Manuscript and Translation

### Page 4 of the Folger Manuscript

1  Discpulus. Hihr we have come. Lt us nw rest for a short tm. I beg to abstract yrself fm all
2  worldy thghts for a shrt space of time and to devote this tme to the cnsdrtn of yourslf and such things as may
★See Note [on page 86]
3  her occr to you. To the place f wh this is a symbol we must all snr or later come. The ruls f r rder have made
4  me brng you hr. Let me make you acquntd with these things. The [hourglass]. An mblm f tme. Turns it.
5  Bhold how rapidly the particles of sand run. It wil soon run out and then if no externl pwer set it in
6  motion agin its movemnts will never renewed. Forgt this not. Here is watr f your refrshmnt.
7  Her is an img of death and mblm f mortality. No human philoshy or thinkng can divne what lies on the
8  other side of this veil or what shll hpn to us there yet it is crtain we shall all thence and it is certn
9  that duration beyond the grave in comparison to the period of hmn life is infinite. This subjct is
10 intrsting then. See here is the only light by whh we can learn how to ntr the G so as to
11 enjo hapns herft. It is the bk of wsdm and cntns a rvltion of the dn will. P First. 12.6.

12 Mn ws crtd n the image of God bt who cn knw hm whn he defrms himslf. Scnd Round.
13 He who is ashamed of rlgn and of truth is unfit for and unwrthy of frtrnty. Third. That
14 mn whse ear is deaf to the cries and the dstrsses of his fllw mn is a monstr in the assmbly of the
15 Brthrn. Let hm nw ascnd the three first mystrous stps leading to the Tmple to try his
16 strngth and then brng hm to the east to mke his vow. Sir your patnce has enabled
17 you to reach an altr at whh by the rules of our order you are rqrd to mak a solmn and irrevocable
18 oath or covnnt never unlwfly to reveal any of the scrts smbls sgns or ceremns blngng to the
19 Ordr of F and Acpd Msns you hve lredy pn bn assurd tht the ordr does nt cntn anythng cntrary
20 to our duties tward Gd, our cntry, our nghbours or ourslves. This assurnce I nw rpeat to you and ask
21 you if you are wllng to mk the oath or cvnant rqrd what do you nswer. But sir bfre you can
22 mke a cvnnt it is necessary that you be well cqntd with its tnure we holding it to
23 be wrng to mak a cvnt with any unlss they be well cqntd with its cndtns ther
24 efore you will please to kneel on the left knee on the [square] and let your rght hnd rest upn the Bible on
25 whh lies the [square] and [compasses] cvrd wth a sword. Sir the book on whh your hdn now rsts is the H Ble opnd
26 at the frst chptr St Jhn and the fifth vrse whre thre is wrtn and so frth. Do you believe that
27 your hnd thus rsts upn the B? And why do you blve it. Thus you cncve that a man
28 upn the serious assurance can blv the thng of whh he has no other evdnce thn ths surnce.
29 Nw I desre you to be atenteve to the voice of the SW who wll rpeat to you the covnt whh you
30 are rqrd to mk evn in the prsnce of the Sprm Arktct f the Unvrse and whh wn made cn

31 not be rcld. Pg Five at the top. | it is here n rmbrnce f the cord. pge second. whh

32 Here repstd. And n the cntre is the blazng str whh we view wtth rvern tial slnce. and fnlly the [cord]

*Page 121*

# The Manuscript and Translation

*Page 5 of the Folger Manuscript*

## The Manuscript and Translation

## Page 5 of the Folger Manuscript

1 Man who is stripd of all sensual and false decorations and ornamnts and covrngs of vanity cannt be knwn and distingshd frm others
2 but by rightousnss and virtue. It is absolutely necessary that you henceforth b cnvncd of your own weknss andthat it
3 is impossible to go forward toward the Tmple of Truth without help and guidance. In order to give us a plain
4 to kn of your want of confidence in yourself you must permit us to deprive you of the light. It is an emb
5 lem of the false views whh are the lot f that man who is lft to his own guidance. Bndge. Tell me can you see any
6 thing on your honor. Be carefull not to use deception with him who shall guide you you will else presntly
7 certnly rpnt. You are now in drkness but fear not those who guide you go on in light and will not lead you stray.
8 hold your hands before you and gurd agns the hndrncs cn meet you. You are now lft aln strve to go forwd
9 bt use the utmost prudence in order to avoid srndng dngr. Tks [3] steps forwrd. I acknowldge you as one
10 who (?)sks I mark wll your srous desre bt in thick darknss and alone you wold undbtdly go astray. Tks his lft hnd and says.
11 As such I will brng you to the [Lodge]. I pry b cnstnt and cnfdnt lrn to suffer wth ptnce and abstnce and thrby mak yourslf
12 worthy to obtn in tme what at presnt ask fr. Fllw me fr nt [3 gavels] D. Who cms h. [1] in drk
13 nss wh seks light and wshs to be acptd Hs nme. Age. Fthrs n whre brn. Prfsin. Relgn and he hs made any vow
14 that frbds hs jng the Msnc fra. Ntr. sir. H i h brght you my tsk is nw fnshd you are in sfe hnds. Evn wth thm who
15 desrve you prfct cnfdnce. Pg one sctn secnd. Whn in the wst and the G hs lft hm M sas thus sir you have sought

16 that the profne are remov'd and the hall in safety. Please to perform that office. The P are rmoved and so on
17 since the P and so on are removed we will pursue that path f duty whh is pointed out to us and strive to
18 consummate our work. [3 raps(?)] Br. Look twrd the east. It was there the light arose by whh we are enbled to
19 work let us be ppd to cntnue our lbours at the sign f the Mastr. M [1 rap(?)]. N order [3 tapers] may the clearst lght
20 shne for us during our lbours [2 tapers]. Prayer. By the mastr as follows

21 Th Creator God of Heaven and Earth
22 Th Thckest Darkness hides not from thy sight
23 In mrcy view and purify our hearts
24 Bless us that we may learn & do thy will
25 Wisdom itself Almighty King is thine
26 And thou alone hast Strength, others are weak
27 In all thy works beauty effulgent shines.
28 We humbly pray thee in this hall of peace
29 Send down thy blessing on our labours here
30 That we may be wise, beautiful and Strong.

31 Br J what is the tme. It is pst high twelve. Br
32 Sn is it the right tme to bgn to work. It is. Thn
33 assist me Br to opn this Disciples [Lodge].

34 [X X(?)] Let us live together in unity. To the honour f J. In the name f fratnry and by virtue
35 of the powr f my office I declare this D [Lodge] opnd. Brethrn be attntive to
36 the work [X X(?)] [1 rap(?)]. The work now proceeds in the usul form the candidate is introduced

37 The next section will occupy the sixth page and thus begns. Closing. Br J what is the tme
38 toward low twelve. Br S is the labour fnshd. It is.
39 Have any f the Br any thing to offr as the labour is

Page 123

## The Manuscript and Translation

*Page 6 of the Folger Manuscript*

# The Manuscript and Translation

## Page 6 of the Folger Manuscript

1  Oblgatn. I do prmse slmlnly and sncrly in the prsnce of G and [this] [Lodge] f Fm that I wll be fthfll
2  and true to the holy Chn rlgn and to the gvrnmnt f the cntry in whh I live and that I wll strve to gn the
3  stmm and love f my fllow mn by prctcng vrtue and shunng vice and by ncourgng othrs so to
4  do and I prmse that I wll as fr as I cn hlp the dstrsd and that I wll cncl frm every
5  one who is not a F and Acc M all the scrts sgns smbls and usages of ths ordr and every prt thrf
6  and I wil nt unlwflly reveal any of thse thngs nor write thm on any thng or mke them
7  legible so tht the scrts of our ordr cn thrby be nlwfly tevld and I will strve to chrsh
8  and love all worthy and good Brthrn f and acc m as Brthrs and should I violte this oth the keepng
9  of whh I slmly prmse I am wllng to be lookd upn dy all hnst and good mn and all Fm
10 as a mn wthout hnr and every prsewrthy quality and dsrvng their cntmpt and dsdn and I now rpeat my
11 wsh to be mde a m so help me God. Hve you heard and rghtly inderstood ths slmn covnt.
12 Are you wllng to mke it and to snctn it ccrdng to the custms of our order I ask you fr the lst tme.
13 [1 gavel]. In rdr B and whle ths mn mkes ths cvnnt It us gve a tokn f our accrdnce wth it.
14 You are now bnd to us and we to you by this your oth but the trial of your sncrty whh is the hardst trial
15 is now at hnd. You have said that you would snctn ths cvnant accordng to the custms of the ordr are you wllng
16 to snctn it with your blood if it should be rqrd of you. Page Two. Secnd Sectn. It is done.

---

17 Brs are you a Dscple. I am. Frm whnce cme the Dscpls. Frm the west. And whither are they
18 going. Towrd the east. Why. In search f lght. What are your duties as a Dscple. To cntnue
19 dignity the work I did begn as cmmded by the Master on the rough stone with what did
20 you work. With the smbol f powr. Why. To shew the prpr use f the pwr with whh I ws intrustd
21 how is a Msn to be known. By sgns words grips. How so. His manners must be gntl and unassumng. His
22 cnversatn brudnt and discreet he bng rather a hearer thn a speaker bng wllng to hear yet apt to teach and
23 shun
   ing foolish dsputes. He dsdns to pollute hmslf by doin any mean fraudulnt act or crmnl
24 he dscountnances lbrtnsm commnds and practices virtue he encourages benovolnce and charity
25 by precept and example. Whre do the D lbour. In the outer court f the Trmple. Have you recived your wages
26 Yes. What are they. I gt food and raimnt and many othr things. Where do you receive your pay. At
27 the ntrnce f the Trmple. Who pays you. The Mstr. Are you satisfied with you wages. I am wll satisfied and
28 know the word. What tme do you dgn to work. Pst high twlve. Whn is the tme f rest. Twrd midnght.
29 are the dmnsns f your Lodge. Its lngth is and so forth. Why this xtnt. Becus Masnry
30 includs all thngs it is unlmtd. What do the [3] tprs rprsnt. The sun and moon and the
31 Master f the [Lodge] and as the sn and mn regulrly dsnse lght and heat and lfe to the erth. Page seven. 2.

---

Page 125

# The Manuscript and Translation

> O Thou Great maker on the throne of Heaven
> Thy word from nothing did call forth the whole
> Thy new foreunneth every thing that is
> and thou forcadeth all in Heaven & Earth
> Look down in mercy from thy holy Heavens
> tho us the Creatures of thy Gracious Will
> Great Wisdom. We are ignorant and blind
> Great Strength. Without they aid we lost are in
> Lord: with thy blefsing beutify our Souls
> And O thy Honour may our work to done
> That Brethren live in Peace. tacking god will
> this may our Brother this Autom. Bring it

*Page 7 of the Folger Manuscript*

# The Manuscript and Translation

## Page 7 of the Folger Manuscript

1   see who it is and if a Br lt hm ntr. It is our nw mde Br. Brng hm to the e by the nw. My Br prmt
2   me to clthe you wth ths lmbskn and n the nme of the ordr I prsnt you wth these whte gloves. The whte
3   clthng you are nw dcrtd wth is mblemtc of burty and innocnce worn honorbly it is a very hnorble badge.
      Brserve thm
4   frm stns. Wear them and nver appr wthuot them in the [Lodge]. The ordr of good Msns does nt prmt wmn to its ass
5   mblies yet we profss and chersh estm fr the vrtus and good amng the othr sx. In tokn f this I prsnt you
6   wth [these] glves whh you cn gve to such a one as merts your stm hre is your mney (?) tke thm
7   my Br n gvng you bck [these] we would admnsh you to bear n mnd tht it is a mst crtn truth that
8   the love f gld slvr and the lke hs producd more evils than any thng else in ths world. Ys. Cvtsnss avarce hve led mn
9   much astray. Have nducd thm to cmmt the mnst acts of cwardce and most atrocus cts f njstce and oprsn and violnce.
10  Cts so mean and so atrocious s to xcte dsdn and horror n vry hnst and fllng mn. Cts whh cuse the sign of sorrow
11  to burst frm the breasts of the really pious and whh alas it is to be feard have brght down the thunder f dmnatn
12  on the heads of the guilty perpetrtrs therfre respctng the prncious nflnce of [these] thngs we should watch. Here is
13  your hat n dlvrng it to you I must remark that none xcpt they be Masters st cvrd n [Lodge]. Tke your swrd
14  use it carflly whn calld upn by your country fr its dfnce but br n mnd that a mn f blood s deemd unft
15  to buld a tmple to the nme f G and nver frgt hs cmmndmnt who gve law to mn n order to mke thm hyp syng thou
16  shlt not kll. Pg Eight I will nw lrn you the tsts of this dgree. Go to the Wrdns and mk yourslf known.

17  Br almoser please perform your duty. [1 rap]. In ordr Br. Before we part Brn let us form a tie f fra
18  trnl union and offr up our dutifull acknowljdgmnts to the great Mastr whose goodnss has enbld us thus
19  fr to do the work f Msnry and supplicate his blessing. Here the Brn all jn hands and the Mastr prays thus

20  O Thou Great mastr on the throne of Heavene
21  Thy word from nothing did call forth the whole.
22  Thy view perceiveth every thing that is.
23  And thou pervadest all in Heaven & Earthe
24  Look down in mercy from thy holy Heaven
25  On us the creatures of thy gracious Wille
26  Grant Wisdome we are ignorant and blind
27  Grant Strengthe without thy aid our toils are vain
28  And with thy blessing beautify our Soulse
29  And to thy Honour may our work be done
30  The Brethren live in peace teaching good will
31  And may our Brother Tie Continue Strong (?) five
32  Brn assst me to close this [Lodge] let us be unimous [X X(?)] I declare
33  this D [Lodge] closed to the honor f J in the name f Fr and by virtue of my
34  offce. Br be attntve IX(?)]. [3 tapers]. E. That lght whh shined
35  durng our labours cannot be seen by the profane. Brn when you
36  seek for light wherewith you would perfct your works remember that
37  that light is in the e and only there to be found. Dsmss. Page Five. See.

# The Manuscript and Translation

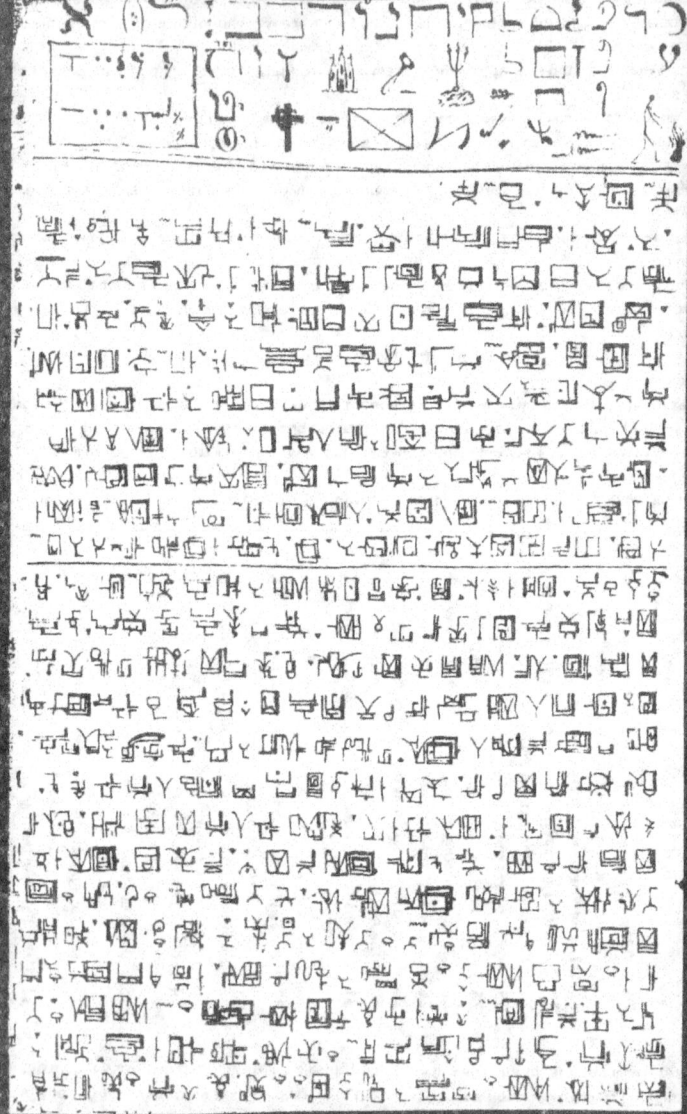

*Page 8 of the Folger Manuscript*

# The Manuscript and Translation

## Page 8 of the Folger Manuscript

| 1 | | [aleph] ( : ) [?] . [beth] [?] [daleth] ō [gimel] [heth] [yod] [qoph] [lamed] [?] [?] [?] [samekh] |
|---|---|---|
| 2 | ā ē ī ō ū | [tauv] th [zayin] [?] [temple] [gavel] [candelabra] [lamed] [mem] [?] [?] [ayin] |
| 3 | ā ē ī ō ū | [tet] t [tet] t key [?] [?] [?] [figure] |

Pge One at the foot.

4  so does the Master dispense knowlge and discipline to the [Lodge] and all Masters f [Lodges] should strive so to do.

5  What is the emblem f a Dsceple. A brokn pillar with the inscrpt adhoc state. How is it xplaind. As by the rmnant f

6  the pllr that is yet stnding we can ascertan to what ordr it blngs and determne what its proportns and rnamnts were whn it was entre and thus be enabld to form another p l knss f the brokn one so from

7  

8  what we know relatve to man we hope and believe that he may be restored to a state aproachng to that first prstne purity and happiness. Why is Solomons Tmple used mblematically n Fm. It was a highly fnshd

9  

10  and splndd building and the first Tmple erected by man publicly sacred to the name f the only wise and true God and Fm

11  teaches us to be built up lvng tmples as perfect and beatifll as the Slmnc Tmple was to the service

12  and to the honour f the Supreme Architect f Heavn and Earth. Flose f the catechism. Nekt follows the catechsm

13  wark. Page Nine at the Top. Work.

14  Then we reprocting the cnfdnce you had hither to placed in us blveld you and you commncd a journy on whh you learnd frm the est some

15  truths on whh the tnets of our ordr n a great measure rest. You thn scnded the mysterious steps f the Tmple ws drught to the

16  altr to mke a very serious promse. On the whole f this journy reciprocl cnfdnce supportd you. Cnfdnce between you and us

17  tr f you had nt had cnfdnce n us you wold have refusd to follow our dretcns and if we had not have believed

18  you to have been upright we would not have reveld you amng us. You was joind to us by a solmn tie and aftwrds you saw a blazing and unstedy lght whch

19  was only sufficient to dscover surroundng apparnt dngers finally the vel was removed wholly you saw the light you bmeld

20  Brn armed for your dfnse and welfre all hostile appearnces wre dne away and everything bore appearnce f love

21  [those] scnes are mblamatical f the dffrnt states f man the unenlghtnd state in whh man makes scirfces and oblatrs tr

22  obtng favours from heavn or for the atonement f atrocious deeds he may have cmmittd in whh state nearly all the

23  objects he perceivs were hostle in appearnce and hs fllows seemd stngrs to him and their arms apred to threatn hm their

24  powr to place hm in dnger he shuns fears or even hates them but n a more enlghtnd state he prcieves that

25  hevn rathr accpts a sncre and cntrite heart thn burnt offrngs and oblations he then acknowldges his fllow men as his

26  Brn and he looks upn their power as means tr his own dfnce and welfare he joins them relies upon them and loves them

27  you ws invested with the badges f innocnce ad admnshed by good conduct to keep them unsulied.

*Page 129*

## The Manuscript and Translation

*Page 9 of the Folger Manuscript*

## The Manuscript and Translation

### Page 9 of the Folger Manuscript

1. to them and to the Br who pledg hmslf n your bhlf. As a m. Ftrwards the S W will teh you the smbll work upn the
2. rough stne. My Br the rough stone n mblm f whh you here see is a smbl f man dfrmd by prjdcs
3. and passns to erdicate and to subdue [them] is the duty and the work of every Masn. The gvl s smblical f pwer. T is used by
4. hwers f stne to strke f the asprties f the shlr and to rdce t to the frm whh the Mstr has prscrbed it should have and we are
5. rmnded by t to strve to sbdue our passions and eradcat our prjudices to ft ourslvs for that sprtul tmple not made
6. wth hnds etrnl n the heavens. In tokn f your wllngnss to do this wrk whh the great Mastr has ordnd we(?)
7. should do stoop hmbly dwn twrd the earth and strke the rugh stone as I do [3 gavels] cntnue cnstntly in the
8. wrk you there begn to do that the Suprm Rchtlt may not be dsplsd wth your labours and that you may strve to merit
9. rward. Hs aprobatn. Nw let the frst work you do as a m be a good work. Do a deed f chrty gve a pttance
10. to help the dstrsd. Bottom f ths page begns the lecture and the rmndr wll be wrtn lkewse turn round

---

11. be attry to a rctn f the rite f ntitn whh nw is endd the smbls usages and custms f our ordr are n your
12. tndd to lead the mnd to the crumptn f thngs f the greatst importnce to that man who is wshfll
13. to lrn and to mditate upn that whh may promote his wlfare. You was first led into a dark and nrrw chmbr whre you was speratd frm the world and from your friend who brght you there. Altho the sprtn
14. was but short yet the thngs there led you to mditate upn subjects however commn yet f a very serious nature
15. to your
16. meditatns were disturbd by the comng f a Br who nquired f you your motves fr jng our order for none(?) but
17. [those] actuated by right motves should be admitted amng us. He who was dputd to guide you hthr n
18. company with your frnd causd you to be dvstd f all money jwls and the lke othrwse ppd you fr introductn nto our
19. Lodge. That you might know that wrldly dstnctns cn not gve rank and must nt create dffrnces amng Masns. In
20. the [Lodge] we all meet upn the lvl and p in fact amng the good and imprt nothg amng but virtue and mnrl acquirements
21. cn gve preemnence amng men n the world and nothing lse cn dstnguish brthrn in the [Lodge]. N the chmbr
22. f ppn it s hoped you spend the tme profitbly. You ws abstrcted from the world and for a momnt prhaps ws
23. ngaged
24. n the cnsdratn f yourself and that xtrnl objects might not ntrely ngage your attntn or dstrb the mprssion whh you there recvd and
25. that you should remve cnfdnce n your guide you ws deprivd f the light and thus led to the door of the [Lodge] whre
26. you ws recvd by the Wardn he dmnd your rlgion nme age and othr prtculars fr none but a profssor f relgn and one who
27. is free and who we know a m arrvd at the years f real mnhood cn be admittd to our [Lodge]. The three blws
28. the [Lodge] shld remnd you that fr hm who seeks with humility and who knks rghtly f the door f
29. f the tmple f frantry and peace shall be opnd. You was cnductd to the care f the wardn and stood then upn the this
30. hold f the [Lodge] your frmr g levng you wth assurnces that you wre n the hnds f [those] who wld nt misld you but
31. bfre you could by the assrne f your new cnduct proceed on your way the M addrsd you and your motvs fr cmng here were cknwldgd to the Br by hm who best cld nfrm us therf by yourself. Bottom f pge seven

# The Manuscript and Translation

*Page 10 of the Folger Manuscript*

# The Manuscript and Translation

## Page 10 of the Folger Manuscript

1  Opening of the Fellows [Lodge]. Senior calls to order [3 raps] Master. In order Brethren [2 raps] Br
2  Wardens what is the duty of all good Masons before the Temple is opened [1 rap] to see that the profane are removed
3  and the [Temple] in safety [2 raps(?)] you will please to perform that duty [man] Senr answers the profane are removed and the
4  [Temple] in safety. Then follows the lighting as in the Disciples G with the address. Then the xhibition of the
5  Brethren behold an emblem of the guide of the wise. Let me persuade [you] to retain this emblem in [your] memory and if un
6  happily passion should tempt [you] from the path of duty may a remembrance of what was seen serve to
7  lead [you] from error if unhapily avarice or ambition should stop [you] on [your] way and a recollec
8  tion of that bright emblem should happily arouse [you] again to pursue [your] journey o return not
9  to the vicious betray not the good. Br Senior what is [your] orders name Giblem Br Jun what time is it.
10  Toward low 12 Br Sen is it right time to begin the work. It is. then please to be in order assist me in open
11  ang [1 gavel]. Sign prayer [1 gavel] be seated. Br Sn for what purpose are we here assembled. To
12  learn to know ourselves and to inspect work done already on [the rough stone] and to strive complete it according to the designs
13  of the Master and to make farther progress in Masonry. My Br let us strive deeply to impress upon our minds that it is high
14  ly important to labor diligently in order to complete the work according to the designs of the Master. Let us henceforth abstain
15  from all foolish and vain pursuits and use the time allotted to us here to labor in discharge of our duty that haply we may be deemed
16  fit for the [Temple] and not be rejected and that we may hope to meet the reward remempering that time flies swiftly away
17  and is irrecoverable for mortals but to the view f the Great Master on high the past the present and the future are all opn?
18  he perceives all the actions of men and knows all their thoughts • Br Senior when does the work end in the [Temple]
19  Fellows [Lodge]. Closing. Br Senior are [you] a F. I have been accepted as such. Where, in a perfect [Lodge] of F.
20  Who accepted [you] the M how shall I know [you] to be a Fellow. By the sign what is the work of the Fellow on
21  the [square stone] and [rough stone] and to finish it according to the Masters designs where have [you] worked as a Fellow in the Temple
22  Why was [you] accepted as a F to lean the letter G what did [you] perceive in the F D that you had not before seen
23  [blazing star] what did it represent or is a symbol of the guide of the wise and faithful where did it arise in the east from whence did [you] see it from the
24  steps of the [Temple] did you go toward it yes I was brought toward it whither did it guide [your] steps towards the Master what else did you
25  perceive the I G what does it signify I know but little about it but it has been said to me to signify geometry was any thing else shwen to you yes [one] of the subjects on which I was to labour have you commenced [your] labours how can you complete them
26  
27  yes how by following the directions given by the Master and by his assistance when will [your] labours as a F cease when I am admitted to the Masters [Lodge] and mave
28  passed through the inner chamber have [you] received wages yes at the [pillar] Jakin I have met with encouragement and the promise of ample reward what is the symbol
29  of a F the [sqare stone] with the inscription DO what is the meaning of this symbol that the Master discovers and points out the defects of the work and has given us the means
30  of rectifying these and it should remind us of our duty to strive to conform to the rules given us thereby endeavouring to fit ourselves for a place in the [Temple]

*Page 133*

# The Manuscript and Translation

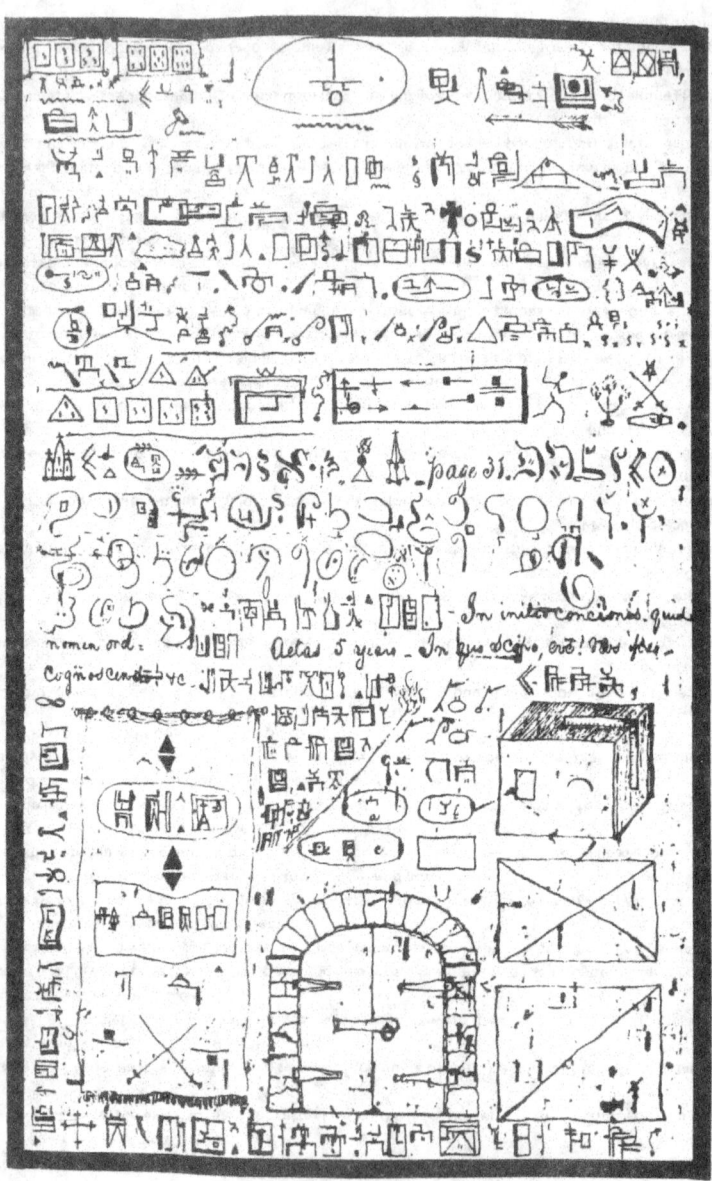

*Page 11 of the Folger Manuscript*

## Page 11 of the Folger Manuscript

1. one two three and so on we or they   Fellow   Begin on the opposite page. seven eight
2. Opening (1 gavel)
3. What is the duty of every good man and so on as in D [Lodge]. What is your orders name. Giblem
4. Br Senior. For what purpose are we here assembled. To learn to know ourselves and to inspect the work
5. already done on the [rough stone] and so on as in the D [Lodge] a b c d e f g h i j k l m n o p q r s t u,v,w x y z .
6. a e i o u y and the. I. thou. he she it. tense as thus love. nothing
7. love  B signifies two or second. he. his. you. your. three or third. numbers
8. him. he.
9. numbers. [Figure lighting candelabra] [crossed swords with star over and coffin under]
10. [Temple] nothing *page 31*
11. d c d a f g j k l m n p r s th o z
12. a o e e u o u y y e u
13. e y At midnight closing as in the Disciples D●  *In initio conciones quid*
14. *nomen ord* = Giblem *Aetas 5 years* ● *In quo Scopo eve! Nos ipso*
15. *cognoscendo!* &c *sic transit gloria mundi*. the Grade of           you     here these within
16. Fellow is written regul            your
17. arly or from page to            we th they
18. page & with many
19. abbreviations      am was
20. characters        have been        26   d o
21. And the
22. light shined in the darkness
23. and the
24. darkness comprehended
25. it not

The Grade of Disciple is written promiscuously on the first pages

27

29 † When thou hast passed to the place of which this a symbol thy destiny will be fixed forever●

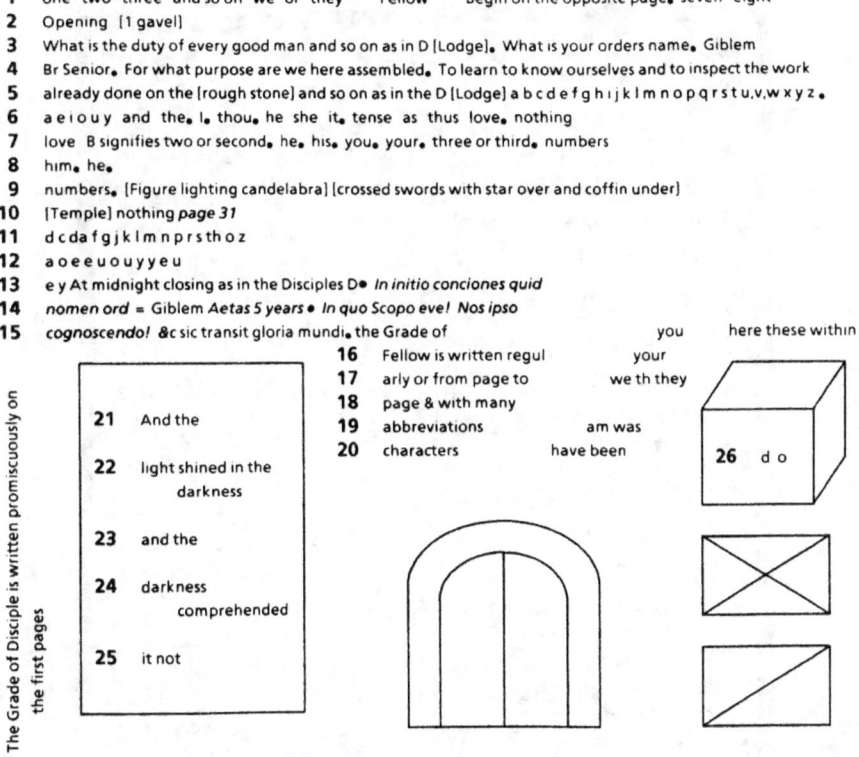

## The Manuscript and Translation

*Page 12 of the Folger Manuscript*

## The Manuscript and Translation

## Page 12 of the Folger Manuscript

1  Address frm the Mastr. Br you re welcome. [gavel]. The F and Masters present have givn their unanimous
2  consent to [your] being accepted as a F and I am well satisfied that in the charactr of a f [you] will use [your] best endeavours to
3  discharge your duties as such. Yet it is my duty to inform [you] that the work of a F not only requires
4  good application but that it is difficult yet it undoubtedly has its reward. [You] are frm hence forth
5  carefully to inspect the work done already on the [man bent over rough stone] and strive to complete it according to the designs
6  of the Master Grt Architect that they may haply nvr be deemed unfit for the temple. We are prepared
7  and willing to assist [you] with advice and rules for [your] work but the work [you] must do [your]self. No man can
8  do it for [you]. And we desire ever that [your] honest endeavours will meet a reward a [Temple and a man]
9  formerly on [your] symbolic journey [you] was blindfolded you was in darkness. At the present time [you] wander in the light
10  yet my Br you would undoubtedly go astray unless [you] were assisted by a guide who knew the way and is willing to shew it to [you]. 5 & 17 =
11  if [you] will go to our Br Second Overseer he will conduct [you] in paths on which [you] can learn
12  things relative to the duty of a Fellow. [His] hand holding [your]s and by which you will be lead forward should remind
13  [you] that a Br should assist another in good and laudable pursuits while the sword
14  resting on [your] breast should impress [you] with a sense of the irregularity and precipatancy
15  in the strvng to consumate our views at the same time it teaches one of the important duties of a F 23
16  viz that of checking all imprudent hastiness but especially when [he] is going upon a way where [he] is a stran
17  ger 83. G makes the [first] [round(?)] [Temple] [man looking at cord containing skull, sprig of acacia, crossed swords, cross (on its side), and blazing star]
18  [gavel] Man was originaly pure upright undefiled happy. How comes it then that
19  [he] so often wars with his own welfare and makes [he]mself miserable. [Your] passions lead [you] astray [and]
20  sensual enjoyments entice him from the garden of happiness into the wilderness of vice and into the labyrinth
21  of error. But presen often alas too late it is feared he is undeceived. Or what is worse he is satiated
22  a feeling of duty or of shame rouses [him] to view [his] present state and [he] sees with remorse that [he] is far from
23  where [he] should be but the ways [he] has wandered through are so winding and intricate
24  that [he] can perhaps never retrace [his] steps and [he] stands like the fool [man] not knowing
25  from whence [he] came or whither [he] went. [Man] [5] [candelabra] [book] [two gavels]
26  [man] [inverted cross with Xs]  [gavel]. He who has begun to go forward in the path of wisdom and virtue and turns back is a thousand times more deplorable
27                [gavel] than [he] who never went that way for [he] never knew what duty was nor did [he] take the pleasu
28  tecond round. res arising from virtous actions such a man has brought a dangerous enemy to war

*Page 137*

# The Manuscript and Translation

*Page 13 of the Folger Manuscript*

## The Manuscript and Translation

## Page 13 of the Folger Manuscript

1. against his welfare viz himself. His own self [stop (from page 22)] [1 gavel]. [man by fire] [aleph] [third] round
2. [1 gavel]. Br we believe that [you] are willing and ready to undertake the task of the F the subject on which you are to labour is
3. deserving of [you]r attention and [you] ought never to neglect it Br Warden lead the Br to the image of the
4. pillar of beauty and let him consider it well that he forget it not. G. If [you] desire to view the obj
5. ect of [you]r labours then draw the veil aside see [you]rself [man] see emblem. Br the F are generally well pleased
6. with [the]ir own work but if [the]y behold [the]m with the eye oc the Master [the]y would be astonished to see how imperfect that
7. is which [the]y think so finished and [the]y would be very much alarmed on beholding how much yet remains to be
8. done in order that [the]y may not be rejected by him who is apointed to inspect [the]m and who will dispose of [the]m according to their merits
9. even the most finished work a man who follows his own thoughts of perfection can produce will perhaps be found very
10. imperfect and full of error and deemed unfit and unuseful yet it a consolation to know that a good artist is able to make of the most
11. unfinished block of [rough stone] an indusputable likness of one of the most beautiful and perfect creatures but in order to do this [he] must
12. be well instructed by and must follow the rules of a great and good Master. Br Sen let our Br ascend the [five] first
13. steps of the [Temple] that [he] may from thence behold an emblem of the light which guided wise men and from [the]nce conduct [him]
14. to the east to make [his] vow      Br when [you] where before at this altar although blindfolded
15. [you] had so much confidence in us    [beth] [mem]    that [you] did not hesitate to give [you]r consent to a covenant the ten
16. ure of which [you] was unacqua     inted with but before [you] took it it was wholly made known to [you]
17. now [you] are in light and [you] have in some measure become acquainted with us and with the order therefore we can expect
18. more confidence of [you] than when [you] was the stranger among us wherefore I ask of [you] if [you] are willing to
19. make the covenant belonging to this D. Answer. My Br we expected of [you] this xpression of confidence
20. and thank [you] for it but Br take our admonition in good part never consent to a serious engagement without first having heard
21. its contents and without having understood [the]m Br Snior please read the covenant to our Br. Br have [you] heard
22. this covenant and are [you] willing to take it kneel then on the [square] and hold the [square] to [your] breast now read it
23. [you]rself Brn while our Br reads the oath let us give a signal of our accordance [altar] [cross on its side]
24. covenant is here taken we hail [you] as a Fellow [open book] I present [you] with this blue ribbon which
25. [you] will hereafter wear it denotes constancy and is the colour of the heavens. Learns the grip
26. sign and word. [aleph] boaz [man throwing spear over fire] [man falling onto something] [unknown symbols, same as on page 7] [gavel] [sword] this sign is
27. a pledge of constancy and good faith it is lake pledging the heart thus in pledging our words as Fellows
28. we point at the heart as thet hing pledged for the sincerity of what we say now make [you]rself known to the W and to our F

*Page 139*

# The Manuscript and Translation

*Page 14 of the Folger Manuscript*

## The Manuscript and Translation

### Page 14 of the Folger Manuscript

1. who has pledged [him]self in [your] behalf are [you] a F. Answer. By what shall I know [you].
2. Answer. As often as [you] make [the]s sign remember that [you] pledge [your] heart your life for the truth of what [you]
3. say salutes him. Covenant. I do voluntary and without deceit in addition to my former covenant most seriously
4. promise and vow never to reveal to any one whatever not even to a Br D any of the secrets symbols or anything
5. appertaining to the D of a Fellow which I am now receiving xcept it should be in a just and legal [Lodge] of Fellows
6. such as I am now in and I vow carefully to conceal all things belonging to [the] Deg from every one xcept I am convinced
7. after strick trial inquiry and xamination that [he] or [the]y are entitled to receive the same and [the]t I can without a breach of covenant in
8. the least deg communicate respecting [the]se things. [He] or [the]y having been accepted as a F in a just and perfect [Lodge]
9. of F such as I am now in and as a token of my sincereity I pledge my heart. then proceed as in Disciples vow.
---
10. Lecture. The well instructed quide who brought [you] to the door of the [Lodge] and properly ppd [you] fom [you]r en
11. trance here and assurance that [you] had laboured diligently procured [you] admission and the welcome of the Master [you] came to the W
12. [your] guide might follow [you] no longer [you] was then to seek another guide and the address from the east must have con
13. vinced [you] how necessary directions and instructions are in things to wh we are strangers [you] could not possibly
14. guess at what was intended to be done or how [you]were to be disposed of yet [your] believing that [they] wished to do
15. well toward [you] prompted [you] to follow the directions given [you] thus when [they] believe in the good intentions of
16. fellow beings [they] are easy and [they] willingly enter into [the]ir views that altho xperience and reason teach us that men are very
17. frail and feeble creatures if [the]y were perfect how much more easily willingly should [they] follow [the]m [you] went again
18. on a symbolic journey and [you] learned on the way the causes of much of the unhappiness and misery to which man could
19. be subjected [your] attention was called to [one] who could become [your] most dangerous enemy [you] was made acquai
20. nted with the error which could make [him] such finally the subject on which [you] was to labour with constancy and care was
21. presented to [you] and the imperfection of human works taught was the rule for removing those imperfections from a more
22. elevated situation than [you] before had [you] could view an emblem of the guide of the wise my dear Br let me persuade
23. [you] to retain that emblem in [your] memory and if unhappily passion should tempt [you] from the path of duty
24. may the remembrance of what was seen serve to lead [you] from error if unhappily avarice or ambition should stop
25. [you] on [your] ~~journey~~ way and the recollection of that bright emblem should happily arouse [you] again to pur
26. sue [your] journey o return not to the vicious betay not the good at the altar [you] made a voluntary vow and rece
27. ived the tests of this D. We hope [you] will often call [these] things to mind with pleasure
28. our order has as [you] already know adopted the implements of operative masons ★ *(see next page)* such

*Page 141*

# The Manuscript and Translation

*Page 15 of the Folger Manuscript*

## The Manuscript and Translation

## Page 15 of the Folger Manuscript

1  instruments were used in ereecing the [Temple] in Jerusalem which was sacred to the name of deity
2  and [the]y have been moralised those peculiar to this D are the [square] plumb and level by help of [the]se the rough stone
3  becomes a good square stone if a stone be so wrought that by neither of [the]se instruments defects can be
4  found it is fitted for the builders use but the square is applied to [two] sides at once but it will not rest evenly on the superficies
5  if the stone is defective hence it is called the symbol of truth and discoverer of error and we hail the love of truth as [one] of the greatest virtues the
6  plumb admonishes to righteousness see its unerring line it directs from earth to heaven and from the heavens to the earth the
7  level is only applicable to the upper superfices of the stone when placed on the building by it undue eminences or depre
8  ssions are discovered which tequire the gavels use to be removed hence it is taken as a symbol to remind us of that equality
9  which should xist among all good Masons the builders of the holy [Temples] in the days that are past were well acquainted
10 with the proportions necessary to the constructing of [the]se beautifull and well contrived edifices and hence [they] ought not to be
11 unacquainted with the dimensions and proportions of architecture and it is certain that in the places where wisdom beauty
12 and strngth characterise the buildings [the]re we not only find science cultivated and the social virtues encouraged but heaven
13 born charity is [the]re xtendin the hand to the assistance of the needy. [Sprig of acacia] the doric ionic and corinthian orders are [those] which in our
14 times are generally esteemed originals [the]y are here in the [Lodge] instead of our more ancient pillars as monuments of human ge
15 nius and of the high degree of taste and love of splendour which already xisted among the people of the old world but most of the magnificent
16 monuments of antiquity are destroyed or ruined sic transit gloria mundi the liberal arts and sciences deserve our attention and
17 ★ encouragement [the]se distinguish a polite people from savages and the capacity for acquiring a knowledge of [the]m leads man
18 to contemplate upon the works and perfections of diety and enables [the]m to lead others from many pernicious errors and to shun
19 [the]m [him]self on on both sides at the entrance of the [Temple] [you] see [two] pillars the [one] formed and ornamented like the other
20 [these] stood before the entrance of the sanctuary and no one could enter [the]herein without passing [the]m Boaz and Jakin is the name
21 of the [two] pillars the meaning of the word [he] shall establish it [the]hese pillars were taken from the Temple by Nebuchadnezzer
22 [the]y were cast by Hiram the widows son of brass were hollow eighteen cubits high and [four] cubits thick [the]y stood here ornamented with the symbols of
23 peace wealth and plenty like twins no difference in [the]m but [the]ir names my Br if [you] will meditate upon [the]se things and upon the mysteries of [the]is [Lodge] [you] will find a wide
24 field for the xercise of the mind the subjects are usefull in a high degree and full of interest and particularly those
25 relating to [you]rself [these] demand [your] most serious attention [man standing] here ends the lectur of the fellow [Lodge] [3 gavels]

26 [hourglass] [sword & flag] closing [curtain] [crossed trumpets, altar with flame] [First] / John / Chaptr
27 ★ as hieroglyphs

# The Manuscript and Translation

*Page 16 of the Folger Manuscript*

## The Manuscript and Translation

## Page 16 of the Folger Manuscript

1. JS. Closing the Fellows Grade [1 gavel]. Br Sr are [you] a F. I have been accepted as such. Where. In a perfct [Lodge] of F
2. who accepted [you] the M how shall i know you to be a F by the sign what is the work of the F to square the smooth [stone *(hill with cross on top and sprig on side)*] and to finish it acco
3. rding to the Masters designs where have [you] worked as a F in the [Temple] why was [you] accepted as a F to learn the letter G what did [you] perceive in the F D
4. that [you] did not before see the [blazing star] what is it the guide to the wise and faithfull where did it rise in the east frm whence did [you] see it from the steps of the Temple
5. did [you] go towards it yes i was brought towards it whither did it guide [your] steps towards the M what else did [you] perceive the letter G
6. what does it signify I know but little about it but it has been said to me to signify geometry was anything else shewn [you] yes one of the subjects on which I was to
7. labour have [you] commenced [your] labours I have can you complete [the]m yes how by following the doctines given me by the Master and by his assistance when will [your]
8. labours as a F cease when I am admitted to the Masters [Lodge] and have passed to the inner chamber have [you] received wages yes at the pillar Jakin I have met with encourage
9. ment and the promise of ample reward what is the symbol of a F [a square stone with "DO" engraved on it] what is the meaning of this symbol that the M discovers and points out the
10. defects of the work and has given us the means of rectifying [them] and it should remind us of our duty to strive to conform to the rules g
11. iven us thereby endeavouring to fit ourselves for a place in the [Temple] Br S when does the work end at midnight here follow
12. closing as in the Disciples [Lodge] xhibiting [star] with the address then questions as in opng f [F lodge] [3 tapers] [2 men with sticks?] [3 gavels]

| Obligation for all members also all candates for the Scots Ritus and visiting Masons | |
|---|---|
| 13 | I promise and swear sincerely and without deceit that i will not reveal speak about or |
| 14 | commmunicate in any manner whater to any person in the world not even to any F and acc Mason |
| 15 | any of the forms symbols doctrnes or ceremonies or any other things practised |
| 16 | n this body xcpting to such as are members of the same or of a [Lodge] acknowledged by the |

17. Master of this body to be working according to the wrk done in this [Lodge] unless the Master of this body grant me per
18. mission so to do as far as it respects any F and Acc Mas and I will not suffer the works to be altered neither will I do the work
19. which is practised here in any other [Lodge] or cause or allow it to be done unless i have the consent of the Master for so
20. doing or the permission of the bresent G M of [Grand Lodge(?)] so helb me God amen    **Disciples Vow**

21. I do promise faithfully and sincerely in the prescence of God and this [Lodge] that I will    **in full form**
    be faithfull and true
22. to the holy Christian religion and to the government of the country in which I live and that I will strive to gain the love and esteem of my fellow
23. men by practising virtue and shunning vice and by encouraging others so to do and I promise that I will as far as I can
24. help the distressed I also promise that I will conceal from everyone who is not a Mason all the s. s. s and usages of this
25. order and every part thereof and I will not reveal unlawfully any of these things nor write [these] on anything nor make [the]m legi
26. ble to o[the]rs whereby the things and matters or secrets or usages shall be unlawfully revealed and i will strive to cherish and love
27. all worthy and good Br of the order as Br and should I violate this oath the keeping f wh I solemnly promise I am willing to be looked upon by all honest

Page 145

# The Manuscript and Translation

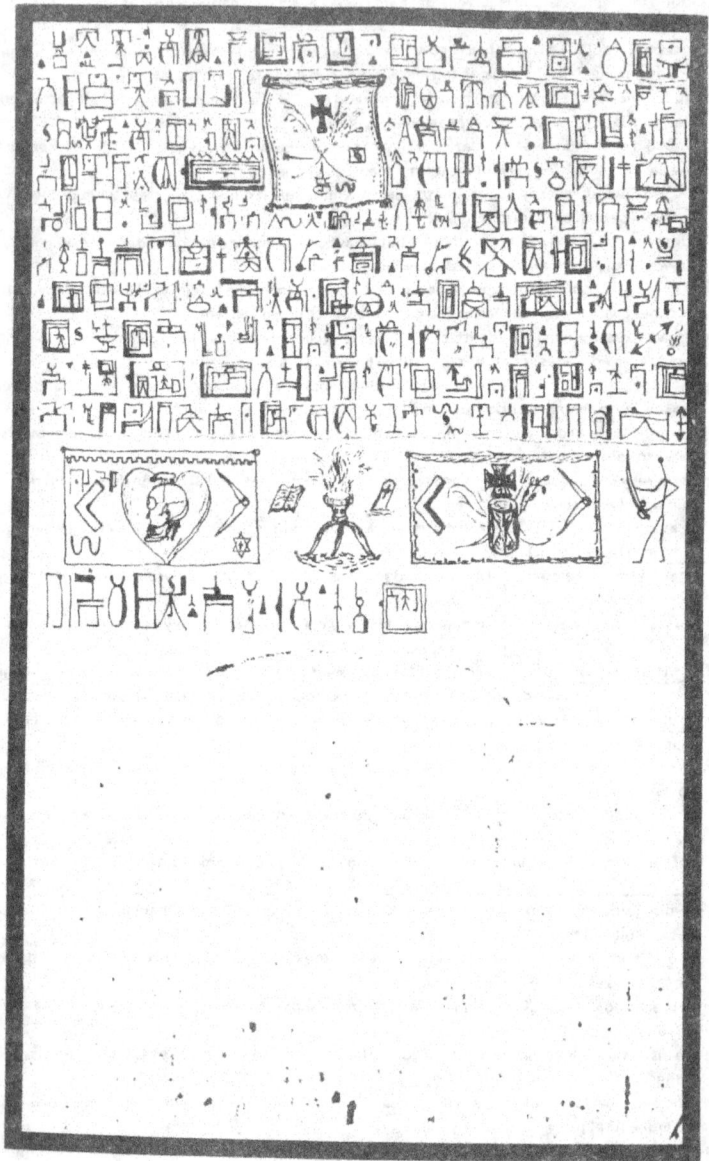

*Page 17 of the Folger Manuscript*

## The Manuscript and Translation

## Page 17 of the Folger Manuscript

1. and good men and all Masons as a man without honour and every praiseworthy quality and deserving [the]ir contempt and disdain and I now repeat my wish
2. to be made a Mason so help me God
3. I do voevluntarily and without any deceit in addition to my
4. symbols mysteries or any thing apperta
   
   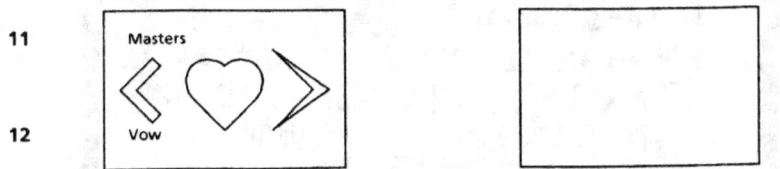
   
   former covenant most solemnly promise never to reveal to
   any one whatever not even to a Br Disciple any of the secrets
   ining to this dg of a F which I am now receiving xcepting
   
   Fellows Vow

5. it should be in a legal [Lodge] of F such as i am now in and I promise carefully to conceal all things belonging to this [Lodge] from every one xcept
6. I am convinced after strict trial inquiry and xamination that [he] or [the]y are entitled to the same [he] or [these] having been accepted as a D and F in a just
7. and perfct [Lodge] such as this I am now in and that I can without a breach of covenant in the least degree communicate respecting the things with each
8. person I likewise promise that I will aid and assist to the best of my ability all worthy F who may claim my help and to be faithfull.
9. With the xceptions above mentioned I promise to keep the secrets of this [Lodge] enclosed in my heart and as a pledge of my sincerity I declare
10. that I will have my heart torn from my breast rather than violate this vow I now make so help me God amen.

11. Masters
12. Vow

13. Masters vow begins in the same way as the F with the following additions

*Page 147*

# The Manuscript and Translation

*Page 18 of the Folger Manuscript*

# The Manuscript and Translation

## Page 18 of the Folger Manuscript

1  Preparation for the Masters Grade. Tablet.

2  We should while we live prepare for death and we should constantly be at this work because we know not
3  when we shall die. But it is certain we shall die and we shall give up our bodies to the dust from whence [they] came
4  our souls die not [they] are to xist forever but how shall this xistance be miserable unhappy.
5  Could we determine it we should choose the happy state but [the]n we ought to be ppd for its enjoyment. And what
6  is necessary to ppre the soul for its hpy state and what will make it fit for its enjoyments whoever saw the vicious hapy
7  even in [this] gross bodily state [they] are not so [they] can clo[the] [the]mselves in purple [they] can live in palaces [they] can own
8  piles of gold [they] eat of dainties and become drunk of rich wines but is this happiness or is it not rather
9  the source of unhappiness if deprived of [these] things would [they] not be miserable.
10  In the grave none of [these] things follow with [the]m. If [the]y think but on death and futurity it is agony to [the]m
11  what [the]n would realization be

12  Br [you] wish to be accptd as a M come follow me. [locked door] [five] [gavels] [2 x 2 raps(?)] At the door.
13  Who is here a F who wishes to be accptd as a M gives the pass he is over [five] years old and has worked in the inner court of the [Temple]
14  on the bolished stone [he] has served [his] time and [his] M is well pleased with [him]. Admits [him] and says are [you] worthy
15  to wear [this] badge takes it from [him] and places [him] in the west (Giblem)

16  Address from the Master

17  Br [you] are now brought to the inner chamber when [you] are passed to z place of wh this is
18  an emblem [the]ere no art nor deception can hide any error or any imperfection the judge
19  who [the]re presides views the [hearts] of men and knows [the]ir most hidden secrets wherefore in reverence
20  to [these] solemn truths be sincere my Br we are here assembled to commerate and to lament the death of our G M
21  [his] loss we may justly sorrow for and as justly deplore the cause of [his] death and debloring [the]em shun [them] [he] was killed
22  by unfaithfull F no guile was in [his] heart nor evil in [his] ways yet [they] set [his] goodness at nought and [the]er
23  ruffian hands murdered [him] Br Wardn shew our F the horrid spectacle before us and watch [him] well and see if [he] appears to
24  be one of the conspjrators against the G M W our F does not apear to be among the guilty and [he] is moved we be
25  lieve at [this] sight M we are glad that [you] do not apear greatly concerned in [this] work
26  of death and we hope [you] never will join [those] who are guilty bring [him] on the Masters path for instruc
27  tion that [he] can join us in seeking the Master. Symb journey

28  tria formant alienuum deponit [et] ascendit in unum

*Page 149*

The Manuscript and Translation

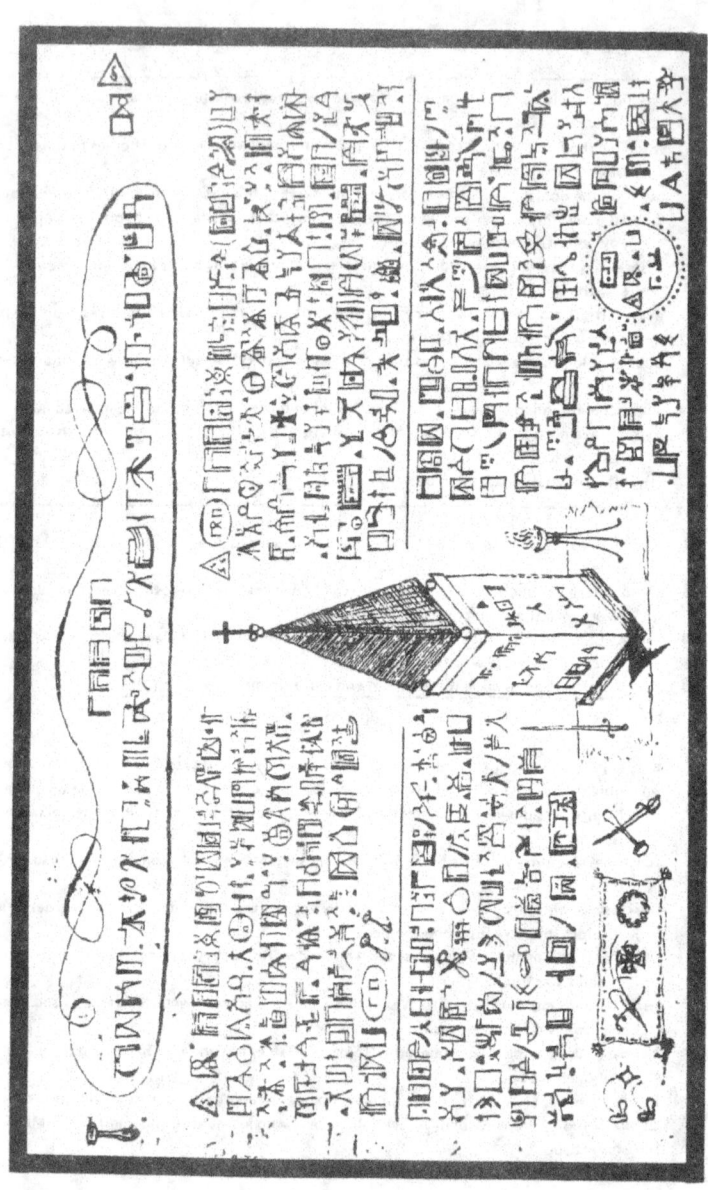

*Page 19 of the Folger Manuscript*

# The Manuscript and Translation

## Page 19 of the Folger Manuscript

First round

1 Remember Death

2 [1 Gavel] That man who has a sense of [his] own frailty and who has laerned to observe [his] own imperfectons has made the first step toward the light

3 [Second] Round Remember Death it is unavoidable how dangerous it is to venture upon the far
4 distant journey without a knowledge of the way we are going how foolish to refuse
5 to attend to the infallible doctrines wh point out the way would one who thus ventures and
6 thus refuses not easily err and not find the city he sought but instead [the]reof faint among
7 the sands of the desert where [the]re is no water to allay burning thirst and bread to keep
8 from starving R D [Two Gavels]

9 [Third] Round Remember Death it is unavoidable it may be very near (perhaps it is near at hnd) let us
10 incline our [heart]s to instruction and our minds to understanding and learn the way to the habitation of
11 rest and comfort let us seek the way thi[the]r with earnestness let us knock at its door with confidence
12 and with all humility let us ask alms for our wants of the good M of the house and believe me [he] will not
13 reject our prayer and will even grant us much more than we xpected and more than we can
14 dispose of let [him] now ascend the seven steps of the [Temple] and bring [him] with Mas seps to the east

15 My Br before [you] can be accepted as a M it is required of [you] to make a solemn covenant
16 with us the Warden reads it [gavel & sword] [3 raps(?)] Now Br [you] are to receve the word and grip
17 of [this] D and in future when [you] use [these] things call to mind the situation [you] were in
18 just before [you]received [them] [one gavel] Br Warden lead our F to the blace where
19 we shall all assemble accepts [him] hymn and procession

20 behold Brn the pall covers the coffin contains a Br God give [you] may
21 hence forth be dead to sin and ever may [you] bear in mind that [you] shall
22 die may [you] have firm hope of being raised from the Fellow to the M
23 from darkness to light from dust to heaven from mortality to eternal
24 life and may this hope cheer [you] and make [you] faithful Brn let us seek to
25 find our M who was slain        Pass    Lord help us children
26 of the dust here is acacia sprig    [once] round    nd [this] has the
27 a grave let us look into [this]        the grave    apearance of G next page continues

28 et
29 Tria formant
30 alienum
31 deponent
ascendit
in
unum

*See pp. 7–8 for a discussion of the triangular monument.*

Page 151

# The Manuscript and Translation

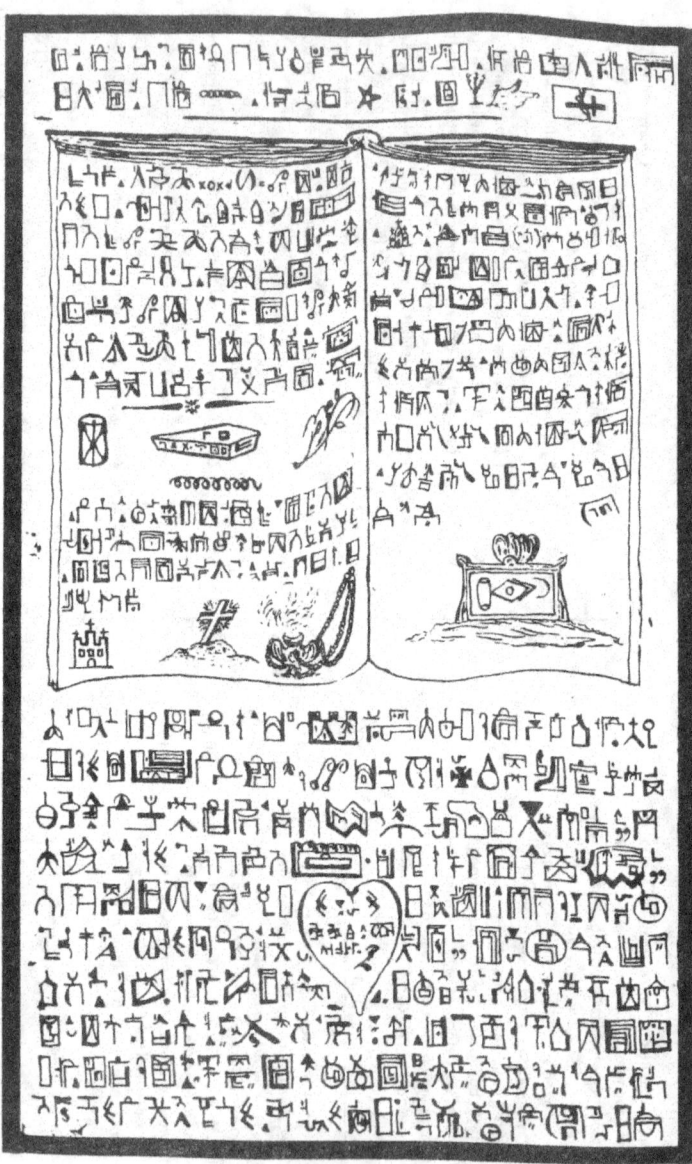

*Page 20 of the Folger Manuscript*

## The Manuscript and Translation

### Page 20 of the Folger Manuscript

1. Br as the word was lost at the death of our M let us now agree that when the body is raised the first spoken shall hereafter
2. be considered as the M word. The flesh is corrupt ★ Raises the body [three tapers] [finger pointing to broken tombstone with cross]

| | | | | |
|---|---|---|---|---|
| 3 | Lecture and instructions XOX [?] [you]r being advanced | 15 | the neccesity of mutual confidence in each other must be |
| 4 | to [this] D the objects can no longer strange to [you] but permit | 16 | aparent to all who have wandered from the court of |
| 5 | me to call [you]r attention to some of the things wh are incul | 17 | the [temple] to the *inner chamber (*its) who would follow |
| 6 | cated by our symbols and ceremonies independant of [your] | 18 | on in strange paths blind or in darkness or seeing |
| 7 | obligations [you]r mind was at an early period of [you]r connection | 19 | where the sword point rests against the naked |
| 8 | with our institution called upon to consider the very importa | 20 | breast xcept [he] had confidence in the directions of |
| 9 | nt and interesting subjects viz time death and imortality | 21 | [those] with whom [he] went and who would conduct any to the sanctuary |
| 10 | R D    It's unavoidab    le | 22 | of fraternity and make an indissolvable covenant of friend |
| 11 | and our aim in the course initiation has been symbolically and directly to point | 23 | ship with [him] unless [he] had confidence in [his] honesty |
| 12 | subjects for meditation whh could in lead men to live virtuously | 24 | and was convinced that [he] would betray not and would not be |
| 13 | and happily to meet death with serenity and to cheer this hope of a bl | 25 | come an enemy    TH |
| 14 | issful futurity | | |

26. Confidence grows however out of the good opinions we may have conceived of others ei[the]r arising from a knowl
27. edge of [those] good principles or our observation of [their] good acts thus if we know men who live blameless lives who s shun
28. covetousness and o[the]r vices and who ncourage truth and virtue who protect innocence and who do good [the]n we should certainly have
29. confidence in [the]se if [they] at the same time strive to propagate rules of life or doctrines tending professedly
30. to make men happier than [the]y otherwise would  [the]y we  be [the]n considering the character of [these] men should
31. at least xamine the things [they] hold out to us and if we even wi  these those and anything necessary  ll not readjly admit [the]m we ought not to neglcte try
32. ing with [the]m and if upon a fair trial and proper xamination  [the]y be found to be useful as having a salutary efect upon indivi
33. duals and upon society in general if [the]y are in unjson with the truth if [the]y answer the great ends of making men better qualifie
34. d for the discharge of duties if [the]y make men really hapier [the]n it would undoubtedly be very contrary to our ideas of duty if not very foolish
35. to reject [them] or even to neglect [them] and that if even [they] should be a little at varianc with our customary thoughts or be somew

# The Manuscript and Translation

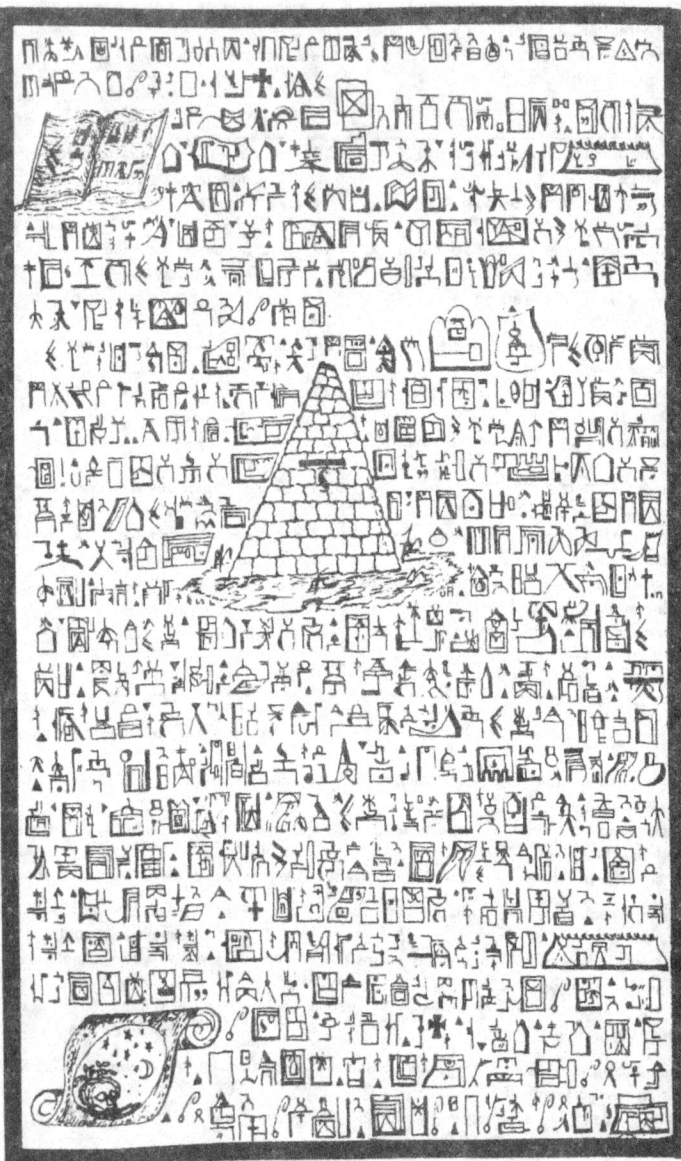

*Page 21 of the Folger Manuscript*

## The Manuscript and Translation

### Page 21 of the Folger Manuscript

1  hat inconventient because f our habits such men and such rules or doctrines as I have alluded to are to be found and it is believed that every[one] who
2  has strove to do [his] task as a D and F will seek and find [them]
3  [This] gre light of   is evr open in a proper [Lodge] to that end that we should be reminded of the duty that of learni
4  at Masonry   ng and practising the xcellent precepts it contains and if we as far as we can scrupulously
5  xamine both the character of [those] who gave the precepts and the influences [they] have had upon society
6  and still have upon it if we xamine the great ends and views of the doctrines here writen and thus become acquainted with [this] volume we shall
7  xperience that [this] volume is an inestimable treasure and should be viewed as such by all good men it is in fact the book that
8  contains the rules of life pointing out to man [his] whole duty
9  [this] volume is of great antiquity and splendid monumnts of the ancients have decayed and nations who peopled the countries where [these] things were written
10  have vanished or are scattered over the face of the earth [the]ir former   places of abode are desolate the languages the book was written in are dead
11  yet the book survives and the enemies of order and opposers   of the good precepts [this] volume contains have sought with astonishing
12  obduracy and unwearied pains with jests with philoso   E   J   phy falsely so called with misaplied learning with every
13  effort of [the]ir genius to bring [this] volume into contempt   but [the]y have been engaged in a foolish work all [the]ir pains have been
14  taken in vain it stands deservedly   now in higher estimation than ever [?]
15  considering the character of the writers for [this] vol   ume and finding [the]m to be good even inimitably so xam
16  ing [the] doctrines contained in [this] volume and observing [the]ir unison with truth and [the]ir beneficent influence upon society and upon individuals thinking upon the great antiquity of [these]
17  writings and the many revolutions which [the]y have survived and [the]ir complete victory over the efforts of enemies [the]re with continually increasing in the estimation of the world at large
18  of the friends of good order and of truth [the]n it can be said even if [the]re were no other reasons for so saying that [this] volume is not to be neglected but
19  on the contrary that it ought to be xamined and should be made the subject of our attention and study and see how correct is its philsophy how interesting the history how
20  sublime and beautiful the poetry how acceptible the doctrines of religion and morality contained in [this] volume it is calculated in every point of view to engage our attention and if attended to the truths it con
21  tains make men better wiser and happier and the benefits arising from [these] sacred truths are not limited to the period of human life [they] point not forward to the grave as the boundary of our
22  xistance as the place where men shall cease to be no the thick gloom of death is dissipated by divine truth a ray of sacred light makes visible to the eye of faith a state
23  of xistance beyond the grave a state of xistance at the approach of which all must fear for it lasts to all eternity for it is a state of rewards and x punishments
24  for it is dependant upon divine mercy for no man can claim a place [the]re hapy indeed is [the] man who has strove to subdue [his] passions and to lay aside
25  [his] prejudices and thus is fitted for the task of the F and studying and xecuting the designs and rules
26  of the M by contemplating upon the image of the pillar of beauty [he] may have observed [his] own weakness
27  and [his] own inability to make [his] work according to the pattern given [him] by the M if [he] is sensible of his own incapacity and imperfections

*Page 155*

The Manuscript and Translation

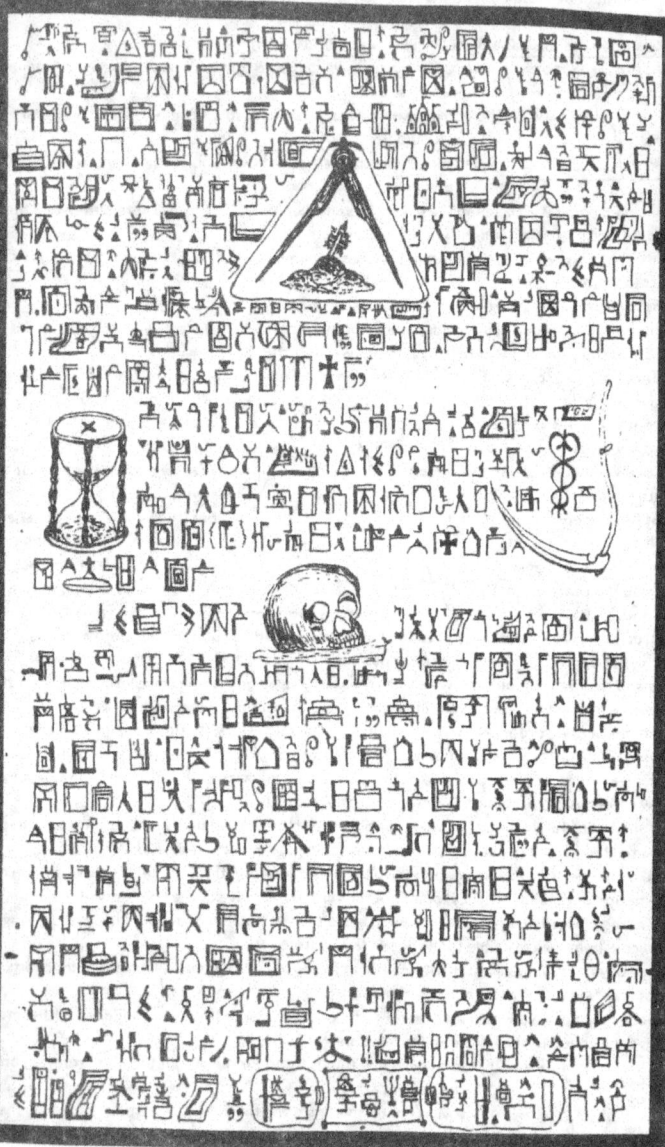

*Page 22 of the Folger Manuscript*

# The Manuscript and Translation

## Page 22 of the Folger Manuscript

1. [He] has in truth made the [first] step toward the light and has thus become more susceptible of the truth than [he] was then [he] will have the trestleboard in
2. [his] hands and use all proper means for becoming acquainted with the designs whh are drawn and no doubt [he] will not only direct o[the]rs how to xert
3. [the]m but [he] will participate in the labour in the erection of the truly noble edifice a [Temple] sacred to the name of God and in [this] work [he] will use the
4. implements of the M the compasses will remind [him] to set proper limits to [his] ~~duties~~ desires and actions not to be eccentric in be-
5. haviour but to preserve any even line of conduct without iregularities we should by xample and persuasion try to exact and encourage
6. fraternal love [this] is the very cement of the Temple if it is wanting the whole becomes a heap of rubbish
7. and is of no worth but on the contary is an obstacle to [those] who pass where it lies and nuisance to [those] who may
8. have a habitation near it where fraternal love is not [the]re must be many evils [the]re the ruffian passions are enthroned and virtue is driven
9. out or spurned with contempt or bound with thorns there folly derides wisdom and truth is obliged to hide her fair
10. face [the]re religion or morality can not be found [the]re all is but mockery
11. Time we cannot recall but we can and we ought to use [that] aright wh is to come see the sand the particles run rapidly
12. and for aught we know with the passing of [one] of [them] [you] or I shall die it is uncertain we
13. should not [the]n neglect a moment but from henceforth do all we can do to the great [caduceus] end
14. of being hapy [realy] for we shall die and in the grave [the]re is no working [the]re is no
15. device no knoweledge no pardon [the]re

16. See [this] emblem [this] monitor t is silent vacant dead yet it speks to our minds the good
17. hear a sound that even make [the]m tremble to some it can be a great cause of terror it reminds all to remember death
18. we have crowned it with a green sprig for we hope in partaking of immortality immortality and hapiness through faith in the giver of every
19. good and perfect gift and by an earnest striving to do [his] wil remembering [that] man was created in [his] image and although
20. much deformed can be again restored to [his] pristine state be made fit for blissful enjoyments remembering [that] we should
21. not be ashamed of truth and religion for [that] would make us unfit for fraternity on earth and disqualify us utterly for the enjoyments of a
22. future state where love is the most essential requisite remembering [that] we should be charitable and sensible of the wants of our fw
23. men for else we are monsters even here as althou assocated as Brn and [the]refore would be hereafter unfit for lasting joys we
24. must have hope to be restored to pristine purity we must have faith we must confes the truth we must xercise love and charity
25. with all our might [these] are the rounds of the mysterious ladder [that] reaches from earth to heaven and charity is the upper round
26. salutation and so forth Br S W are [you] a Master M yes I know the acacia sprig where do M M hold [the]ir [Lodges] in the inner chamber what
27. is [that] place a place of perfect silence where is it situated in a deep valley
28. furniture jewels ornaments symbols [candelabra] numbers colours signs gs and words in each D same as in the o[the]rs

*Page 157*

# The Manuscript and Translation

Thy word is truth & we shall surely die
From Dust we came, to Dust we shall return
But thou hast given us the fond desire
The Hope, Belief of Life - even after Death
For as thy Mighty Word formed us of Dust
So canst thou raise us from the Grave again
And place us in a Pardise Divine
Or drive us out to Sorrow & to Pain
But how can we Almighty King obtain
Thy blessing — or Eternal life & Joy.
Lead us from Evil — Lord. or else we err.
Shield us from Danger. Lord. or else we fall
Lead us to Learn & Do thy holy will
Save us from perishing or else we're lost.
Thou King of Mercies. Great, Almighty God.

*Page 23 of the Folger Manuscript*

## The Manuscript and Translation

## Page 23 of the Folger Manuscript

1 From whence come the Ms and how do [the]y journey fr the east why to dispense light and truth when [one] of our Brn is missing where shall we hope
2 to find [him] between the compass and square him your you stop  Z [?] I thou h[e] sh[e] it
3 and th the and th numbers [the]se you [the]se those he his he he him him you you temple
4 we ye or you [th]ey tenses as
5 love st thee thee

6 *Thy word is truth & we shall surely die*
7 *From Dust we came, to Dust we shall return*
8 *But thou hast given us the fond desire*
9 *The Hope, Belief of Life - even after Death*
10 *For as thy Mighty-Word formed us of Dust*
11 *So canst thou raise us from the Grave again*
12 *And place us in a Paridise Divine*
13 *Or drive us out to Sorrow & to Pain*
14 *But how can we Almighty-King obtain*
15 *Thy blessing - or Eternal life & Joy -*
16 *Lead us from Evil - Lord - or else we err -*
17 *Shield us from Danger - Lord - or else we fall*
18 *Lead us to Learn & Do thy holy will*
19 *Save us from perishing or else we're lost*
20 *Thou King of Mercies - Great, Almighty-God.*

## The Manuscript and Translation

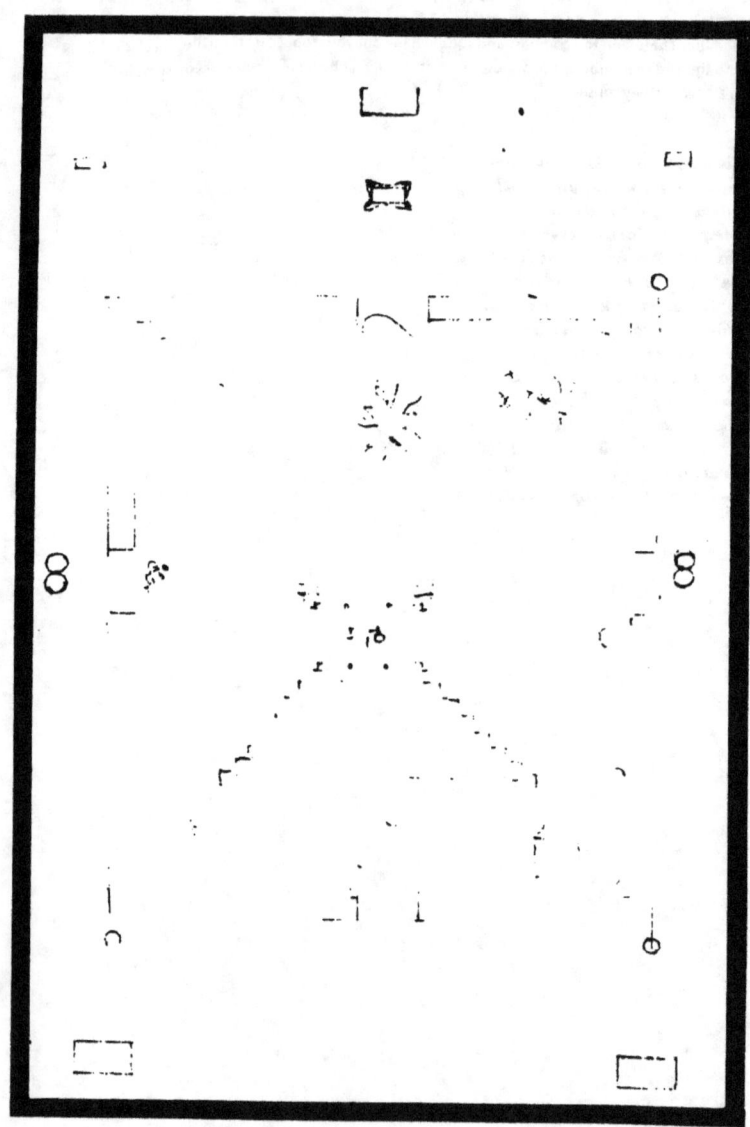

*Page 25 of the Folger Manuscript*

## Page 25 of the Folger Manuscript

# The Manuscript and Translation

*Page 77 of the Folger Manuscript*

## Page 77 of the Folger Manuscript

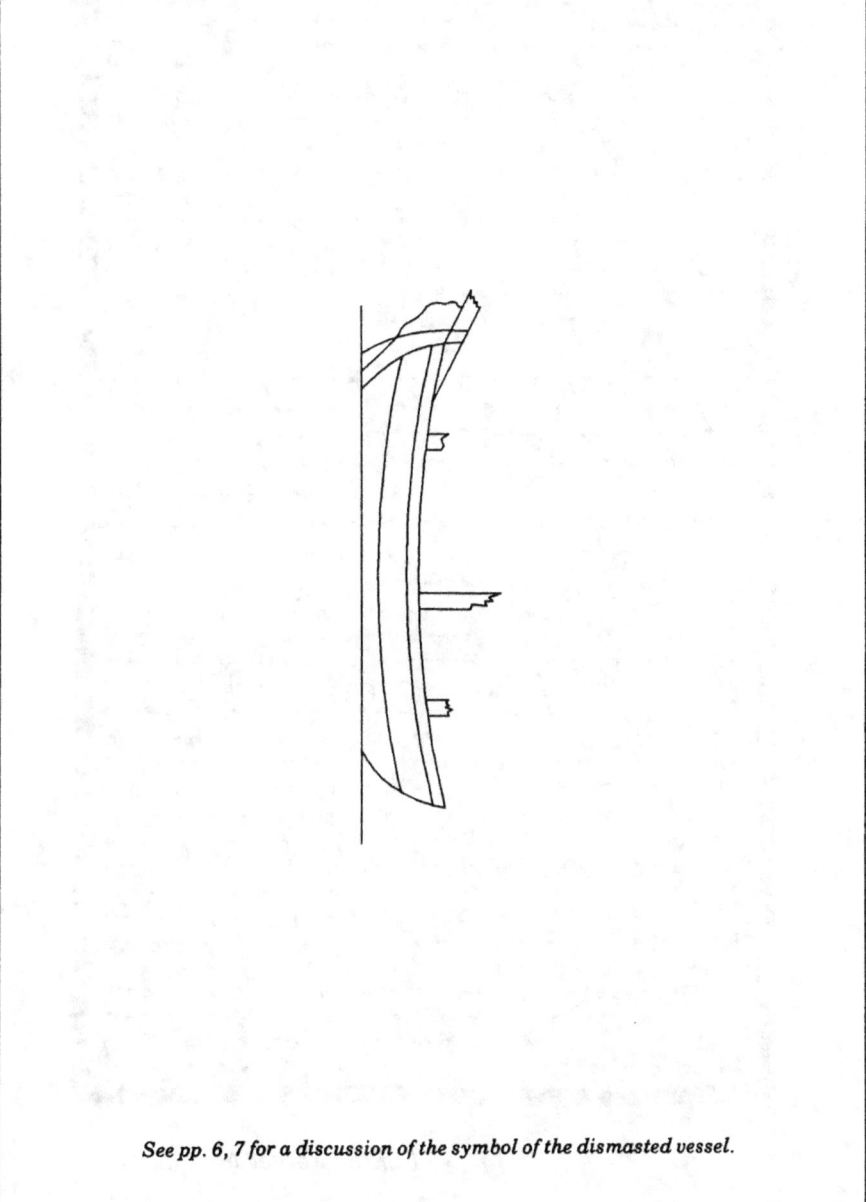

See pp. 6, 7 for a discussion of the symbol of the dismasted vessel.

## The Manuscript and Translation

*Page 81 of the Folger Manuscript*

## Page 81 of the Folger Manuscript

1  [Mons] was erected in [France] &c the monks joined the order and the of the Temp
2  lars originated. Now the statutes were published in England & the English Lodges (1705)
3  formed a Grand Lodge and usurped the Supremacy &c. The Jesuits – Mystics – Illu
4  minati joined the order & by entirely influencing altering and adding to it it got to
5  the shape is now has & the most of those who tried the reformation of the work (1779
6  1788] knew not the ancient forms & objects the work then became what it now is an
7  essentially & entirely different from what it originally was in the same kingdom as
8  other places.
9  Before the inquiry by [Rome] from a short time after the X there remained in [Jerusalem]
10 several of the brethren, among them [John] he & they a short time before the destruction re
11 -tired to Ephesus at ? ? they taught the sublime doctrines of C and joined to them sev
12 -eral [men of Jerusalem] who were in possession of the rites & of the Temple. They had assemb
13 introduced many christians into the mysteries – these serving rather as an exaltation
14 of knowledge & shewing that the real doctrines of Christ had long been known and
15 cultivated in the world even from very ancient times. But Justin the High Priest and
16 many of the Jews were opposed to the doctrines of the Cross and had got a wrong imp$^r$ as
17 to the myst & all these & all who were not Christians were not admitted among the Brethren
18 From Ephesus many went into Greece & to Achaia in particular were they taught C
19 In some places they privately learned the brethren the Mys. Shewing them who were
20 acquainted with these things that the new doctrine did not contradict but rather
21 confirmed the Myst & the precepts of Life which these contained. But soon after the
22 destruction by Titus some of the dispersed Brethren returned to [Jerusalem?] and their keeping to
23 landmarks of the holy places in view & many of them were desirous to search the vaults
24 of the Temple & the graves of the Kings thinking not only that it was possible that
25 there were treasures there but that they should in time be able to find some things be
26 -longing to the Temple of which only tradition existed & which were deposited by Z acc$^d$ g
27 to their acct. But the Roman Soldiers & many uninvited Jews & infidels being generally
28 present hindered them in their researches & as the infidel Jews in the year 105 made a
29 kind of revolution Adrian utterly destroyed the buildings which had been repaired in ? ?
30 & the 3 towers & the Brethren fled. But they were well acquainted with the landmarks
31 and a description of this if of the Temple &c formed hereafter a
32 part of the mysterious instruction. In the 2$^d$ century [121 : 30] many Brethren ret$^d$
33 with associates & devoted themselves to acts of Piety dwelling in secret places & praying
34 fasting & doing acts of charity of which there was much new. But they also kept
35 communion with each other & as far as circumstances would permit propagated the
36 mysteries. However many of the church were opposed to these things & the Brethren were
37 obliged to be very discreet & their number sometimes was very small. Yet in other parts
38 of the world there appear to have been numerous assemblies of the same kind tho under diff$^t$
39 denominations as in Greece. In 613 there were many in ? ? ? & many persons in 613 - 680
40 joined them. Bldgs were now build in the holy places one of which was called Sol Temple.
41 being a church built on the found$^n$ of the Temples sanct with flat roofs on the West
42 side & a kind of shelter with a stone wall & steep roof on the East side. By these
43 buildings the place of the Sanc$^y$ was afterwards known – times

## The Manuscript and Translation

*Page 82 of the Folger Manuscript*

# The Manuscript and Translation

## Page 82 of the Folger Manuscript

1. The regular formation of ? ? ? was uncoubtedly affected by ? & at his time
2. but this was ? ? ? ? & no other is in the first regular [Lodge] was undoubtedly
3. formed in [Europe] not in other places as in ? ? ? ? ? &
4. ? ? ? was born 1590 – lived 61 years [in ?s time C] was likened upon fig•g
5. by the courtiers as the murdered master – his mother was yet living as a
6. widow & his masonic subjects called themselves her children &c &c] During ?s
7. time there were many Lodges in England Ireland & Scotland & masonry was generally
8. adopted & flourishing throughout these kingdoms but also in other places yet out of Eng
9. Mas was something also in form & object & in these places it was not popular and
10. connected with wrong speculations ?s Lodges admitted all kinds of people without respect
11. to Religion Morality or Cultivation & it appears that he only used the order as a means
12. by which he expected to effect some certain more political views. He pretended to advocate
13. Equality & Freedom but this appears to have been all a sham. He found the doctrines
14. of Masonry convenient with a little feebl alterations to his republican & afterwards to
15. his despotical views. The rebuilding of the Temple was made a figure in all its parts
16. subservient to the circumstances & to the political views of & many of his English Coa
17. -djutors. In England about this time the order had many names one after the
18. other as Free Masons – then Nivelleur – then members of the 5th Monarchy and finally
19. were again called Free Masons ? appointed † for Secretaries for the 4 Quarters of
20. the Globe &c. Genl Rainsborough was the master of the Nivelleurs. Sons of his
21. Companions were concerned in the death of the king. Their ostensible object was
22. as a society to the establishment of Freedom &c. Harrington was Master of the
23. 5th Monarchy & a friend & connection of ?. Their professed object was freedom and
24. equality & not to acknowledge any other Regent than ? ? ? They called the form of a
25. Flag with a Lion Sleeping with this motto – "Who will wake him. They conspired
26. however against ? & were persecuted afterwards by him. Hereafter ? sought to give
27. to free Masonry in England a more Religious Tendency that it had before had in
28. that land & it is said that the oath now has received quite another form & a more
29. political one than before & several Nivelleurs were during this alteration severely pun-
30. ished even with Death [see Parchards History 1736. When the order had got a more
31. f oath &c] it is however to be remarked that Williberts Architects & Masons
32. Societies [in 600] was one of the first formular appearances of M in Europe & it
33. there after a short time got the name of F & A.M. The murdering of Charles of
34. England gave the Society another form. The flight of James 2 produced the higher
35. degrees. Here is the secret of the Dagger with which the Usurper should be killed
36. [truth] & this ?s arrival in ? ? and the institution thereabouts of an order is a sub
37. ject much connected with the Mas History yet it is certain that several
38. hundred years before this time in which ? ? ? institution existed that there was an order
39. established or introduced on one of the western isles & flourished there prior to 1118•. M
40. was not denominated any such thing as M but was the real Masonry which altho
41. now but little known among Masons but is known to some few. On the restoration of
42. the Royal family after the republic ? was adopted insted of other things [? ? ? ? ?] & knight

Page 167

The Manuscript and Translation

*Page 83 of the Folger Manuscript*

## Page 83 of the Folger Manuscript

1 my Br in times of old it was ordained even by god that those who entered the sanctuary (into the our a) should [aleph]
2 wash [the]mselves cleansing [the]mselves from uncleannes it was a symbol and it impressed upon the mind the necessity of holiness in those
3 who went into the sancetuary my Br it is a token of [you]r sincere wish and intention henceforth to live undefiled wash your
4 hands and remember god is a witness to the berformance of his ordinances

5         Vow
6         of the
7        Anc Scotch Master
8 I promise

# The Manuscript and Translation

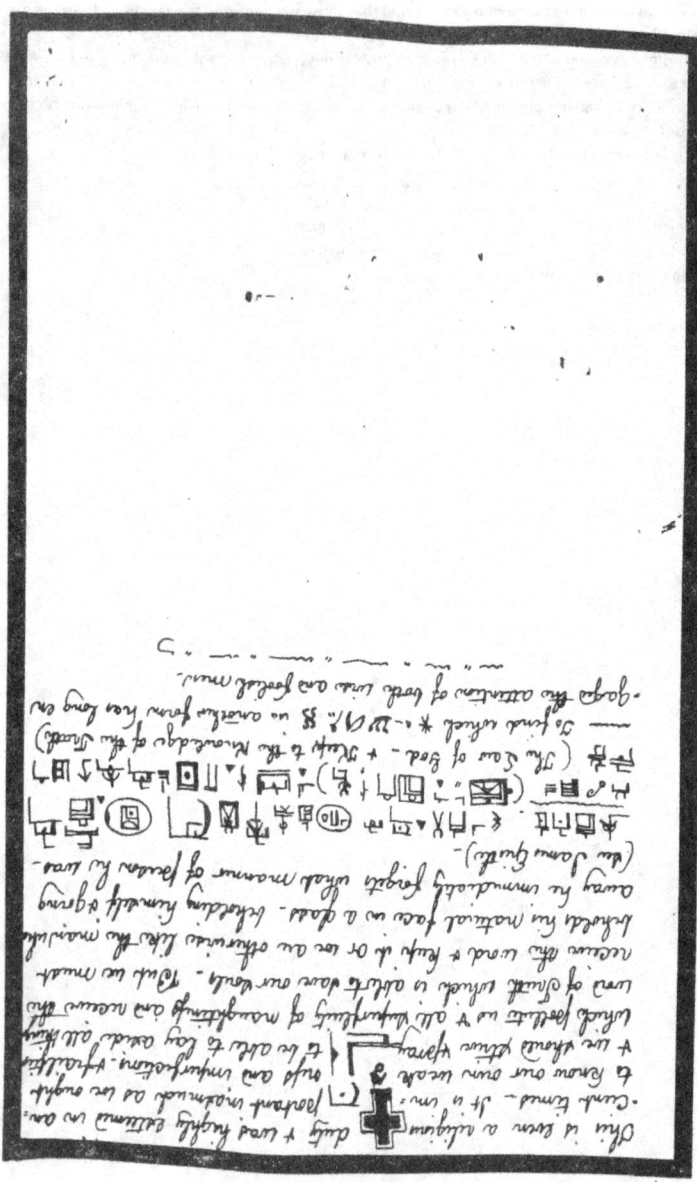

*Page 84 of the Folger Manuscript*

## Page 84 of the Folger Manuscript

1   This is even a religious         K         duty & was highly esteemed in an
2   -cient times. It is im-        thy
3   portant inasmuch as we ought
    to know our own weak
4   ness and imperfections & frailties
8   & we should strive & pray to     self      be able to lay aside all things
5   which pollute us & all superfluity of naughtiness and receive the
6   word of Truth which is able to save our souls. But we must
7   receive the word & keep it or we are otherwise like the man who
8   beholds his natural face in a glass - beholding himself & going
9   away he immediately forgets what manner of person he was.
10  (See James Epistle)
11  Consider thyself. [this] is shewn and that thou shouldst often think upon this duty and remember that
12  wh [you] here see (aparently at the bottom of a vault) is the image of the receptacle that contains great
13  treasures (The Law of God - & keeps to the Knowledge of the Truth)
14  —To find which " [shin ? vau aleph] in another form has long en-
15  gaged the attention of both wise and foolish men.

# The Manuscript and Translation

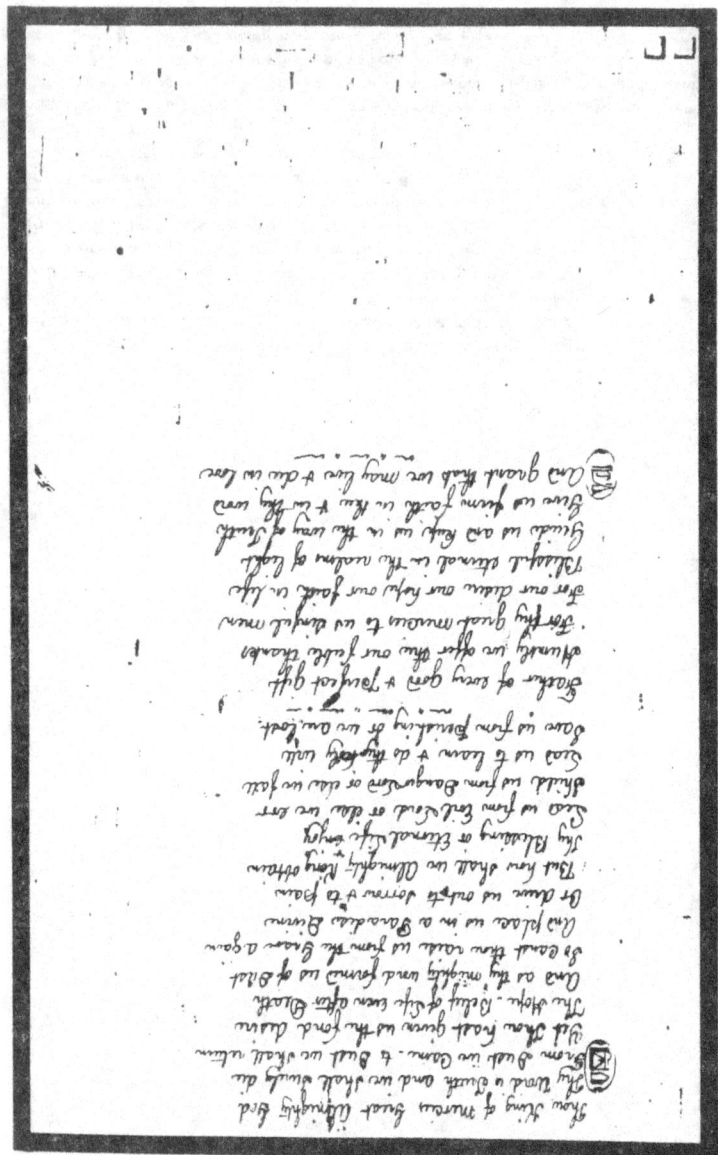

Page 85 of the Folger Manuscript

# The Manuscript and Translation

## Page 85 of the Folger Manuscript

| | | |
|---|---|---|
| 1 | Opening | 2  Thou King of Mercies Great Almighty God |
| | | 3  Thy Word is Truth and we Shall Surely die |
| | | 4  From Dust we Came - to Dust we shall return |
| | | 5  yet Thou hast given us the fond desire |
| | | 6  The Hope - Belief of Life even after Death |
| | | 7  And as thy mighty word formed us of Dust |
| | | 8  So canst thou raise us from the Grave again |
| | | 9  And place us in a Paradise Divine |
| | | 10 Or drive us out to Sorrow & to pain |
| | | 11 But how shall we Almighty-King obtain |
| | | 12 Thy Blessing or Eternal Life & enjoy |
| | | 13 Lead us from Evil Lord or else we err |
| | | 14 Shield us from Danger Lord or else we fall |
| | | 15 Lead us to learn & do thy holy will |
| | | 16 Save us from perishing or we are lost |
| | | 17 *Father of every good & perfect gift* |
| | | 18 Humbly we offer thee our feeble thanks |
| | | 19 For thy great mercies to us sinful men |
| | | 20 Humbly we offer thee our feeble thanks |
| | | 21 Blissful eternal in the realms of light |
| | | 22 Guide us and keep us in the way of Truth |
| | | 23 Give us firm faith in thee & in thy word |
| 25 | Closing | 24 And grant that we may live & die in love |

*Page 173*

# The Manuscript and Translation

*Page 86 of the Folger Manuscript*

# The Manuscript and Translation

## Page 86 of the Folger Manuscript

1  Prptns gsian Tblt. Mn ws orgnly pure nfld hppy hw coms it thn that he wrs wth
2  hs own wlfre and oftn mks hmslef msrable ths s a sbjct whh ndbtly dmnds our hghst attentn n as mch
3  s we oght to stdy to void nhpnss secnd the fool wndrs hs whle lfe thragh wthat cnsdrng or
4  knwng frm whnce he come or whthr he wnt Br the wse mn stus to know wht he is about and cnsdrng evry
5  stp its end and intntn and by clsly pursung the objcts of hapns he avoids all that can stop him in his way and knowing his own
6  wknss and ignornce he receives wth hmlty the doctrns tht are gvn him and wth grattude proffd
7  support when he is wrong and whn his own strngth would not bear him farthr. Guide. Masnry is progrssve. It is ncssary in evry pursuit
8  of knwldge grdually to advance in ordr to undrstnd thngs arght whrefore you ws not at all at once mde cqntd with all the arts of our ordr
9  but are advnced grdully through thm and indeed as nerly evrythng n our rites is smblical it requires previous previ
10 ous ppn to undrstnd thm and to mke thm usefll to ourslvs. Permit me to ask you wht is your opnion
11 of the tndcy of our ordr. Ths D is to be considered partly as a recompnse for your labours past but princpally
12 as tndng to ppre you for the Mastrs D. I cn assure you my B that your constncy and fortitude in this D must stnd
13 vry serious tsts. If you are detrmnd and fxd to go frwrd thn follow me like a man but if you wavr thn I advise
14 you rthr to remn in the D of Dscple untll you by the easier duties required in the D you hve tkn have becme
15 strng. Now B dcide yet do not decieve yrslf will you follow me. [three gavels]. Who kncks it is a D
16 who wishes to be accptd as a Flwl. His nme he hs lboured in the outr court of the Tmple on the rough stne
17 Pass. Hithr I hve brought you as you desired to the p whthr you durst not app my wrk is now fnshd try to
18 find yourslf a new G. Pg the thrd frm this. M. B you are wlcme. Page Eleven [man turned away from fire]

---

19 Covenant before entering a scotch [Lodge] I solemnly promise and vow that I will not converse about so as in
20 any manner to communicate or reveal to any person whatevr not even to F and acceptd Mason
21 any of the forms doctines symbols or ceremonies or any other things practised or done in the
22 xcepting it be to a member of the same or to such as are members of a [Lodge] acknowledged by the M
23 or his successors to be working according to the work done here unless our M or his successors grant
24 me permission so to do nor will I reveal the time and qlace of meeting to any but members
25 of the same amen

---

26  ★It is dark dlack seperated from the world see page [two] Disciples preparation
[man facing candelabra]   27   Thus vanisheth the splendor of the world like a flame kindled suddenly before [your] eyes and suddenly xtinguished when [you] seek for it nor a vestige of
28 it is to be found not withstanding its aparent splendour it shall utterly vanish
29 Br when [you] look for [light/flame(?)] remember it is only to be found in the east

# The Manuscript and Translation

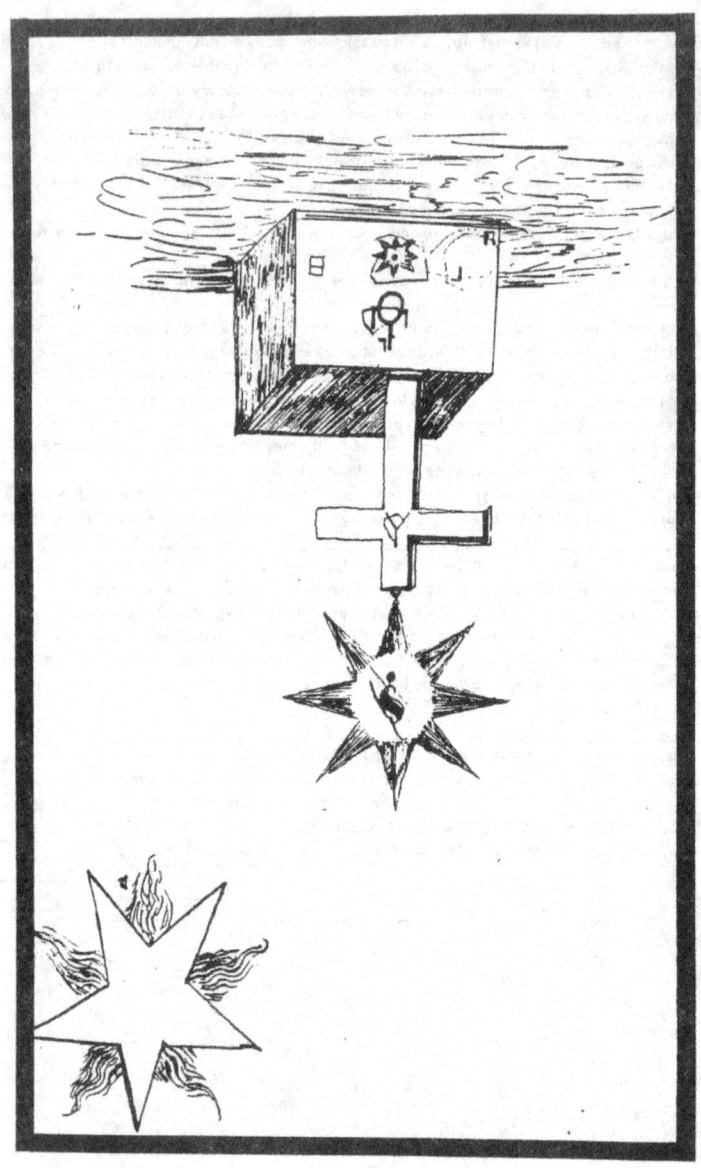

*Page 88 of the Folger Manuscript*

## Page 88 of the Folger Manuscript

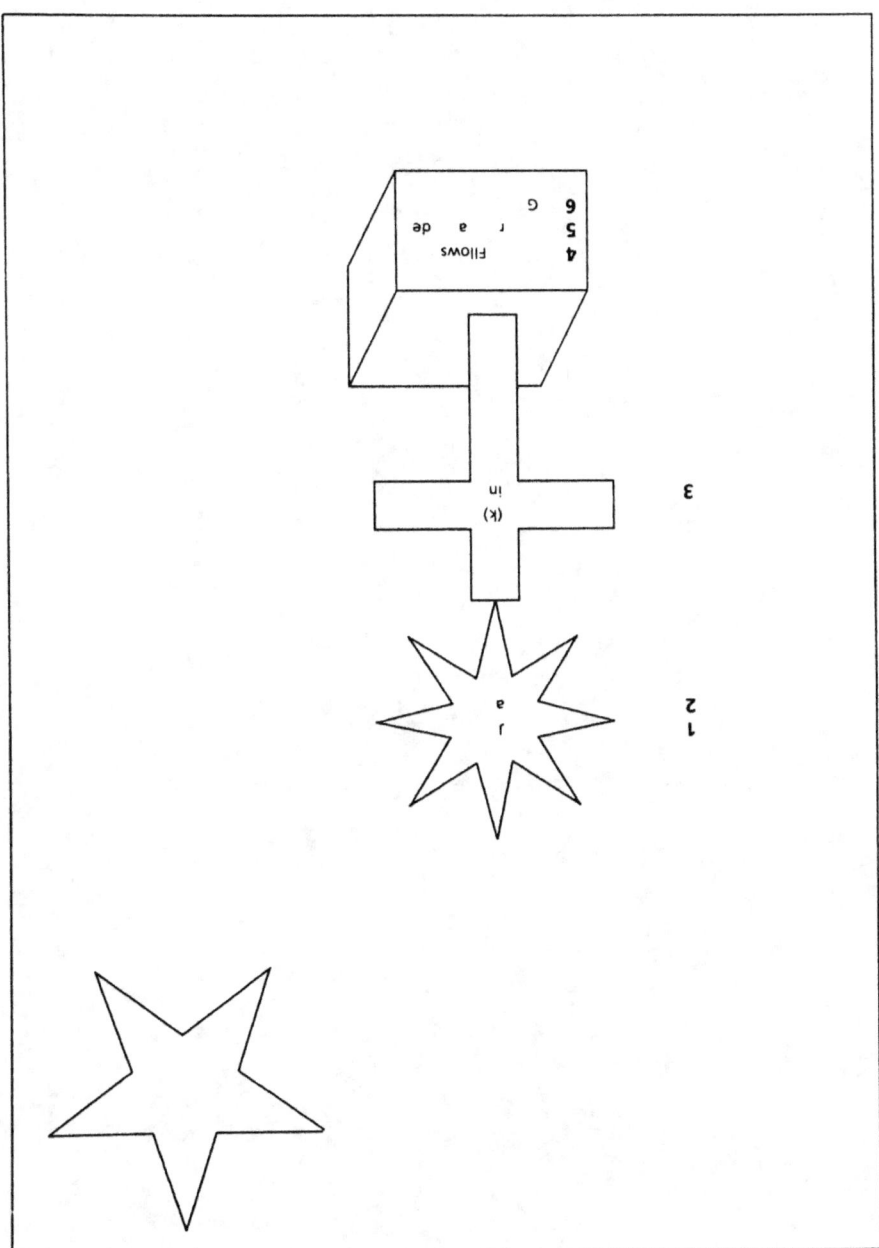

# THE RITUALS AND THE HISTORY

THE RITUALS IN THE *MACOY BOOK* are quite complete, even with their maddening blanks. The ceremonies are printed here with modern spellings and an attempt at punctuation (which Folger seemed to abandon after about page 14). The rubrics are printed in italics, and any text enclosed in brackets has been added to clarify the original. Few speakers were identified in the manuscript, and thus most identifications are only reasonable estimates. Not all of Folger's special symbols have been deciphered, so it is entirely possible that rubrics indicating signs or gavels have been inadvertently left out.

## OBSERVATIONS

Most of the differences between the ceremonies in the *Macoy Book* and standard American workings are simply the differences between the Régime Ecossais Rectifié and the Preston-Webb-Cross rituals used by most American Grand Lodges. The *Folger Manuscript*, however, is not a perfect rendition of the R.E.R. rituals (probably caused by poor memory or translation on the part of Hans B. Gram). Some features in the *Macoy Book* are interesting enough to warrant individual comment.

## THE OBLIGATIONS

For reasons unknown, Folger encrypted two nearly identical versions of the Disciple's Obligation (pages 6 and 16) and of the Fellow's Obligation (pages 14 and 17). The very first clause of the Disciple's Covenant ignores the religious universality of Masonry, but is consistent with the R.E.R.: "I will be faithful and true to the holy Christian religion." The Disciple's penalty in each version is "to be looked upon by all honest and good men and all Masons as a man without honour and every praiseworthy quality and deserving their contempt and disdain." A new Fellow promises in one version, "I will have my heart torn from my breast rather than violate this vow I now make." In the other, he makes the less gruesome promise, "and as a token of my sincerity, I pledge my heart." No complete version of the Master's Obligation is given.

## WORDS

The Disciple's word is *Boaz* and the Fellow's word is *Jakin*, which follows English Antient Grand Lodge workings. Among French exposés, only *La Réception Mystéieuse*, 1738, has *Boaz* for the first degree; the others use the English Modern Grand Lodge system with *Jakin* for Apprentices. The manuscript has no explicit passwords for any degree and no word for Masters, but on page 20, lines 1 and 2, the following is written: "Let us now agree, when the body is raised, the first word spoken shall hereafter be considered as the Master's word. The flesh is corrupt ★ Raises the body." This follows the wording of many English and French exposures for giving the Master's word.

The following question appears out of context on page 11, line 3, in cipher: "What is your order's name? *Giblem*." Then further down is a Latin reference in plain to one of the questions used in opening a Fellow's Lodge with the answer in cipher, "In initio conciones, quid nomen ord. = *Giblem*" [In the beginning of the meeting, what is your order's name = *Giblem*]. The reception of a Fellow for advancement to Master begins on page 18, line 15, and *Giblem* appears to be the "pass."

The word *Giblem* and variants appear in several early Masonic manuscripts and exposures: *Giblin*, the Jerusalem Word in *The Grand Mystery of Free-Masons Discover'd*, 1724; *G[iblin]*, the Jerusalem Word in *Institution of Free Masons*, ca. 1725; *Gibboram*, the $3^d$ Word in *The Whole Institutions of Free-Masons Opened*, 1725; *Gibboam* and *Gibberum*, the name of the second

Temporal Sign in *The Grand Mystery Laid Open*, 1726; *Giblin*, the name of a Mason in the *Wilkinson Manuscript*, ca. 1730-90; *Giblim*, the Master's Password in *L'Ordre des Francs-Maçons Trahi*, 1746; *Giblos*, the Password of a Master in *La Desolation des Entrepreneurs Modernes*, 1747; *Giblin*, the Password of a Master in *L'Anti Maçon*, 1748; *Giblim*, the Password of a Master in *Le Maçon Démasqué*, 1751.

## THE CORD

New Disciples are shown a carpet or tracing board containing the principal symbols of the order. Most of the emblems are common to Masonic ceremonies, but the explanation of the cord, which begins on page 4, line 32, merits special note.

> And finally, the Cord. It is here in remembrance of the Cord which the veil of the tabernacle was drawn aside with, and it is emblematical of the tie which unites all good men and Masons, and we should remember ever that silence is the veil which keeps our sanctuary in safety.

Prichard's *Masonry Dissected* of 1730 had as the furniture of a Lodge the "mosaick pavement, blazing star, and indented tarsel." "The latter is defined as the 'Border round about' the Lodge. This is the first appearance of the indented border in our modern Tracing Boards and carpets."[1] It is generally thought to be an indented tessellated border, either decorating the floor or drawn around the various symbols sketched there. Perau, in *Le Secret des Francs-Maçons*, 1744, translated Prichard's obscure term as *houpe dentelée*, which means indented tuft or tassel, and then succeeding French authors included a *houpe dentelée* in their workings.[2] Louis Travenol included the first illustrations of floor drawings in *Catéchisme des Francs-Maçons*, 1744, and he there depicted the *houpe dentellée* as a Tasselled Cord bordering the drawing. Then in his

---

[1] Samuel Prichard, *Masonry Dissected*, analysis and commentary by Harry Carr (Bloomington, IL: The Masonic Book Club, 1977), p. 86.

[2] Harry Carr, ed., *The Early French Exposures* (London: Quatuor Coronati Lodge, No. 2076, 1971), pp. 72-73.

The Rituals and the History

1747 work, *La Desolation des Entrepreneurs Modernes*, he further describes the *houpe dentellée* as a *cordon de veuve* or widow's cord, which Carr discovered is a term from French heraldry describing an intertwined cord surrounding the arms of a widow.[3] The linguistic circle has now been completed from English to French and back to English, as succeeding ritualists tried to clarify the obscure: the *indented tessellated border* became Prichard's *indented tarsal* which became Perau's *houpe dentelée* and then Travenol's *cordon* and finally Folger's *cord*.

## ODE TO A SKULL

Page 22 has a drawing of a skull and a brief lecture similar to the American Knights Templar "Ode to a Skull." In a letter to Enoch T. Carson in 1881, Folger stated, "The degree of Knights Templar, as we now have it, was instituted & manufactured by Cerneau, & is a perfect transcript of the Rose Croix, with some little additions."[4] The Cerneau Supreme Council established the Grand  Encampment of New York in 1814 and played a role in forming the General Grand Encampment in 1816. It is interesting to speculate what influence Templary may have had upon the Folger Manuscript, especially if Folger felt compelled to improve or complete Gram's possibly fragmentary ceremonies. On the other hand, the influence may have been in the other direction, as Folger was active in the Knights Templar.

## THE ABLUTION

An unattached ceremony of ablution appears on page 83. The candidate is reminded "that those who entered the sanctuary

---

[3] Carr, *The Early French Exposures*, p. 320.

[4] Robert B. Folger, New York, to Enoch T. Carson, [Past Lt. Grand Commander], [Ohio], Nov. 9, 1881, Typescript, Archives, Supreme Council, A.A.S.R., N.M.J., U.S.A., Lexington, Mass.

should wash themselves," and he is instructed to wash his hands as "a token of [his] sincere wish and intention henceforth to live undefiled." The incomplete "Vow of the Ancient Scotch Master" then follows, but the degree in which the hand washing occurs is not specified. The candidate is addressed as "My Brother" for the ablution, which eliminates the first section of the Disciple's Grade. A Fellow labors symbolically in the inner court of the Temple, and so has not yet been admitted to the sanctuary. This could be a ceremony for Ancient Scotch Masters, but it would be the only part of their work written by Folger. In the Grade of Master, however, the candidate is told, "Brother, you are now brought to the inner chamber," and we thus conclude that the ablution is part of the preparation of a candidate before he enters the inner chamber or sanctuary.

# [5]DISCIPULUS

## [FIRST SECTION]

*[The candidate is conducted by the Introductor to the Chamber of Preparation[6] where he is seated.]*

**Introductor**[7] Hither we have come. Let us now rest for a short time. I beg you to abstract yourself from all worldly thoughts for a short space of time and to devote this time to the consideration of yourself and such things as may here occur to you.

*[Shows cross[8]]* To the place of which this is a symbol we must all sooner or later come. [9]It is dark, black, separated from the world. [10]The rules of our Order have made me bring you here. Let me make you acquainted with these things.

*[Shows Hourglass]* The hourglass, an emblem of time. *Turns it.* Behold how rapidly the particles of sand run. It will soon run out, and then, if no external power set it in motion again, its movements will never be renewed. Forget this not.

Here is water for your refreshment.

*[Shows skull[11]]* Here is an image of death and an emblem of mortality. No human philosophy or thinking can divine what lies on the other side of this veil or what shall happen to us there, yet it is certain we shall all thence, and it is certain

---

[5] Page 4, line 1.

[6] The phrase "Chamber of Preparation" does not appear here, but it is mentioned on page 9, lines 21-22.

[7] The speaker is not identified, but the text which follows this on page 3, line 1, begins, "Introductor: The Lodge have commanded me . . . ," thus the Introductor seems to be an officer of the Lodge responsible for conducting candidates to the Chamber of Preparation.

[8] No object is identified, but on page 11, line 29, is written, "† When thou has passed to the place of which this is a symbol, thy destiny will be fixed forever."

[9] Page 86, line 26.

[10] Page 4, line 3.

[11] No object is identified.

that duration beyond the grave, in comparison to the period of human life, is infinite. This subject is interesting then.

*[Shows Bible[12]]* See, here is the only light by which we can learn how to enter the grave so as to enjoy happiness hereafter. It is the book of wisdom and contains a revelation of the Divine will.

[13]Question first: Do you believe in the existence of a Jehovah, perfect and good, the creator of all things?

Second: Do you believe in the immortality of the soul?

Third: What do you believe is your duty toward Jehovah, your neighbor, and yourself?

*Here it is proper for a Deputy to return to the Master the aspirant's answer.*

[14]**Introductor** The Lodge have commanded me to inform you respecting some of our customs and to prepare you in a proper manner to be brought to the Lodge in order to be accepted a Disciple. Permit me to advise you: I would encourage you to exercise fortitude in the trials you are about to endure and to place confidence in those who shall conduct you on the way in which you have concluded to enter upon. The first sign of your ready determination to join us is to deliver me your hat and sword.

*[Speaking to the Deputy]* Brother, please deliver this to the Lodge and return hither to me again.

Sir, will you please to lay from you all money, jewels, metal, and other signs of distinction; uncover your left breast and expose the knee; tread down the left shoe. Now, Sir, you are externally prepared to be presented to the Lodge, and it is

---

12 No object is identified.

13 Page 2, line 1. The manuscript reads, "in the xstnce of a J, perft and good." The letter *j* (which is sometimes read as *i*) could be interpreted as *Jehovah* or *Jesus*. The overt Christian nature of the obligation argues for *Jesus*, but it does not fit in the context of this question.

14 Page 3, line 1.

## The Grade of Disciple

pleasing to me to believe that your heart and thoughts correspond with this external preparation, and that you have taken, and will continue to take, all possible pains to eradicate all prejudices and emotions of the mind which militate against your proper duties as a man.

But Sir, you must be convinced that a [15]man who is stripped of all sensual and false decorations and ornaments and coverings of vanity cannot be known and distinguished from others but by righteousness and virtue. It is absolutely necessary that you henceforth be convinced of your own weakness and that it is impossible to go forward toward the Temple of Truth without help and guidance.

In order to give us a plain to know of your want of confidence in yourself, you must permit us to deprive you of the light. It is an emblem of the false views which are the lot of that man who is left to his own guidance.

*Bandage [is placed over candidate's eyes].*

Tell me, can you see any thing? On your honour? Be careful not to use deception with him who shall guide you. You will else presently certainly repent.

You are now in darkness, but fear not. Those who guide you go in light and will not lead you astray. Hold your hands before you and guard against the hindrances that can meet you. You are now left alone. Strive to go forward, but use the utmost prudence in order to avoid surrounding danger.

*[The candidate] takes three steps forward.*

I acknowledge you as one who seeks. I mark well your serious desire, but in thick darkness and alone you would undoubtedly go astray.

---

[15] Page 5, line 1.

*[The Introductor] takes his left hand and says:*

As such I will bring you to the Lodge. I pray, be constant and confident, learn to suffer with patience and abstinence, and thereby make yourself worthy to obtain in time what at present you ask for. Follow me. Fear not.

*Three knocks [at the door]*[16]

**Deacon**[17]  Who comes here?

**Introductor**  One in darkness who seeks light and wishes to be accepted.

**Deacon**  His name? Age? Father's name? Where born? Profession? Religion? And has he made any vow that forbids his joining the Masonic fraternity?

Enter, Sir.

**Introductor**  Here I have brought you. My task is now finished. You are in safe hands, even with them who deserve your perfect confidence.

*When in the west and the Guide*[18] *has left him Master says:*

**W.M.**  Thus, Sir, you have sought [19]to be received among us. This your request we have seriously attended to, and from the good opinion we have conceived of your character, and as one of our Brethren has pledged himself for you in a solemn manner, and he who I sent to inquire as to your motives in joining us and your opinion of our institution has reported so favorably of you, we have therefore sent you a Guide who has opened our door to you, and now you are in the midst of us in a state fit for trials which you must endure and which everyone who wishes to be received among us must endure, remembering that the present is a state of trial.

---

[16] Page 5, line 12. Three gavels are drawn in the text, which are translated here as *knocks*. Later translations as *knocks* or *gavels* are made without further comment.

[17] Page 5, line 12. The manuscript reads, "D. Who cms h."

[18] Page 5, line 15. The manuscript reads, "and the G has left him."

[19] Page 2, line 4.

## The Grade of Disciple

But, Sir, before we can proceed further, I have some questions to ask to you which I must require an audible and unequivocal answer. But first, Sir, I must state to you that there is nothing in our Order which is incompatible with religion or with civil or moral duties. For the truth of this we pledge you our honour.

And I now ask you if you are prompted to join us by a desire of being charitable and useful to your fellow man?

Second, are you prompted to join us by a desire of the knowledge of truth and to be associated with those who profess to promulgate it and encourage virtue and laudable pursuits?

Third, will you conform to the regulations of the Freemasons and do you voluntarily request to be made a Mason?

Well then, your request shall be granted you. God give at some future day it may serve to make you happy. You are about to be going on a mysterious journey, and, although you cannot see the way, yet confiding in him who leads you, go forward with firmness, yet with caution, and rest assured that your guide will not bring you in paths where you should not go.

*Three gavels*

Guide  Sir, the naked sword pointing to your heart is but a weak symbol of the dangers which surround one who wanders in darkness, put your trust in God and fear not. Come with me.

**First Round**

[20]Man was created in the image of God, but who can know him when he deforms himself?

**Second Round**

He who is ashamed of religion and of truth is unfit for and unworthy of fraternity.

---

20 Page 4, line 12.

## The Grade of Disciple

**Third Round**

That man whose ear is deaf to the cries and the distresses of his fellow man is a monster in the assembly of the Brethren.

W.M.   Let him now ascend the three first mysterious steps leading to the Temple to try his strength, and then bring him to the East to make his vow.

Sir, your patience has enabled you to reach an altar at which, by the rules of our Order, you are required to make a solemn and irrevocable oath or covenant never unlawfully to reveal any of the secrets, symbols, signs, or ceremonies belonging to the Order of Free and Accepted Masons. You have already been assured that the Order does not contain anything contrary to our duties toward God, our country, our neighbors, or ourselves. This assurance I now repeat to you and ask you if you are willing to make the oath or covenant required? What do you answer?

But, Sir, before you can make a covenant, it is necessary that you be well acquainted with its tenure, we holding it to be wrong to make a covenant with any unless they be well acquainted with its conditions. Therefore, you will please to kneel on the left knee on the square and let your right hand rest upon the Bible, on which lies the square and compasses covered with a sword. Sir, the book on which your hand now rests is the Holy Bible opened at the first chapter of St. John and the fifth verse where there is written, "And the light shineth in darkness; and the darkness comprehended it not."

Do you believe that your hand thus rests upon the Bible? And why do you believe it? Thus you conceive that a man, upon the serious assurance, can believe the thing of which he has no other evidence than this assurance?

Now, I desire you to be attentive to the voice of the Senior Warden who will repeat to you the covenant which you are required to make, even in the presence of the Supreme Architect of the Universe, and which, when made, can not be recalled.

The Grade of Disciple

*[The Disciple's Obligation follows, but later, for reasons unknown, Folger encrypted another, nearly identical version, which is printed with the first for comparison. The small differences may indicate that someone, probably Gram, translated the text from another manuscript.]*

## [Disciple's] [21] Obligation

S.W. I do promise, solemnly and sincerely, in the presence of God and this Lodge of Freemasons, that I will be faithful and true to the holy Christian religion and to the government of the country in which I live, and that I will strive to gain the esteem and love of my fellow man by practicing virtue and shunning vice, and by encouraging others so to do. And I promise that I will, as far as I can, help the distressed, and that I will conceal from everyone who is not a Free and Accepted Mason all the secrets, signs, symbols, and usages of this Order and every part thereof, and I will not unlawfully reveal any of these things, nor write them on anything, or make them legible so that the secrets of our Order can thereby be unlawfully revealed. And I will strive to cherish and love all worthy and good Brethren Free and Accepted Masons as Brothers, and should I violate this oath, the keeping of which I solemnly promise, I am willing to be looked upon by all honest and good men and all Freemasons as a man without honour and every praiseworthy

[21] Page 6, line 1.

## [22] Disciple's Vow in Full Form

S.W. I do promise, faithfully and sincerely, in the presence of God and this Lodge, that I will be faithful and true to the holy Christian religion and to the government of the country in which I live, and that I will strive to gain the love and esteem of my fellow men by practicing virtue and shunning vice and by encouraging others so to do. And I promise that I will, as far as I can, help the distressed. I also promise that I will conceal from everyone who is not a Mason all the secrets, symbols, signs, and usages of this Order and every part thereof, and I will not reveal unlawfully any of these things, nor write these on anything, nor make them legible to others whereby the things and matters or secrets or usages shall be unlawfully revealed. And I will strive to cherish and love all worthy and good Brethren of the Order as Brothers, and should I violate this oath, the keeping of which I solemnly promise, I am willing to be looked upon by all honest [23] and good men and all Masons as a man without honour and every praiseworthy quality

[22] Page 16, line 20.
[23] Page 17, line 1.

## The Grade of Disciple

quality and deserving their contempt and disdain. And I now repeat my wish to be made a Mason. So help me God.

and deserving their contempt and disdain. And I now repeat my wish to be made a Mason. So help me God.

**W.M.** [24]Have you heard and rightly understood this solemn covenant? Are you willing to make it and to sanction it according to the customs of our Order? I ask you for the last time.

*One gavel.*

In order Brethren, and while this man makes this covenant, let us give a token of our accordance with it.

*[The candidate repeats the covenant.]*

You are now bound to us and we to you by this your oath, but the trial of your sincerity, which is the hardest trial, is now at hand. You have said that you would sanction this covenant according to the customs of the Order. Are you willing to sanction it with your blood if it should be required of you?

[25]Then I accept you as a Disciple in Masonry, to the honour of almighty God, in the name of fraternity[26], and by virtue of the power vested in me, Amen.

*Response [by the candidate]*

**W.M.** Arise.

This last trial, your being willing to sanction your vows with your blood, is convincing of your sincerity and I now salute you by the name of Brother, but forget not under what conditions you obtained this name. Brother Wardens, bear him to the West, there to come to light.

**S.W.** He is prepared.

---

[24] Page 6, line 11.

[25] Page 3, line 11.

[26] Page 3, line 11. The manuscript reads, "N the nme of F." This is the same formula as used in the opening of a Disciple's Lodge, where *fraternity* is spelled out.

The Grade of Disciple

**W.M.**   *One gavel.*

*[The new Disciple's blindfold is removed, and in dim light he sees several Brothers apparently threatening him with their drawn swords.]*

**W.M.**   However weak the present light that flames before you may be, yet my Brother it is sufficient to show you our weapons turned against you, threatening you with shame and disdain if ever you should unhappily betray the trust we have reposed in you. Let him be veiled again.

*One gavel. [After the Brethren with swords retire the light is restored, and the blindfold is removed again.]*

Sic Transit Gloria Mundi! For a moment since, you saw our weapons turned against you, apparently hostile. Look at us now, armed for your defense and welfare. Yes, my Brother, the Order will not and shall not forsake you as long as you are faithfully doing your duty and keeping your covenants.

Brother Master of Ceremonies, let our new Brother be clothed and return with him to the Lodge.

## [SECOND SECTION]

**Deacon**[27]   Worshipful Master, one knocks.

**W.M.**   [28]See who it is, and, if a Brother, let him enter.

**Deacon**   It is our new made Brother.

**W.M.**   Bring him to the East by the Northwest.

My Brother, permit me to clothe you with this lambskin, and in the name of the Order I present you with these white gloves. The white clothing you are now decorated with is emblematic of purity and innocence. Worn honorably it is a very honorable badge. Preserve them from stains. Wear them and never appear without them in the Lodge.

[27] No officer is identified here.
[28] Page 7, line 1.

## The Grade of Disciple

The Order of good Masons does not permit women to its assemblies, yet we profess and cherish esteem for the virtues and good among the other sex. In token of this, I present you with these gloves, which you can give to such a one as merits your esteem.

Here is your money. Take them, my Brother. In giving you back these, we would admonish you to bear in mind that it is a most certain truth that the love of gold, silver, and the like has produced more evils than anything else in this world. Yes. Covetousness and avarice have led men much astray, have induced them to commit the meanest acts of cowardice and most atrocious acts of injustice and oppression and violence. Acts so mean and so atrocious as to excite disdain and horror in every honest and feeling man. Acts which cause the sign of sorrow to burst from the breasts of the really pious, and which, alas, it is to be feared, have brought down the thunder of damnation on the heads of the guilty perpetrators. Therefore, respecting the pernicious influence of these things, we should watch.

Here is your hat. In delivering it to you I must remark that none except they be Masters[29] sit covered in Lodge.

Take your sword, use it carefully when called upon by your country for its defense, but bear in mind that a man of blood is deemed unfit to build a temple to the name of God, and never forget His commandment, who gave law to man in order to make them happy, saying, "Thou shalt not kill."

I will now learn you the tests of this degree.

---

[29] This probably means *Master Masons* rather than *Masters of Lodges*. In the Belgian R.E.R., a new Master Mason has his hat returned to him, and is told, "From now on you will always be covered in Lodge, to indicate the superiority that this Degree gives you over Apprentices and Fellows." (*Ritual de Loge de Saint-Jean, 3ᵉ Grade* [Brussels: Grand Loge Réguliére de Belgique, n.d.], p. 41.) In the Amez-Droz translation of the ritual of the Lodge Union des Couers, a new Master Mason is told, "In future you are empowered to don it in Lodge to mark the authority your rank gives you over the Apprentices and Companions." (F. Amez Droz trans, "Ritual of the Third degree [Master Mason], Decreed at the Convent General of the Order in 1782," n.d., p. 23, Archives, Iowa Masonic Library, Cedar Rapids.)

## The Grade of Disciple

Go to the Wardens and make yourself known [30]to them and to the Brother who pledged himself in your behalf, as a Mason. Afterwards, the Senior Warden will teach you the symbolic work upon the rough stone.

S.W.  My Brother, the rough stone, an emblem of which you here see, is a symbol of man deformed by prejudices and passions. To eradicate and to subdue them is the duty and the work of every Mason.

The gavel is symbolical of power. It is used by hewers of stone to strike off the asperities of the ashlar and to reduce it to the form which the Master has prescribed it should have. And we are reminded by it to strive to subdue our passions and eradicate our prejudices to fit ourselves for that spiritual temple, not made with hands, eternal in the heavens. In token of your willingness to do this work, which the Great Master has ordained we should do, stoop humbly down toward the earth and strike the rough stone as I do.

*Three gavels*

Continue constantly in the work you there began to do, that the Supreme Architect may not be displeased with your labors and that you may strive to merit reward: His approbation. Now, let the first work you do as a Mason be a good work. Do a deed of charity, give a pittance to help the distressed.

Turn around, [31]be attentive to a recitation of the rite of initiation which now is ended.

## [LECTURE]

W.M.  The symbols, usages, and customs of our order are intended to lead the mind to the contemplation of things of the greatest importance to that man who is wishful to learn, and to meditate upon that which may promote his welfare. You was first

[30] Page 9, line 1.
[31] Page 9, line 11.

led into a dark and narrow chamber where you was separated from the world and from your friend who brought you there. Although this separation was but short, yet the things there led you to meditate upon subjects however common, yet of a very serious nature.

Your meditations were disturbed by the coming of a Brother who inquired of you your motives for joining our Order, for none but those actuated by right motives should be admitted among us. He who was deputed to guide you hither in company with your friend caused you to be divested of all money, jewels, and the like, and otherwise prepared you for introduction into our Lodge, that you might know that worldly distinctions can not give rank and must not create differences among Masons. In the Lodge we all meet upon the level. In fact, among the good and impartial, nothing but virtue and mental acquirements can give preeminence among men in the world, and nothing else can distinguish Brethren in the Lodge.

In the Chamber of Preparation, it is hoped you spent the time profitably. You was abstracted from the world and, for a moment perhaps, was engaged in the consideration of yourself and, that external objects might not entirely engage your attention or disturb the impression which you there received and that you should shew confidence in your guide, you was deprived of the light and thus led to the door of the Lodge where you was received by the Warden. He demanded your religion, name, age, and other particulars, for none but a professor of religion, and one who is free, and who we know a man arrived at the years of real manhood, can be admitted to our Lodge.

The three blows on the door of the Lodge should remind you that for him who seeks with constancy, who seeks with humility, and who knocks rightly, the door of the Temple of Fraternity and Peace shall be opened. You was conducted to the care of the Warden and stood then upon the threshold of the Lodge, your former guide leaving you with assurances

## The Grade of Disciple

that you were in the hands of those who would not mislead you. But before you could, by the assistance of your new conductor, proceed on your way, the Master addressed you, and your motives for coming here were acknowledged to the Brother by him who best could inform us thereof, by yourself.

[32]Then we, reciprocating the confidence you had hitherto placed in us, believed you, and you commenced a journey on which you learned from the East some truths on which the tenets of our Order in a great measure rest. You then ascended the mysterious steps of the Temple, and was brought to the altar to make a very serious promise. On the whole of this journey reciprocal confidence supported you. Confidence between you and us, for if you had not had confidence in us you would have refused to follow our directions and, if we had not have believed you to have been upright, we would not have received you among us.

You was joined to us by a solemn tie, and afterwards you saw a blazing and unsteady light which was only sufficient to discover surrounding apparent dangers. Finally, the veil was removed wholly, and you saw the light. You beheld Brethren armed for your defense and welfare. All hostile appearances were done away, and everything bore appearances of love. Those scenes are emblematical of the different states of man.

The unenlightened state, in which man makes sacrifices and oblations for obtaining favours from heaven or for the atonement of atrocious deeds he may have committed. In which state nearly all the objects he perceives were hostile in appearance, and his fellows seemed strangers to him, and their arms appeared to threaten him, their power to place him in danger. He shuns, fears, or even hates them, but, in a more enlightened state, he perceives that heaven rather accepts a sincere and contrite heart than burnt offerings and oblations. He then acknowledges his fellow men as his Brethren, and he

---

[32] Page 8, line 14.

looks upon their power as means for his own defense and welfare. He joins them, relies upon them, and loves them. You was invested with the badges of innocence and purity and admonished by good conduct to keep them unsullied.

[33]And then you received the tests of this Degree, by which you can make yourself known to Brother Masons. Do not, my Brother, be among those who strive to publish to the world that they are Masons. Neither countenance anything tending to this end, for the honour and usefulness of the Order are much more extended by concealment and by an intimate acquaintance with the exalted aim of our labours and the probable extent of their influence upon the welfare of the human race. You will be assured that silence and circumspection tend to give our Order force.

The carpet[34] before you, containing the principle symbols of our Order deserves your attention. The Border, including the whole, is a representation of Mason work, and this is the covering to all the other symbols and should remind us of that concealment of which we have already spoken.

The Rough Stone and Square Stone are symbols. The one of the raw and uncultivated man, the other of him which has subjected himself to the discipline of truth and virtue.

The Trestle Board should admonish us carefully to study and to follow the plans of the Master.

You see the Sun and Moon. They are here represented to remind us of application to our duties day and night, for this is all a man can do without erring.

There are the different instruments used by Masons as Plumb, Level, and Square and so forth. They are adopted as hieroglyphs by us, and therefore are [35]here represented.

---

[33] Page 2, line 20.
[34] This probably refers to the drawing on page 25.
[35] Page 4, line 32.

The Grade of Disciple

And in the center is the Blazing Star, which we view with reverential silence.

And finally, the Cord. It is here in remembrance of the cord which [36]the veil of the tabernacle was drawn aside with, and it is emblematical of the tie which unites all good men and Masons, and we should remember ever that silence is the veil which keeps our sanctuary in safety.

Close before you is the Mosaic Pavement, which in Solomon's Temple covered the courts and on which the sanctuary stood. It is emblematical of the foundation which we seek in those we accept among us. They should be men of a firm and fair character, fit for surrounding and supporting a sanctuary.

On the left you see a Pillar with the initial of the word of your degree. Bear in mind the meaning of the word: "In him is strength."[37] You ascended those three first steps of the Temple, but, as your time was not yet come, the door remained shut and you was led back again, and it is recommended to you to wait with patience and to labour diligently yet with meekness, that when the door of the Temple shall be opened to you, you may hope, yes believe, to enter into the inner apartments with great joy.

# END

---

[36] Page 3, line 21.
[37] The word *Boaz* means "In him is strength."

## [38]OPENING THE DISCIPLE'S LODGE

W.M.   Brother Warden, are you a Disciple?

S.W.   I am.

W.M.   Brother Senior and Junior, what is the first duty of every good Mason and, in the Lodge, particularly of the Brother Wardens?

S.W.   To see [39]that the profane are removed and the hall in safety.

W.M.   Please to perform that office.

*The profane are removed and so on.*

Since the profane and so on are removed, we will pursue that path of duty which is pointed out to us and strive to consummate our work.

*3 [gavels]*

S.W.   Brethren, look toward the East. It was there the light arose by which we are enabled to work. Let us be prepared to continue our labours at the signal of the Master.

W.M.   *One [gavel]* In order.

*[The three tapers are lit.]*[40]

May the clearest light shine for us during our labours. Prayer by the Master as follows:

---

[38] Page 3, line 30. The manuscript reads, "Opning the Dscples ☐." Throughout the manuscript, Folger sometimes used the box symbol, ☐, to stand for *Lodge*. However, ☐ is also the symbol for the letter *d*, and thus the line could be read as either "Opening the Disciple's *Lodge*" or "Opening the Disciple's *Degree*." The next line reads, "Br W are you a ☐?", and clearly the proper interpretation here is "Brother Warden, are you a *Disciple*?" While in the next line, ☐ should be interpreted as *Lodge*. The translation of ☐ for *Lodge* or *Degree* or possibly *Disciple* is often a matter of judgment, but will not be elaborated in most later decisions.

[39] Page 5, line 16.

[40] Only a drawing of a three branched candlestick appears in the text, but the Master's comments let us infer the Master's action.

The Grade of Disciple

> Thou Creator God of Heaven and Earth the thickest darkness hides not from thy sight. In mercy view and purify our hearts. Bless us that we may learn and do thy will. Wisdom itself, Almighty King, is Thine and Thou alone hast strength, others are weak, in all thy works beauty effulgent shines. We humbly pray thee in this hall of peace, send down thy blessing on our labours here that we may be wise, beautiful and strong.

**W.M.** Brother Junior, what is the time?

**J.W.** It is past high twelve.

**W.M.** Brother Senior, is it the right time to begin to work?

**S.W.** It is.

**W.M.** Then assist me, Brethren to open this Disciples' Lodge. Let us live together in unity, to the honour of Jehovah[41]. In the name of fraternity and by virtue of the power of my office, I declare this Disciples' Lodge opened.

> Brethren, be attentive to the work.

*One [gavel]*

*The work now proceeds in the usual form. The candidate is introduced.*

---

[41] Page 5, line 24. The manuscript reads, "To the honour f J," and *Jehovah* and *Jesus* seem to be the two most likely choices. *Jehovah* has been chosen to be consistent with the initial questions asked of Candidates.

## [42]CLOSING [THE DISCIPLE'S LODGE]

**W.M.**   Brother Junior, what is the time?

**J.W.**   Toward low twelve.

**W.M.**   Brother Senior, is the labour finished?

**S.W.**   It is.

**W.M.**   Have any of the Brothers anything to offer, as the labour is finished?

[43]Brother Almoner, please perform your duty.

*One [gavel]*

In order Brethren. Before we part, Brethren, let us form a tie of fraternal union and offer up our dutiful acknowledgments to the great Master whose goodness has enabled us thus far to do the work of Masonry and supplicate his blessing.

*Here the Brethren all join hands and the Master prays thus:*

O Thou Great Master on the throne of Heaven. Thy word from nothing did call forth the whole. Thy view perceiveth every thing that is, and thou pervadest all in Heaven and Earth. Look down in mercy from thy holy Heaven on us, the creatures of thy gracious Will. Grant wisdom, we are ignorant and blind. Grant strength, without thy aid our toils are vain. And with thy blessing, beautify our Souls. And to thy Honour may our work be done, the Brethren live in peace teaching good will, and may our Brother tie continue strong.

Brethren, assist me to close this Lodge. Let us be unanimous.

I declare this Disciples' Lodge closed to the honour of Jehovah[44], in the name of fraternity, and by virtue of my office. Brothers be attentive.

---

[42] Page 5, line 31.
[43] Page 7, line 17.
[44] Page 7, line 33. The manuscript reads, "to the honor of J."

## The Grade of Disciple

*[Three tapers in the East are extinguished.]*

[45]Thus vanisheth the splendor of the world, like a flame kindled suddenly before your eyes and suddenly extinguished when you seek for it, nor a vestige of it is to be found. Notwithstanding its apparent splendour, it shall utterly vanish. Brother, when you look for light[46], remember is is only to be found in the East.

[47]That light which shined during our labours cannot be seen by the profane. Brethren, when you seek for light wherewith you would perfect your works, remember that that light is in the East and only there to be found.

*Dismiss.*

---

[45] Page 86, line 27. The drawings and dialogue in the text indicate the importance of the three branched candle stick, referred to as "three tapers." This brief statement, standing alone in the manuscript, seems to describe the extinguishing of a candle and is thus placed here.

[46] Page 86, line 29. A unique symbol is used that looks like a flame, which is interpreted as the word *light*.

[47] Page 7, line 34.

## [DISCIPLE'S CATECHISM]

**Q:** [48]Brother Senior, are you a Disciple?

**A:** I am.

**Q:** From whence come the Disciples?

**A:** From the West.

**Q:** And whither are they going?

**A:** Toward the East.

**Q:** Why?

**A:** In search of light.

**Q:** What are your duties as a Disciple?

**A:** To continue diligently the work I did begin as commanded by the Master on the rough stone.

**Q:** With what did you work?

**A:** With the symbol of power.

**Q:** Why?

**A:** To shew the proper use of the power with which I was intrusted

**Q:** How is a Mason to be known?

**A:** By signs, words, and grips.

**Q:** How so?

**A:** His manners must be gentle and unassuming, his conversation, prudent and discreet. He being rather a hearer than a speaker, being willing to hear, yet apt to teach, and shunning foolish disputes. He disdains to pollute himself by doing any mean, fraudulent, or criminal act. He discountenances libertinism, commends and practices virtue. He encourages benevolence and charity by precept and example.

---

[48] Page 6, line 17.

## The Grade of Disciple

Q: Where do the Disciples labour?
A: In the outer court of the Temple.
Q: Have you received your wages?
A: Yes.
Q: What are they?
A: I got food and raiment and many other things.
Q: Where do you receive your pay?
A: At the entrance of the Temple.
Q: Who pays you?
A: The Master.
Q: Are you satisfied with your wages?
A: I am well satisfied and know the word.
Q: What time do you begin to work?
A: Past high twelve.
Q: When is the time of rest?
A: Toward midnight.
Q: What are the dimensions of your Lodge?
A: Its length is and so forth.
Q: Why this extent?
A: Because Masonry includes all things; it is unlimited.
Q: What do the three tapers represent?
A: The sun and moon and the Master of the Lodge, and as the sun and moon regularly dispense light and life[49] to the earth, [50]so does the Master dispense knowledge and discipline to the Lodge, and all Masters of Lodges should strive so to do.
Q: What is the emblem of a Disciple?

---

[49] Page 6, line 31. The manuscript reads "lght and heat and lfe".
[50] Page 8, line 4.

A: A broken pillar with the inscription "Adhuc stat."[51]

Q: How is it explained?

A: As by the remnant of the pillar that is yet standing we can ascertain to what order it belongs and determine what its proportions and ornaments were when it was entire, and thus be enabled to form another pillar in likeness of the broken one, so from what we know relative to man we hope and believe that he may be restored to a state approaching to that first pristine purity and happiness.

Q: Why is Solomon's Temple used emblematically in Freemasonry?

A: It was a highly finished and splendid building and the first Temple erected by man publicly sacred to the name of the only wise and true God, and Freemasonry teaches us to be built up living temples as perfect and beautiful as the Solomonic Temple was to the service and to the honour of the Supreme Architect of Heaven and Earth.

## CLOSE OF THE CATECHISM

---

[51] Page 8, line 5. The manuscript reads "Ad hoc stat," but this is probably a misspelling or misunderstanding of the motto of the R.E.R. First Degree, "Adhuc stat."

# FELLOW'S GRADE[52]

## [FIRST SECTION]

*[The candidate is conducted to the Chamber of Preparation by the Introductor, and then asked the]* [53]*preparation questions.*

**Introductor** Man was originally pure, undefiled, happy. How comes it then that he wars with his own welfare and often makes himself miserable? This is a subject which undoubtedly demands our highest attention, in as much as we ought to study to avoid unhappiness.

Second, The fool wanders his whole life through without considering or knowing from whence he come or whither he went. Brother, the wise man studies to know what he is about. And considering every step, its end and intention, and, by closely pursuing the objects of happiness, he avoids all that can stop him in his way. And knowing his own weakness and ignorance, he receives with humility the doctrines that are given him and with gratitude proffered support when he is wrong, and when his own strength would not bear him farther.

**Guide**[54] Masonry is progressive. It is necessary, in every pursuit of knowledge, gradually to advance in order to understand things aright. Wherefore you was not all at once made acquainted with all the arts of our order, but are advanced gradually through them, and, indeed, as nearly everything in our rites is symbolical, it requires previous preparation to understand them and to make them useful to ourselves.

---

[52] Page 88, line 4.

[53] Page 86, line 1.

[54] The text clearly shows that the Guide begins speaking here, which seems to indicate that another officer, perhaps the Introductor as in the Disciple's Grade, brought the candidate to the Chamber of Preparation.

Permit me to ask you what is your opinion of the tendency of our Order?

This degree is to be considered partly as a recompense for your labours past, but principally as tending to prepare you for the Master's degree. I can assure you, my Brother, that your constancy and fortitude in this degree must stand very serious tests. If you are determined and fixed to go forward, then follow me like a man, but if you waver then I advise you rather to remain in the degree of Disciple until you, by the easier duties required in the degree you have taken, have become strong.

Now, Bother, decide. Yet do not deceive yourself. Will you follow me?

*[Candidate answers and, if affirmative, gives] three knocks.*

**Deacon** Who knocks?

**Guide** It is a Disciple who wishes to be accepted as a Fellow.

**Deacon** His name?

**Guide** He has laboured in the outer court of the Temple on the rough stone.

**Deacon** Pass.

**Guide** Hither I have brought you, as you desired, to the place whither you durst not approach. My work is now finished. Try to find yourself a new guide.

**W.M.** Brother you are welcome.

*One gavel*

## [55]ADDRESS FROM THE MASTER

The Fellows and Masters present have given their unanimous consent to your being accepted as a Fellow, and I am well satisfied that in the character of a Fellow you will use

---

[55] Page 12, line 1.

## The Grade of Fellow

your best endeavours to discharge your duties as such. Yet it is my duty to inform you that the work of a Fellow not only requires good application, but that it is difficult, yet it undoubtedly has its reward.

You are from henceforth carefully to inspect the work done already on the rough stone and strive to complete it according to the designs of the Master Great Architect, that they may happily never be deemed unfit for the Temple. We are prepared and willing to assist you with advice and rules for your work, but the work you must do yourself. No man can do it for you. And we desire ever that your honest endeavours will meet a reward.

Formerly on your symbolic journey, you was blindfolded, you was in darkness. At the present time you wander in the light. Yet, my Brother, you would undoubtedly go astray unless you were assisted by a guide who knew the way and is willing to shew it to you.

If you will go to our Brother Second Overseer, he will conduct you in paths on which you can learn things relative to the duty of a Fellow. His hand holding yours, and by which you will be lead forward, should remind you that a Brother should assist another in good and laudable pursuits, while the sword resting on your breast should impress you with a sense of the irregularity and precipitancy in the striving to consummate our views at the same time it teaches one of the important duties of a Fellow, viz. that of checking all imprudent hastiness, but especially when he is going upon a way where he is a stranger.

*1 gavel.*

*Guide makes the first round.*

## First Round[56]

2nd O.  Man was originally pure, upright, undefiled, happy. How comes it then that he so often wars with his own welfare and makes himself miserable? His passions lead him astray, and sensual enjoyments entice him from the garden of happiness into the wilderness of vice and into the labyrinth of error. But present, often, alas too late it is feared, he is undeceived or, what is worse, he is satiated. A feeling of duty or of shame rouses him to view his present state and he sees with remorse that he is far from where he should be, but the ways he has wandered through are so winding and intricate that he can perhaps never retrace his steps. And he stands like the fool man, not knowing from whence he came or whither he went.

*Two gavels*

### Second round

2nd O.  *One gavel*

He who has begun to go forward in the path of wisdom and virtue and turns back is a thousand times more deplorable

*One gavel*

than he who never went that way, for he never knew what duty was nor did he take the pleasures arising from virtuous actions. Such a man has brought a dangerous enemy to war [57]against his welfare, viz. himself–his own self.

*One gavel*

### Third round

2nd O.  *One gavel*

Brother, we believe that you are willing and ready to undertake the task of the Fellow. The subject on which you

---

[56] Immediately after this in the text, page 12, line 17, is a drawing of a temple and a man facing a looped cord. Inside the cord is a skull, a sprig, two crossed swords, a cross, and a blazing star (see chapter 3, figure 4).

[57] Page 13, line 1.

## The Grade of Fellow

are to labour is deserving of your attention, and you ought never to neglect it.

**W.M.** Brother Warden, lead the Brother to the image of the pillar of beauty, and let him consider it well that he forget it not.

**Warden** If you desire to view the object of your labours then draw the veil aside. See yourself.

*See emblem. [A curtain is pulled aside to reveal a mirror.]*

[58]Know thyself. This is even a religious duty and was highly esteemed in ancient times. It is important, inasmuch as we ought to know our own weaknesses and imperfections and frailties, and we should strive and pray to be able to lay aside all things which pollute us and all superfluity of naughtiness and receive the word of Truth, which is able to save our souls. But we must receive the word and keep it, or we are otherwise like the man who beholds his natural face in a glass, beholding himself and going away, he immediately forgets what manner of person he was. (See James' Epistle.[59])

Consider thyself. This is shewn and that thou shouldst often think upon this duty and remember that what you here see (apparently at the bottom of a vault) is the image of the receptacle that contains great treasures (the Law of God–and keeps to the knowledge of the truth), to find which, in another form, has long engaged the attention of both wise and foolish men.

**W.M.** [60]Brother, the Fellows are generally well pleased with their own work, but if they behold them with the eye of the Master, they would be astonished to see how imperfect that is which they think so finished, and they would be very much alarmed on beholding how much yet remains to be done in

---

[58] Page 84, line 1. This text stands alone in the manuscript, with no indication where it goes or who speaks it. The text of the Fellow's Grade contains the unexplained instruction "See emblem," but the R.L.R. has a similar mirror ceremony in its Second Degree (see p. 8).

[59] "For if any be a hearer of the word, and not a doer, he is like unto a man beholding his natural face in a glass: For he beholdeth himself, and goeth his way, and straightway forgetteth what manner of man he was." James 1:23-24.

[60] Page 13, line 5.

## The Grade of Fellow

order that they may not be rejected by Him who is appointed to inspect them and Who will dispose of them according to their merits. Even the most finished work a man who follows his own thoughts of perfection can produce will, perhaps, be found very imperfect and full of error and deemed unfit and unuseful, yet it is a consolation to know that a good artist is able to make of the most unfinished block of rough stone an indisputable likeness of one of the most beautiful and perfect creatures, but in order to do this he must be well instructed by and must follow the rules of a great and good Master.

Brother Senior, let our Brother ascend the five first steps of the Temple that he may from thence behold an emblem of the light which guided wise men, and from thence conduct him to the East to make his vow.

**W.M.** Brother when you were before at this altar, although blindfolded, you had so much confidence in us that you did not hesitate to give your consent to a covenant, the tenure of which you was unacquainted with. But before you took it, it was wholly made known to you. Now you are in light, and you have in some measure become acquainted with us and with the Order. Therefore we can expect more confidence of you than when you was the stranger among us. Wherefore I ask of you if you are willing to make the covenant belonging to this degree?

*[The candidate gives his] answer.*

**W.M.** My Brother, we expected of you this expression of confidence and thank you for it, but Brother take our admonition in good part: never consent to a serious engagement without first having heard its contents and without having understood them. Brother Senior, please read the covenant to our Brother.

*[The Fellow's Obligation follows, but later, for reasons unknown, Folger encrypted another, nearly identical version, which is printed with the first for comparison. The small differences may*

The Grade of Fellow

*indicate that someone, probably Gram, translated the text from another manuscript.]*

## [Fellow's] ⁶¹Covenant

S.W. I do voluntary and without deceit, in addition to my former covenant, most seriously promise and vow never to reveal to anyone whatever, not even to a Brother Disciple, any of the secrets, symbols, or anything appertaining to the Degree of a Fellow which I am now receiving, except it should be in a just and legal Lodge of Fellows such as I am now in. And I vow carefully to conceal all things belonging to this Degree from everyone, except I am convinced, after strict trial, inquiry, and examination, that he or they are entitled to receive the same, and that I can, without a breach of covenant in the least degree, communicate respecting these things, he or they having been accepted as a Fellow in a just and perfect Lodge of Fellows such as I am now in. And as a token of my sincerity I pledge my heart.

*Then proceed as in Disciple's vow.*

## ⁶²Fellow's Vow

S.W. I do voluntarily and without any deceit, in addition to my former covenant, most solemnly promise never to reveal to anyone whatever, not even to a Brother Disciple, any of the secrets, symbols, mysteries, or anything appertaining to this Degree of a Fellow which I am now receiving, excepting it should be in a legal Lodge of Fellows such as I am now in. And I promise carefully to conceal all things belonging to this Lodge from everyone, except I am convinced after strict trial, inquiry, and examination that he or they are entitled to the same, he or they having been accepted as a Disciple and Fellow in a just and perfect Lodge such as this I am now in, and that I can, without a breach of covenant in the least degree, communicate respecting the things with each person. I likewise promise that I will aid and assist, to the best of my ability, all worthy Fellows who may claim my help and to be faithful. With the exceptions above mentioned, I promise to keep the secrets of this Lodge enclosed in my heart, and, as a pledge of my sincerity, I declare that I will have my heart torn from my breast, rather than violate this vow I now make. So help me God. Amen.

⁶¹ Page 14, line 3.

⁶² Page 17, line 3.

**W.M.** [63]Brother, have you heard this covenant and are you willing to take it?

*[The candidate answers.]*

**W.M.**  Kneel then on the square and hold the square to your breast. Now read it yourself.

Brethren, while our Brother reads the oath, let us give a signal of our accordance.

*Covenant is here taken.*

**W.M.**  We hail you as a Fellow!

*Open book*

I present you with this blue ribbon which you will hereafter wear. It denotes constancy and is the colour of the heavens.

*Learns the grip, sign, and word.*

*One gavel*

This sign is a pledge of constancy and good faith. It is like pledging the heart. Thus, in pledging our words as Fellows, we point at the heart as the thing pledged for the sincerity of what we say. Now make yourself known to the Wardens and to our Fellow [64]who has pledged himself in your behalf.

**S.W.**  Are you a Fellow?

*Answer*

**S.W.**  By what shall I know you.

*Answer*

**S.W.**  As often as you make this sign, remember that you pledged your heart, your life for the truth of what you say.

*Salutes him.*

---

[63] Page 13, line 21.
[64] Page 14, line 1.

The Grade of Fellow

## LECTURE

**W.M.**  The well instructed guide who brought you to the door of the Lodge and properly prepared you for your entrance here, and assurance that you had laboured diligently procured you admission and the welcome of the Master. You came to the West. Your guide might follow you no longer. You was then to seek another guide, and the address from the East must have convinced you how necessary directions and instructions are in things to which we are strangers. You could not possibly guess at what was intended to be done or how you were to be disposed of.

Yet, your believing that they wished to do well toward you prompted you to follow the directions given you. Thus when they believe in the good intentions of fellow beings, they are easy, and they willingly enter into their views that, although experience and reason teach us that men are very frail and feeble creatures, if they were perfect, how much more easily, willingly should they follow them.

You went again on a symbolic journey, and you learned on the way the causes of much of the unhappiness and misery to which man could be subjected. Your attention was called to one who could become your most dangerous enemy. You was made acquainted with the error which could make him such. Finally, the subject on which you was to labour with constancy and care was presented to you, and the imperfection of human works taught was the rule for removing those imperfections.

From a more elevated situation than you before had, you could view an emblem of the guide of the wise. My dear Brother, let me persuade you to retain that emblem in your memory, and, if unhappily passion should tempt you from the path of duty, may the remembrance of what was seen serve to lead you from error. If unhappily avarice or ambition should

The Grade of Fellow

stop you on your way[65], and the recollection of that bright emblem should happily arouse you again to pursue your journey, oh return not to the vicious, betray not the good. At the altar you made a voluntary vow and received the tests of this degree. We hope you will often call these things to mind with pleasure.

Our Order has, as you already know, adopted the implements of operative masons as hieroglyphs. Such [66]instruments were used in erecting the Temple in Jerusalem, which was sacred to the name of deity, and they have been moralized. Those peculiar to this degree are the square, plumb, and level. By help of these, the rough stone becomes a good square stone. If a stone be so wrought that by neither of these instruments defects can be found, it is fitted for the builder's use.

But the square is applied to two sides at once, but it will not rest evenly on the superficies if the stone is defective. Hence it is called the symbol of truth and discoverer of error, and we hail the love of truth as one of the greatest virtues.

The plumb admonishes us to righteousness. See its unerring line. It directs from Earth to Heaven and from the Heavens to the Earth.

The level is only applicable to the upper superficies of the stone when placed on the building. By it, undue eminences or depressions are discovered which require the gavel's use to be removed. Hence it is taken as a symbol to remind us of that equality which should exist among all good Masons.

The builders of the holy Temples in the days that are past were well acquainted with the proportions necessary to the constructing of these beautiful and well contrived edifices, and hence they ought not to be unacquainted with the dimensions and proportions of architecture, and it is certain that in the places where wisdom, beauty, and strength characterize the buildings, there we not only find science cultivated and

---

[65] Page 14, line 25. The manuscript reads "you on your journey way."
[66] Page 15, line 1.

the social virtues encouraged but heaven born charity is there extending the hand to the assistance of the needy.

The Doric, Ionic, and Corinthian orders are those which in our times are generally esteemed originals. They are here in the Lodge, instead of our more ancient pillars, as monuments of human genius and of the high degree of taste and love of splendour which already existed among the people of the old world. But most of the magnificent monuments of antiquity are destroyed or ruined. Sic transit gloria mundi.

The liberal arts and sciences deserve our attention and encouragement. These distinguish a polite people from savages, and the capacity for acquiring a knowledge of them leads man to contemplate upon the works and perfections of Deity and enables them to lead others from many pernicious errors and to shun them himself.

On on both sides at the entrance of the Temple you see two pillars, the one formed and ornamented like the other. These stood before the entrance of the sanctuary, and no one could enter therein without passing them. Boaz and Jakin is the name of the two pillars. The meaning of the word he shall establish it. These pillars were taken from the Temple by Nebuchadnezzar. They were cast by Hiram, the widow's son, of brass, were hollow, eighteen cubits high, and four cubits thick. They stood here ornamented with the symbols of peace, wealth, and plenty, like twins–no difference in them but their names.

My Brother, if you will meditate upon these things and upon the mysteries of this Lodge, you will find a wide field for the exercise of the mind. The subjects are useful in a high degree and full of interest, and particularly those relating to yourself. These demand your most serious attention.

## Here ends the lecture of the Fellow Lodge

*Three gavels.*

The Grade of Fellow

## [67]OPENING OF THE FELLOW'S LODGE

*Senior [Warden] calls to order.*

W.M.   In order Brethren.

Brother Wardens, what is the duty of all good Masons before the Temple is opened?

S.W.   To see that the profane are removed and the Temple in safety.

W.M.   You will please to perform that duty.

S.W.   The profane are removed and the Temple in safety.

*Then follows the lighting as in the Disciple's Grade, with the address. Then the exhibition of the blazing star.*

W.M.   Brethren, behold an emblem of the guide of the wise. Let me persuade you to retain this emblem in your memory, and, if unhappily passion should tempt you from the path of duty, may a remembrance of what was seen serve to lead you from error. If unhappily avarice or ambition should stop you on your way, and a recollection of that bright emblem should happily arouse you again to pursue your journey. Oh return not to the vicious, betray not the good.

W.M.   Brother Senior, what is your order's name?

S.W.   Giblem.

W.M.   Brother Junior what time is it?

J.W.   Toward low twelve.

W.M.   Brother Senior, is it right time to begin the work?

S.W.   It is.

W.M.   Then please to be in order. Assist me in opening.

---

[67] Page 10, line 1. The previous text, page 8, lines 12-13, reads "Next follows the catechism work," even though the text has the opening and closing of a Fellow's Lodge. Most of the questions and answers of these ceremonies could comprise the catechism.

## The Grade of Fellow

> *One gavel.*
>
> *Sign.*
>
> *Prayer.*
>
> *One gavel*
>
>> Be seated.

**W.M.** Brother Senior, for what purpose are we here assembled?

**S.W.** To learn to know ourselves, and to inspect work done already on the rough stone, and to strive to complete it according to the designs of the Master, and to make farther progress in Masonry.

**W.M.** My Brother, let us strive deeply to impress upon our minds that it is highly important to labor diligently in order to complete the work according to the designs of the Master. Let us henceforth abstain from all foolish and vain pursuits and use the time allotted to us here to labor in discharge of our duty that happily we may be deemed fit for the Temple and not be rejected, and that we may hope to meet the reward, remembering that time flies swiftly away and is irrecoverable for mortals, but, to the view of the Great Master on high, the past, the present, and the future are all open. He perceives all the actions of men and knows all their thoughts.

The Grade of Fellow

*Once again Folger has encrypted two nearly identical passages, this time for the Closing the Fellow's Lodge. They are printed together for comparison.*

## 68 FELLOW'S LODGE CLOSING

W.M. Brother Senior, are you a Fellow?

S.W. I have been accepted as such.

W.M. Where?

S.W. In a perfect Lodge of Fellows.

W.M. Who accepted you?

S.W. The Master.

W.M. How shall I know you to be a Fellow?

S.W. By the sign.

W.M. What is the work of the Fellow?

S.W. On the square stone and the rough stone, and to finish it according to the Master's designs.

W.M. Where have you worked as a Fellow?

S.W. In the Temple.

W.M. Why was you accepted as a Fellow?

S.W. To learn the letter G.

W.M. What did you perceive in the Fellow's Degree that you had not before seen?

S.W. The blazing star.

W.M. What did it represent?

68 Page 10, line 19.

## 69 CLOSING OF THE FELLOW'S GRADE

W.M. *One gavel*

Brother Senior, are you a Fellow?

S.W. I have been accepted as such.

W.M. Where?

S.W. In a perfect Lodge of Fellows.

W.M. Who accepted you?

S.W. The Master.

W.M. How shall I know you to be a Fellow?

S.W. By the sign.

W.M. What is the work of the Fellow?

S.W. To square the smooth stone and to finish it according to the Master's designs.

W.M. Where have you worked as a Fellow?

S.W. In the Temple.

W.M. Why was you accepted as a Fellow?

S.W. To learn the letter G.

W.M. What did you perceive in the Fellow's Degree that you did not before see?

S.W. The blazing star.

W.M. What is it?

69 Page 16, line 1.

## The Grade of Fellow

| | |
|---|---|
| **S.W.** It is a symbol of the guide of the wise and faithful. | **S.W.** The guide to the wise and faithful. |
| **W.M.** Where did it arise? | **W.M.** Where did it rise? |
| **S.W.** In the East | **S.W.** In the East. |
| **W.M.** From whence did you see it? | **W.M.** From whence did you see it? |
| **S.W.** From the steps of the Temple. | **S.W.** From the steps of the Temple. |
| **W.M.** Did you go toward it? | **W.M.** Did you go towards it? |
| **S.W.** Yes, I was brought toward it. | **S.W.** Yes, I was brought towards it. |
| **W.M.** Whither did it guide your steps? | **W.M.** Whither did it guide your steps? |
| **S.W.** Towards the Master. | **S.W.** Towards the Master. |
| **W.M.** What else did you perceive? | **W.M.** What else did you perceive? |
| **S.W.** The letter G. | **S.W.** The letter G. |
| **W.M.** What does it signify? | **W.M.** What does it signify? |
| **S.W.** I know but little about it, but it has been said to me to signify geometry. | **S.W.** I know but little about it, but it has been said to me to signify geometry. |
| **W.M.** Was anything else shewn to you? | **W.M.** Was anything else shewn you? |
| **S.W.** Yes, one of the subjects on which I was to labour. | **S.W.** Yes, one of the subjects on which I was to labour. |
| **W.M.** Have you commenced your labours? | **W.M.** Have you commenced your labours? |
| **S.W.** I have. | **S.W.** I have. |
| **W.M.** Can you complete them? | **W.M.** Can you complete them? |
| **S.W.** Yes. | **S.W.** Yes. |
| **W.M.** How? | **W.M.** How? |
| **S.W.** By following the directions given by the Master and by his assistance. | **S.W.** By following the doctrines given me by the Master and by his assistance. |
| **W.M.** When will your labours as a Fellow cease? | **W.M.** When will your labours as a Fellow cease? |
| **S.W.** When I am admitted to the Masters' Lodge and have passed through the inner chamber. | **S.W.** When I am admitted to the Masters' Lodge and have passed to the inner chamber. |

W.M. Have you received wages?

S.W. Yes, at the pillar Jakin I have met with encouragement and the promise of ample reward.

W.M. What is the symbol of a Fellow?

S.W. The square stone with the inscription "DO."

W.M. What is the meaning of this symbol?

S.W. That the Master discovers and points out the defects of the work and has given us the means of rectifying these, and it should remind us of our duty to strive to conform to the rules given us, thereby endeavouring to fit ourselves for a place in the Temple.

W.M. Brother Senior, when does the work end?

---

W.M. Have you received wages?

S.W. Yes, at the pillar Jakin I have met with encouragement and the promise of ample reward.

W.M. What is the symbol of a Fellow?

S.W. A square stone with "Do" engraved on it.

W.M. What is the meaning of this symbol?

S.W. That the Master discovers and points out the defects of the work and has given us the means of rectifying them, and it should remind us of our duty to strive to conform to the rules given us, thereby endeavouring to fit ourselves for a place in the Temple.

W.M. Brother Senior, when does the work end?

S.W. At midnight.

*Here follow closing as in the Disciples' Lodge, exhibiting star with the address, then questions as in opening of Fellows' Lodge.*

*Three gavels*

# [MASTER'S GRADE]

## [70]PREPARATION FOR THE MASTER'S GRADE

**Introductor**[71] We should, while we live, prepare for death, and we should constantly be at this work because we know not when we shall die. But it is certain we shall die, and we shall give up our bodies to the dust from whence they came. Our souls die not, they are to exist forever. But how shall this existence be–miserable, unhappy? Could we determine it, we should choose the happy state, but then we ought to be prepared for its enjoyment.

And what is necessary to prepare the soul for its happy state, and what will make it fit for its enjoyments? Whoever saw the vicious happy? Even in this gross bodily state they are not. So they can clothe themselves in purple, they can live in palaces, they can own piles of gold, they eat of dainties and become drunk of rich wines, but is this happiness or is it not rather the source of unhappiness? If deprived of these things, would they not be miserable? In the grave, none of these things follow with them. If they think but on death and futurity, it is agony to them. What then would realization be?

**Introductor** [72]Brother, you wish to be accepted as a Master. Come, follow me.

*Five gavels at the door.*

**Deacon** Who is here?

**Introductor** A Fellow who wishes to be accepted as a Master.

---

[70] Page 18, line 1.

[71] No officer is indicated as speaker here, but the Introductor is continued as in the Disciple's and Fellow's Grades.

[72] Page 18, line 12.

# The Grade of Master

*Gives the pass: [Giblem].*

**Introductor**  He is over five years old and has worked in the inner court of the Temple on the polished stone. He has served his time and his Master is well pleased with him.

*[The Deacon] admits him and says:*

**Deacon**  Are you worthy to wear this badge?[73]

Takes it from him and places him in the west.

[74]My Brother, in times of old it was ordained, even by God, that those who entered the sanctuary should wash themselves, cleansing themselves from uncleanness. It was a symbol and it impressed upon the mind the necessity of holiness in those who went into the sanctuary. My Brother, it is a token of your sincere wish and intention henceforth to live undefiled. Wash your hands and remember, God is a witness to the performance of his ordinances.

## [75]ADDRESS FROM THE MASTER

**W.M.**  Brother, you are now brought to the inner chamber.

*[Exhibits a cross.]* When you are passed to a place of which this is an emblem,[76] there no art nor deception can hide any error or any imperfection. The Judge who there presides views the hearts of men and knows their most hidden secrets. Wherefore, in reverence to these solemn truths, be sincere.

My Brother, we are here assembled to commemorate and to lament the death of our Grand Master. His loss we may justly sorrow for, and as justly deplore the cause of his death, and, deploring them, shun them. He was killed by unfaithful

---

[73] Probably an apron, though no object is identified.

[74] Page 83, line 1. This passage stands alone, with no indication of where it goes or who speaks it. However, the salutation, "My Brother," seems to eliminate the Disciple's Grade, and it does appear to come prior to entering the "sanctuary."

[75] Page 18, line 16.

[76] No object is identified, but on page 11, line 29, is written "† When thou has passed to the place of which this is a symbol, thy destiny will be fixed forever."

The Grade of Master

Fellows. No guile was in his heart nor evil in his ways, yet they set his goodness at nought and their ruffian hands murdered him.

Brother Warden, shew our Fellow the horrid spectacle before us and watch him well and see if he appears to be one of the conspirators against the Grand Master.

**Warden** Our Fellow does not appear to be among the guilty, and he is moved, we believe, at this sight.

**W.M.** We are glad that you do not appear greatly concerned in this work of death, and we hope you never will join those who are guilty. Bring him on the Master's path for instruction, that he can join us in seeking the Master.

## SYMBOLIC JOURNEY

[77]**First Round**

**Warden** Remember Death.

*One gavel*

That man who has a sense of his own frailty and who has learned to observe his own imperfections has made the first step toward the light.

[78]**Second Round**

**Warden** Remember Death. It is unavoidable.

How dangerous it is to venture upon the far distant journey without a knowledge of the way we are going. How foolish to refuse to attend to the infallible doctrines which point out the way. Would one who thus ventures and thus refuses not easily err and not find the city he sought, but instead thereof faint among the sands of the desert where there is no water to allay burning thirst and bread to keep from starving?

[77] Page 19 line 1.
[78] Page 19, line 3.

The Grade of Master

Remember Death.

*Two gavels*

### [79]Third Round

Warden  Remember Death. It is unavoidable.

It may be very near; perhaps it is near at hand. Let us incline our hearts to instruction and our minds to understanding and learn the way to the habitation of rest and comfort. Let us seek the way thither with earnestness. Let us knock at its door with confidence and with all humility. Let us ask alms for our wants of the good Master of the house, and, believe me, He will not reject our prayer and will even grant us much more than we expected and more than we can dispose of.

W.M.  Let him now ascend the seven steps of the Temple, and bring him with Master's steps to the East.

W.M.  [80]My Brother, before you can be accepted as a Master, it is required of you to make a solemn covenant with us.

*The Warden reads it.*

W.M.  Now, Brother, you are to receive the word and grip of this degree, and in future when you use these things, call to mind the situation you were in just before you received them.

*One gavel*

Brother Warden, lead our Fellow[81] to the place where we shall all assemble.

*Accepts him. Hymn and procession.*

W.M.  [82]Behold, Brethren, the pall covers. The coffin contains a Brother. God give you may henceforth be dead to sin, and

---

[79] Page 19, line 9.

[80] Page 19, line 15.

[81] Page 19, line 18. The manuscript reads, "lead our F to the blace." This could be *fratre*, but the candidate appears to be considered still a Fellow until he is raised.

[82] Page 19, line 20.

# The Grade of Master

ever may you bear in mind that you shall die. May you have firm hope of being raised from the Fellow to the Master, from darkness to light, from dust to heaven, from mortality to eternal life, and may this hope cheer you and make you faithful.

Brethren, let us seek to find our Master who was slain.

*Pass once round the grave.*

Lord help us children of the dust. Here is acacia sprig, and this has the appearance of a grave. Let us look into this.

**W.M.** [83]Brother, as the word was lost at the death of our Master, let us now agree that, when the body is raised, the first spoken shall hereafter be considered as the Master's word.

The flesh is corrupt.

*Raises the body [on the F.P.O.F.][84]*

## [85]LECTURE AND INSTRUCTIONS

**W.M.** Your being advanced to this degree, the objects can no longer be strange to you. But permit me to call your attention to some of the things which are inculcated by our symbols and ceremonies, independent of your obligations. Your mind was, at an early period of your connection with our institution, called upon to consider the very important and interesting subjects, viz. time, death, and immortality. And our aim in the course of initiation has been, symbolically and directly, to point subjects for meditation which could lead men to live virtuously and happily, to meet death with serenity, and to cheer this hope of a blissful futurity

[86]The necessity of mutual confidence in each other must be apparent to all who have wandered from the court of the Temple to its inner chamber, who would follow on in strange

---

[83] Page 20, line 1.
[84] Page 20, line 2. The manuscript reads, "The flesh is corrupt. ★ Raises the body."
[85] Page 20, line 3.
[86] Page 20, line 15.

## The Grade of Master

paths blind or in darkness or seeing where the sword point rests against the naked breast, except he had confidence in the directions of those with whom he went, and who would conduct any to the sanctuary of fraternity and make an indissolvable covenant of friendship with him unless he had confidence in his honesty and was convinced that he would betray not and would not be come an enemy.

[87]Confidence grows, however, out of the good opinions we may have conceived of others, either arising from a knowledge of those good principles or our observation of their good acts. Thus if we know men who live blameless lives, who shun covetousness and other vices, and who encourage truth and virtue, who protect innocence, and who do good, then we should certainly have confidence in these.

If they, at the same time, strive to propagate rules of life or doctrines tending professedly to make men happier than they otherwise would be, then, considering the character of these, men should at least examine the things they hold out to us. And if we even will not readily admit them, we ought not to neglect trying with them, and if upon a fair trial and proper examination they be found to be useful, as having a salutary effect upon individuals and upon society in general, if they are in unison with the truth, if they answer the great ends of making men better qualified for the discharge of duties, if they make men really happier, then it would undoubtedly be very contrary to our ideas of duty, if not very foolish, to reject them or even to neglect them. And that, if even they should be a little at variance with our customary thoughts or be somew[88]hat inconvenient because of our habits, such men and such rules or doctrines as I have alluded to are to be found, and it is believed that everyone who has strove to do his task as a Disciple and Fellow will seek and find them.

---

[87] Page 20, line 26.
[88] Page 21, line 1.

## [ADDRESS ON THE BIBLE]

**W.M.** This great light of Masonry is ever open in a proper Lodge, to that end that we should be reminded of the duty, that of learning and practicing the excellent precepts it contains. And if we, as far as we can, scrupulously examine both the character of those who gave the precepts and the influences they have had upon society and still have upon it, if we examine the great ends and views of the doctrines here written, and thus become acquainted with this volume, we shall experience that this volume is an inestimable treasure and should be viewed as such by all good men. It is in fact the book that contains the rules of life pointing out to man his whole duty. This volume is of great antiquity, and splendid monuments of the ancients have decayed and nations who peopled the countries where these things were written have vanished or are scattered over the face of the earth, their former places of abode are desolate, the languages the book was written in are dead, yet the book survives.

And the enemies of order and opposers of the good precepts this volume contains have sought with astonishing obduracy and unwearied pains, with jests, with philosophy falsely so-called, with misapplied learning, with every effort of their genius to bring this volume into contempt. But they have been engaged in a foolish work. All their pains have been taken in vain. It stands deservedly now in higher estimation than ever.

Considering the character of the writers for this volume and finding them to be good, even inimitably so, examining the doctrines contained in this volume, and observing their unison with truth and their beneficent influence upon society and upon individuals, thinking upon the great antiquity of these writings and the many revolutions which they have survived and their complete victory over the efforts of enemies, therewith continually increasing in the estimation of the world at large of the friends of good order and of truth,

## The Grade of Master

then it can be said, even if there were no other reasons for so saying, that this volume is not to be neglected, but, on the contrary, that it ought to be examined and should be made the subject of our attention and study.

And see how correct is its philosophy, how interesting the history, how sublime and beautiful the poetry, how acceptable the doctrines of religion and morality contained in this volume. It is calculated in every point of view to engage our attention, and, if attended to, the truths it contains make men better, wiser, and happier, and the benefits arising from these sacred truths are not limited to the period of human life. They point not forward to the grave as the boundary of our existence, as the place where men shall cease to be.

No, the thick gloom of death is dissipated by divine truth. A ray of sacred light makes visible to the eye of faith a state of existence beyond the grave, a state of existence, at the approach of which all must fear. For it lasts to all eternity, for it is a state of rewards and punishments, for it is dependent upon Divine mercy, for no man can claim a place there. Happy indeed is the man who has strove to subdue his passions and to lay aside his prejudices, and thus is fitted for the task of the Fellow.

And studying and executing the designs and rules of the Master, by contemplating upon the image of the pillar of beauty, he may have observed his own weakness and his own inability to make his work according to the pattern given him by the Master. If he is sensible of his own incapacity and imperfections, [89]he has in truth made the first step toward the light and has thus become more susceptible of the truth than he was. Then he will have the trestleboard in his hands and use all proper means for becoming acquainted with the designs which are drawn, and no doubt he will not only direct others how to exert them, but he will participate in the labour

---

[89] Page 22, line 1.

in the erection of the truly noble edifice—a Temple sacred to the name of God.

And in this work he will use the implements of the Master. The compasses will remind him to set proper limits to his duties, desires, and actions, not to be eccentric in behaviour, but to preserve any even line of conduct without irregularities.

We should, by example and persuasion, try to exact and encourage fraternal love. This is the very cement of the Temple. If it is wanting the whole becomes a heap of rubbish and is of no worth, but on the contrary is an obstacle to those who pass where it lies and nuisance to those who may have a habitation near it. Where fraternal love is not, there must be many evils. There the ruffian passions are enthroned and virtue is driven out or spurned with contempt or bound with thorns. There folly derides wisdom, and truth is obliged to hide her fair face. There religion or morality can not be found. There all is but mockery.

Time we cannot recall, but we can and we ought to use that aright which is to come. *[Exhibits hourglass.]* See the sand. The particles run rapidly, and, for aught we know, with the passing of one of them you or I shall die. It is uncertain. We should not then neglect a moment, but from henceforth do all we can do to the great end of being really happy. For we shall die, and in the grave there is no working. There is no device, no knowledge, no pardon there.

*[Exhibits skull.]* See this emblem, this monitor. It is silent vacant dead yet it speaks to our minds. The good hear a sound that even make them tremble. To some it can be a great cause of terror. It reminds all to remember death. We have crowned it with a green sprig, for we hope, in partaking of immortality, immortality and happiness through faith in the giver of every good and perfect gift, and by an earnest striving to do His will.

Remembering that man was created in His image and, although much deformed, can be again restored to his pristine state, be made fit for blissful enjoyments. Remembering that we should not be ashamed of truth and religion, for that would make us unfit for fraternity on earth and disqualify us utterly for the enjoyments of a future state, where love is the most essential requisite. Remembering that we should be charitable and sensible of the wants of our fellow men, for else we are monsters even here, as although associated as Brethren, and therefore would be hereafter unfit for lasting joys.

We must have hope to be restored to pristine purity. We must have faith. We must confess the truth. We must exercise love and charity with all our might. These are the rounds of the mysterious ladder that reaches from earth to heaven, and charity is the upper round.

The Grade of Master

## [OPENING OR CLOSING OF THE MASTER'S LODGE][90]

**W.M.** [91]*Salutation and so forth.*

Brother Senior Warden, are you a Master Mason?

**S.W.** Yes, I know the acacia sprig.

**W.M.** Where do Master Masons hold their Lodges?

**S.W.** In the inner chamber.

**W.M.** What is that place?

**S.W.** A place of perfect silence.

**W.M.** Where is it situated?

**S.W.** In a deep valley.

*Furniture, jewels, ornaments, symbols, 3 tapers, numbers, colors, signs, grips*[92], *and words in each Degree same as in the others.*

[93]**W.M.** From whence come the Masters and how do they journey?

**S.W.** From the East.

**W.M.** Why?

**S.W.** To dispense light and truth.

**W.M.** When one of our Brethren is missing, where shall we hope to find him?

**S.W.** Between the compass and square.[94]

---

[90] The following questions and answers appear in the text without any heading and end abruptly, followed by a prayer. As the dialogue is between the Master and the Senior Warden, it is assumed to be the Opening or Closing rather than the Master's Catechism.

[91] Page 22, line 26.

[92] Page 22, line 28. The manuscript reads, "signs, gs, and words."

[93] Page 23, line 1.

[94] The "Wilkinson Manuscript" of *ca.* 1730-90 has "Q. If a Mason be lost where is he to be found? A. Between the Square & the Compass." Douglas Knoop, et al., *The Early Masonic Catechisms*, 2nd ed., Harry Carr, ed., (London: Quatuor Coronati Lodge, No. 2076, 1975), p. 138. *Le Maçon Démasqué* of 1751 has on its title page "D. Si un Franc-Maçon se perdoit, ou le trouveriéz vous? R. Entre l'équerre, & le Compas." Harry Carr, ed., *The Early French Exposures*, p. 417.

# [PRAYERS]

*[The prayer on the left, written in the clear, follows the previous questions (with three intervening lines of special symbols). Later Folger wrote a similar version, marked "Opening," which is printed with the first for comparison; it could be used to open any degree. Below the later opening prayer is a prayer marked "Closing."]*

## [Prayer]

[95]Thy word is truth and we shall surely die. From dust we came, to dust we shall return, but Thou hast given us the fond desire, the hope, belief of life, even after death. For as Thy mighty word formed us of dust, so canst Thou raise us from the grave again and place us in a paradise divine or drive us out to sorrow and to pain. But how can we, Almighty King, obtain Thy blessing, or eternal life and joy? Lead us from evil, Lord, or else we err. Shield us from danger, Lord, or else we fall. Lead us to learn and do Thy holy will. Save us from perishing, or else we're lost, Thou King of Mercies, Great, Almighty God.

## [96]Opening [Prayer]

Thou King of Mercies, great Almighty God, Thy word is truth and we shall surely die. From dust we came, to dust we shall return. Yet Thou hast given us the fond desire, the hope, belief of life, even after death. And as thy mighty word formed us of dust, so canst thou raise us from the grave again and place us in a paradise divine or drive us out to sorrow and to pain. But how shall we, Almighty King, obtain Thy blessing or eternal life and joy. Lead us from evil, Lord, or else we err. Shield us from danger, Lord, or else we fall. Lead us to learn and do Thy holy will. Save us from perishing, or we are lost.

## Closing [Prayer]

[97]Father of every good and perfect gift, humbly we offer Thee our feeble thanks for Thy great mercies to us sinful men for our desire, our hopes, our faith in life, blissful, eternal in the realms of light. Guide us and keep us in the way of truth, give us firm faith in Thee and in Thy word, and grant that we may live and die in love.

---

[95] Page 23, line 6.
[96] Page 85, line 1.
[97] Page 85, line 17.

## SCOTTISH OBLIGATIONS

*[The following "Scotish" obligations stand alone in the text.]*

### [98]Covenant Before Entering a Scotch Lodge

I solemnly promise and vow that I will not converse about, so as in any manner to communicate or reveal to any person whatever, not even to a Free and accepted Mason, any of the forms, doctrines, symbols, or ceremonies, or any other things practiced or done in the Scotch Degree, excepting it be to a member of the same, or to such as are members of a Lodge acknowledged by the Master or his successors to be working according to the work done here, unless our Master or his successors grant me permission so to do. Nor will I reveal the time and place of meeting to any but members of the same. Amen.

### [99]Obligation for all Members also all Candidates for the Scots Ritus and Visiting Masons

I promise and swear, sincerely and without deceit, that I will not reveal, speak about, or communicate in any manner whatever to any person in the world, not even to any Free and Accepted Mason, any of the forms, symbols, doctrines, or ceremonies, or any other things practiced in this body, excepting to such as are members of the same or of a Lodge acknowledged by the Master of this body to be working according to the work done in this Lodge, unless the Master of this body grant me permission so to do as far as it respects any Free and Accepted Mason. And I will not suffer the works to be altered, neither will I do the work which is practiced here in any other Lodge, or cause or allow it to be done, unless I have the consent of the Master for so doing, or the permission of the present Grand Master of the Grand Lodge.[100] So help me God, amen.

[98] Page 86, line 19.

[99] Page 16, line 13.

[100] The manuscript uses a unique symbol here, ⊠. Since the covenant refers to the *G M*, the consistent interpretation is *Grand Lodge*. However, this is the covenant for the "Scots Ritus," and perhaps the special symbol stands for *Supreme Council*, or *Grand Consistory*.

# [THE HISTORY]

[101]The regular formation of {? ? ?}[102] was undoubtedly affected by Cromwell[103] and at his time, but this was {? ? ? ? ?} and no other and in _____. The first regular {Lodge} was undoubtedly formed in {Europe} not in other places as in {? ? ? ? ?}, etc.

{? ? ?} was born 1590–lived 61 years. (In Cromwell's time Charles I was likened upon figuratively[104] by the courtiers as the murdered master–his mother was yet living as a widow and his Masonic subjects called themselves her children, etc., etc.) During Cromwell's time there were many Lodges in England, Ireland, and Scotland, and Masonry was generally adopted and flourishing throughout these kingdoms but also in other places. Yet out of England, Masonry was something also in form and object, and in these places it was not popular and connected with wrong speculations.

Cromwell's Lodges admitted all kinds of people without respect to Religion, Morality, or Cultivation, and it appears that he only used the Order as a means by which he expected to effect some certain more political views. He pretended to advocate Equality and Freedom, but this appears to have been all a sham. He found the doctrines of Masonry convenient with a little feeble alterations to his republican and afterwards to his despotical views. The rebuilding of the Temple was made a figure in all its parts subservient to the circumstances and to the political views of many of his English coadjutors.

101 Page 82, line 1.

102 In many places, Folger used Hebrew letters to spell phonetically certain words, indicated here by braces. When his intentions are not clear, braces containing question marks are used, one question mark for each Hebrew letter. In a few places in the text, large blanks appear, as if Folger was intending to later fill in some word or characters. These blanks are indicated by underlining in the text.

103 The manuscript has an ill formed *beth* or *kaph*, but later a *kaph* is deduced to stand for *Cromwell*, because of the similarities to Larudan's *Les Franc-Maçons Ecrasés* (see chapter 1). Therefore all occurrences of the *kaph/beth* letter are interpreted as *Cromwell*.

104 Page 82, line 4. The manuscript reads, "C I was likened upon fig.y."

The History

In England about this time, the Order had many names one after the other as Free Masons–then Nivelleurs–then members of the Fifth Monarchy and finally were again called Free Masons. Cromwell appointed priests[105] for Secretaries for the four Quarters of the Globe etc. General Rainsborough was the Master of the Nivelleurs. Some of his Companions were concerned in the death of the King. Their ostensible object was as a society to the establishment of Freedom, etc. Harrington was Master of the Fifth Monarchy and a friend and connection of Cromwell. Their professed object was freedom and equality and not to acknowledge any other Regent than {Jesus}. They had the form of a flag with a Lion sleeping with this motto –"Who will wake him?" They conspired however against Cromwell and were persecuted afterwards by him.

Hereafter Cromwell sought to give to Free Masonry in England a more religious tendency that it had before had in that land, and it is said that the oath now has received quite another form and a more political one than before. And several Nivelleurs were during this alteration severely punished, even with death (see Parchard's *History*, 1736, when the Order had got a more fearsome[106] oath, etc.). It is however to be remarked that Williberts Architects and Masons Societies (in 600) was one of the first formular appearances of Free Masonry in Europe, and it thereafter a short time got the name of Free and Accepted Masons.

The murdering of Charles of England gave the society another form. The flight of James II produced the higher degrees. Here is the secret of the Dagger with which the Usurper should be killed.

{? ? ? ?} and this {?}'s arrival in {? ?} and the institution thereabouts of an order is a subject much connected with the Masons' History, yet it is certain that several hundred years before this time in which {? ? ?} institution existed that there was an order

---

[105] Page 82, line 19. The manuscript reads, "*kaph* appointed † for Secretaries."
[106] Page 82, lines 30-31. The manuscript reads, "the order dad got a more *f* oath &c."

established or introduced on one of the western Isles and flourished there prior to 1118. Masonry was not denominated any such thing as Masonry but was the real Masonry, which altho now but little known among Masons but is known to some few. On the restoration of the Royal family after the republic {?} was adopted insted of other things {? ? ? ? ? ?} and Knight.

[107](Mons) was erected in {? ? ? ?}, etc. The monks joined the order and the _____ of the Templars originated. Now the statutes were published in England, and the English Lodges (1705) formed a Grand Lodge and usurped the Supremacy, etc. The Jesuits–Mystics–Illuminati– joined the order and by entirely influencing, altering, and adding to it, it got to the shape is now has. And the most of those who tried the reformation of the work (1779-1788) knew not the ancient forms and objects. The work then became what it now is, an essentially and entirely different from what it originally was in the same kingdom as other places.

Before the inquiry by {Rome}, from a short time after the crucifixtion[108], there remained in {Jerusalem] several of the Brethren, among them {? ? ?}. He and they, a short time before the destruction, retired to Ephesus. At Jerusalem they taught the sublime doctrines of Christ[109] and joined to them several {? ? ? ?} who were in possession of the rites of the Temple. They had assembled and introduced many Christians into the mysteries–these serving rather as an exaltation of knowledge and shewing that the real doctrines of Christ had long been known and cultivated in the world even from very ancient times.

But Justin the High Priest and many of the Jews were opposed to the doctrines of the Cross and had got a wrong impression as to the mysteries and these and all who were not Christians were not admitted among the Brethren. From Ephesus many went into Greece, and to Achaia. In particular were they taught Christianity,[110] and

---

[107] Page 81, line 1.
[108] Page 81, line 9. The manuscript reads, "a short time after the ×."
[109] Page 81, line 11. The manuscript reads, "sublime doctrines of C."
[110] Page 81, line 18. The manuscript reads, "were they taught C."

The History

in some places they privately learned the Brethren the Mysteries. Shewing them who were acquainted with these things that the new doctrine did not contradict but rather confirmed the Mysteries and the precepts of Life which these contained.

But soon after the destruction by Titus some of the dispersed Brethren returned to {Jerusalem} and their keeping to landmarks of the holy places in view, and many of them were desirous to search the vaults of the Temple and the graves of the Kings, thinking not only that it was possible that there were treasures there, but that they should in time be able to find some things belonging to the Temple of which only tradition existed and which were deposited by Zerubabel[111] according to their account. But the Roman Soldiers and many uninvited Jews and Infidels being generally present hindered them in their researches.

And as the Infidel Jews in the year 105 made a kind of revolution, Adrian utterly destroyed the buildings which had been repaired in {Jerusalem} and the three towers, and the Brethren fled. But they were well acquainted with the landmarks _____ and a description of this and of the Temple, etc. formed hereafter a part of the mysterious instruction. In the second century (121-30) many Brethren retired with associates and devoted themselves to acts of Piety, dwelling in secret places and praying, fasting, and doing acts of charity of which there was much new. But they also kept communion with each other and as far as circumstances would permit propagated the mysteries.

However many of the church were opposed to these things and the Brethren were obliged to be very discreet, and their number sometimes was very small. Yet in other parts of the world there appear to have been numerous assemblies of the same kind tho under different denominations, as in Greece. In 613 there were many in {? ? ?}, and many persons in 613-680 joined them. Buildings were now built in the holy places, one of which was called Solomon's Temple, being a church built on the foundation of the

---

[111] Page 81, line 26. The manuscript reads, "deposited by Z."

ings were now built in the holy places, one of which was called Solomon's Temple, being a church built on the foundation of the Temple's Sanctuary with flat roofs on the West side, and a kind of shelter with a stone wall and steep roof on the East side. By these buildings the place of the Sanctuary was afterwards found.–times

# References

## BOOKS AND ARTICLES

Anderson, James. *The Constitutions of the Freemasons.* London: 1723.

Atwood, Henry C. *The Master Workman or True Masonic Guide.* New York: Simons & Macoy, 1850.

———. "The Supreme Grand Council of the Northern Masonic Jurisdiction." Published in 14 parts. *The Masonic Sentinel*, Vol. I, No. 1, Aug. 16, 1851–Vol. I, No. 18, Dec. 13, 1851.

Barlow, S. B. "Miscellaneous: Dr. Gram." *The American Homeopathic Review*, Vol. III, No. 4, Oct. 1862, p. 185.

———. "Obituary: Hans B. Gram." *The United States Medical and Surgical Journal*, Vol. II, July 1867, pp. 449–452.

Baynard, Samuel H., Jr. *History of the Supreme Council, 33°.* 2 vols. Boston: Supreme Council, 33°, N.M.J., 1938.

Bradford, Thomas. *The Pioneers of Homeopathy.* Philadelphia: Boericke & Tafel, 1897.

Brockaway, Charles A. *One Hundred Years of Aurora Grata: 1818–1908.* Brooklyn: Waverly Press, 1908.

Caldwell, John D. *Cerneauism a Poison to Masonry.* N.p.: [1885.]

Carr, Harry, ed. *The Early French Exposures.* London: Quatuor Coronati Lodge No. 2076, 1971.

Carson, Enoch T. "History of Ancient and Accepted Scottish Rite Masonry in the United States." *The History of Freemasonry.* 4 vols. R. F. Gould et al., eds. New York: John C. Yorston, 1889.

Cartwright, E. H. *A Commentary on the Freemasonic Ritual.* 2nd, revised ed. Tunbridge Wells, Kent: Fenrose, Ltd., 1973.

References

Coil, Henry W. et al. *Coil's Masonic Encyclopedia.* New York: Macoy Masonic Publishing and Supply Co., Inc., 1961.

*The Collected Prestonian Lecturers 1975–1987.* Shepperton, England: Lewis Masonic, 1988.

*Columbia University Alumni Register: 1754–1931.* New York: Columbia University Press, 1932.

[Diterlé, E.] *Précis Historique de La Sincérité No. 373.* [New York: 1955.]

Drummond, Josiah H. "Ancient and Accepted Scottish Rite of Freemasonry." *History of Freemasonry and Concordant Orders,* H. L. Stillson et al., eds. Boston: Fraternity Publishing Co., 1912.

Duncan, William J. *History of Independent Royal Arch Lodge No. 2, F. & A.M., of the State of New York.* New York: Charles S. Bloom, 1904.

Engel, Alfred. *Die freimaurerischen Geheimschriften.* Bayreuth: Quatuor Coronati Lodge, 1972.

Folger, Robert B. *The Ancient and Accepted Scottish Rite in Thirty-Three Degrees.* 2nd ed. New York: The Author: 1881.

———. *A History of the Ancient and Accepted Scottish Rite in the United States,* 1877, Typescript, Collection No. SC087, Archives, Supreme Council, 33°, N.M.J., Lexington, Mass.

———. *Information for the Members of the Ancient, Accepted Scottish Rite.* New York: Edward O. Jenkins' Sons, [1884.]

———. "Recollections of a Masonic Veteran." *New York Dispatch.* Published in 42 parts (two numbered "Part 3" and Part 31 taking two issues). Apr. 20, 1873–Sept. 20, 1874.

———. "Reply to John D. Caldwell." in *Rites and Supreme Councils.* Cincinnati: *Masonic Review,* October 1885.

———. "Reply to the 'War Whoops' of Enoch T. Carson." Columbus, Oh.: Hann & Adair, 1886.

Foulhouze, James. *Mémoire à Consulter sur L'Origine du Rite Ecossais Ancien Accepté.* New Orleans: L. Marchand & Cie., 1858.

Gardiner, William Sewall. *A History of the Spurious Supreme Councils in the Northern Jurisdiction of the United States.* Washington: Pearson's Steam Press, 1884.

Gardner, William L. *Historical Reminiscences of Morton Commandery No. 4, Knights Templar.* New York: J. W. Keeler, 1891.

Gilbert, Robert A. "The Masonic Career of A. E. Waite." *Ars Quatuor Coronatorum*, Vol. 99, 1986, pp. 88–110.

Hamill, John M. "The Sins of our Masonic Fathers." *Ars Quatuor Coronatorum*, Vol. 101, 1988, pp. 133–159.

"Hans B. Gram. M.D." *The U.S. Medical and Surgical Journal*, Vol. II, July 1867, pp. 449–452.

Hays, Edmund B. "Hays Register." Archives, Supreme Council, 33°, N.M.J. Lexington, Mass.

"A Historical Note of Dr. Gram." *The Hahnemannian Monthly*, Vol. VII, No. 1, 1871, p. 84.

King, William H. *History of Homeopathy. 2 vols.* New York: Lewis Publishing Co., 1905.

Knoop, Douglas et al. *The Early Masonic Catechisms*, 2$^{nd}$ ed. Harry Carr, ed. London: Quatuor Coronati Lodge, No. 2076, 1975.

———. *Early Masonic Pamphlets.* Manchester: Manchester University Press, 1945.

———. *The Two Earliest Masonic Manuscripts.* Manchester: Manchester University Press, 1938.

Lachmann, Heinrich. *Geschichte und Gebräuche der maurerischen Hochgrade und Hochgrad-Systeme.* Brunswick: Herzoglich Waisenhaus-Buchdrukerei, 1866.

Larudan. *Les Francs-Maçons Ecrasés.* Amsterdam: 1778.

## References

"The Late Dr. Gram." *The Homeopathic Examiner*, Vol. I, No. 2, Feb. 1840, p. 101.

"The Late Henry C. Atwood." *The Masonic Messenger*, Vol. V, No. 12, Sept. 15, 1860, pp. 110–111.

Lenhoff, Eugen and Oskar Posner. *Internationales Freimaurerlexikon*. Munich: Amalthea-Verlag, 1975.

Mackey, Albert Gallatin and William R. Singleton. *The History of Freemasonry*. 7 vols. New York: Masonic History Co., 1906.

McClenachan, Charles T. *History of the Most Ancient and Honorable Fraternity of Free and Accepted Masons in New York from the Earliest Date*. 4 vols. New York: Grand Lodge F. & A.M., 1892.

"Obituary, Ferdinand L. Wilsey." *The American Homeopathic Review*, Vol. II, No. 9, June and July 1860, pp. 431–432.

Oppenheim, Samuel. *The Jews and Masonry in the United States Before 1810*. Reprint of the publications of the American Jewish Historical Society, No. 19. Bronx, N.Y.: Samuel Oppenheim, 1910.

"Pen Pictures of the Active Members of the Ancient Council, A.&A.S. Rite [Robert B. Folger]." *Masonic Chronicle*, Vol. VI, No. 10, Sept. 1884, p. 147.

Peterson, Norman D. *Annotated Book of the Lodge*. Portland, Oreg.: N. D. Peterson, November, 1990.

———. "Broad Characteristics of the A.&A.S.R. Blue Degrees." Portland, Oreg.: N. D. Peterson, Aug. 1990 draft.

[Pike, Albert.] *Beauties of Cerneauism. No. 1*. [ Washington, D.C.: Supreme Council, 33°, S.J., U.S.A., 188–.]

Prichard, Samuel. *Masonry Dissected*. Reprint. Commentary by Harry Carr. Bloomington, Ill: The Masonic Book Club, 1977.

Ross, Peter. *A Standard History of Freemasonry in the State of New York*. New York: Lewis Publishing Co., 1899.

Runkel, Ferdinand. *Geschichte der Freimaurerei in Deutschland.* 3 vols. Berlin: Verlag von Reimar Hobbing, 1931.

"Scottish Rite Testimony [Wm. A. Hershiser, et al. vs. S. Stacker Williams, et al., Franklin, Co., Oh., 1889]." Published in several parts. *Masonic Chronicle,* Vol. XIV, No. 7, June 1892,-.

Singer, Herbert T. and Osian Lang. *New York Freemasonry: A Bicentennial History, 1781-1981.* New York: Grand Lodge F.&A.M., 1981.

Smith, Henry M. "Homeopathic Directory: New York Historical Sketch." *The New England Medical Gazette.* Vol. VI, No. 2, Feb. 1871, pp. 91-94.

*Statement of Proceedings Relative to Grievances Existing in the Grand Lodge of the State of New York, and the Reasons for Reviving St. John's Grand Lodge.* New York: Charles Shields, 1853.

Speth, G. W. "Two New Versions of the Old Charges." *Ars Quatuor Coronatorum,* Vol. 1, 1886-1888, pp. 127-129.

"The Spurious Council 33d, New York." *The Freemason's Monthly Magazine,* Vol. XII, No. 8, June 1, 1853, p. 240.

Supreme Council for the United States, their Territories and Dependencies [Thompson-Folger revived Cerneau Supreme Council]. *Official Manifesto.* New York: Isley & Marx, 1881.

Voorhis, Harold V. B. "Henry Clinton Atwood-A Connecticut Yankee in New York." *Transactions of the American Lodge of Research* [New York], Vol. III, No. 1, 1960, pp. 89-96.

Worts, F. R. *The "Yokshire" Old Charges of Masons.* York: Installed Masters' Association, Leeds, 1935.

References

## ARCHIVAL MATERIALS

Baden, Wil. "Decryption of the Folger Manuscript, [ca. 1955]." Typescript. Archives, Macoy Publishing and Masonic Supply Co., Inc., Richmond, Va.

Jacobs, Abraham. "Register, Rules & Status. of the Sublime Degrees of Masonry, [ca. 1809]." Archives, Supreme Council, 33°, N.M.J., U.S.A., Lexington, Mass.

Droz, F. Amez, trans. *Ritual of the Second Degree (Companion) for the System of the Rectified Masonry Decreed at the Convent General of the Order in 5782.* N.d. Archives, Iowa Masonic Library, Cedar Rapids.

——. *Ritual of the Third Degree (Master Mason), Decreed at the General Convent of the Order in 5782.* N.d. Archives, Iowa Masonic Library, Cedar Rapids.

Folger, Robert B. "Cipher Manuscript [*The Macoy Book*]," July 12, 1827. Transcript in the hand of R. B. Folger. Archives, Macoy Publishing and Masonic Supply Co., Inc., Richmond, Va.

Hays, Edmund B. "Hays Register," Archives, Supreme Council, 33°, N.M.J., Lexington, Mass.

Minutes, Supreme Council in and for the Sovereign and Independent State of New York [Second Atwood Supreme Council]. Transcript in the hand of Robert B. Folger. Collection No. SC012. Archives, Supreme Council, 33°, N.M.J., U.S.A., Lexington, Mass.

*Rituel de Loge de Saint-Jean, 2e Grade.* Brussels: Grande Loge Régulière de Belgique, n.d.

*Rituel de Loge de Saint-Jean, 3e Grade.* Brussels: Grande Loge Régulière de Belgique, n.d.

*Rituel du Rite Ecossais Ancien et Accepté d'après les Rituels Anciens.* New York: La Sincérité No. 373, n.d.

# INDEX

### Prepared by Norman D. Peterson

**A**

ablution, 103, 182, 223
acacia sprig, 152, 209n
Achaia, 238
"Ad hoc stat." 5, 205n
"Adhuc stat." (Thus far it stands.), xvi, 5, 205n
Adrian, Emperor of Rome, 238
Albany, N.Y., xxiii
*aleph*, backward, Hebrew letter, 107
All-Healing Balsam (patent medicine), 93
altar, 9, 107
American Lodge of Research, 33
American Metropolitan College of the Grand Professed, 4
Amez-Droz, F., 6, 193
Ancient & Accepted Scottish Rite. *See* Scottish Rite
*The Ancient and Accepted Scottish Rite in Thirty-Three Degrees* (Folger, 1862, 1881), 86n, 102, 102-A*n*, 102-F*n*
Ancient and Primitive Rite, xxvi, 102-D
Ancient Chapter, R.A.M., 86
"Ancient Council," Scottish Rite S.C., 102-F
Ancient Scotch Master. *See* Scottish Master
Ancient, Free, and Accepted Scottish Rite. *See* Scottish Rite
Anderson, James, xvi
Andrew in the East Lodge, 93
*Annotated Book of the Lodge* (Peterson, 1990), 16n
Antient Grand Lodge workings, 180
antimasonic movement, xxvi–xxviii, 1, 51, 54, 60; conspiracy theory of xxvii
*The Antimasonic Party in the United States* (Vaughn, 1983), xxviii*n*
apron, 223
ashlar. *See* stone
Ashmole, Elias, xv
Atwood Lodge, 76
Atwood, Edward W., 80
Atwood, Henry C. (1801–1860), 4, 27, 85, 87, 102; becomes a Mason, 55–56; biography, 55–82; disliked by J. Herring, G.S., 61; established classes in "Cross work," 56; expelled from Masonry, 61, again, 73; failing health, 78; Grand Officer of schismatic bodies, Cerneau S.C., 27, Cerneau S.C. revived, 64, St. John's G.L., 62; last "hurrah," 81; *Masonic Sentinel*, published by, 67; memorial, 82; personality difficult, 62, 64, 65, 69, 82; position on Scottish Rite and Lodges, 70; receives 32° and 33°, 59; vocational & business history, 80
Austin, James M., Grand Secretary, N.Y., 73

**B**

Baden, Wil, 3, 18, 21, 33
"Balsam, All-Healing" (patent medicine), 93
Barker, John, 85
Barthe, Dr., 75
Batavia, N.Y., xxvii
Baynard, Samuel H., Jr., xxiv*n*, xxv*n*, 63n, 66n, 87n
*Beauties of Cerneauism* (Pike, 188–), 76n
Benevolent Lodge, 60
Bennett, Donald H., 3, 34
*beth*, Hebrew letter, 139, 235
Bible, 185, 228
Bideaud Supreme Council, xxiv, 86
Bideaud, Antoine, xxi, xxiii, 86
biographies
  Atwood, Henry C. (1801–1860), 55–82
  Folger, Robert B. (1803–1892), 83–102-G
  Gram, Hans B. (1786–1840), 47–52
  Wilsey, Ferdinand L. (1797–1860), 53–55
blazing star, 3, 109, 181, 209n
Blitz, Edouard, 4
blood, 191
blue ribbon, 213
Boaz, 107
Boudreau, Allan, 53n
box symbol, 199n
box with an *x*, 107
boxed-in cipher symbols, 38
Bradford, Thomas, 48n, 50n, 52n
broken pillar, 5, 7, 205; used for toast by Folger, 25
Brown, William Moseley, 4

**C**

C.B.C.S. (Chevalier Bienfaisant de la Cité Sainte), 4
Canandaigua, N.Y., 54
candelabra, 108, 202
Carr, Harry, xvi*n*, 181n, 232n

*Page 247*

# Index

Carson, Enoch T. (1822–1899), Lt. Gr. Commander, N.M.J., 66n, 67n, 68n, 69n, 76n, 79, 80n, 102
Cassard, Andres, 77
*Catéchisme des Francs-Maçons* (Travenol, 1744), 11, 181
Cerneau Sov. Grand Consistory, 86
Cerneau Supreme Council, 4, 27, 59, 102-B; revived, 63
Cerneau, Joseph (??–1827+), founder & Gr. Commander, Cerneau S.C., xxi, xxiv, 83, 86, 182
Cerneauism xxiii–xxvi; defended by Folger, 102-A
chain of union, 201
chamber of preparation, 184
Chapters, Rose Croix. *See* Rose Croix Chapters
Chapters, Royal Arch. *See* Royal Arch Chapters
Charles I, King of England, 235, 236
Charleston origin of A.A.S.R. denied by Folger, 102-B
Charleston Supreme Council. *See* Supreme Councils: Southern Jurisdiction
chartering of Lodges by Scottish Rite, 94
Chéreau, Antoine G., 105
Chevalier Bienfaisant de la Cité Sainte, 4
Christ, 200n, 236, 237
Christianity, 238; basis of R.E.R., 180
Church of the New Jerusalem, 52
cipher text only attack, 34
ciphers, representative Masonic, 105
Clay, Henry, xxviii
clef des lettres, 105
Clinton, De Witt (1769–1828), Governor & Gr. Master, N.Y., xix, xxiv, 59
coadjutors of Robert B. Folger, 47
Cohen, Moses, 58
Coil, Henry W., xixn, xxiin, xxviiin, 59n
*Coil's Masonic Encyclopedia* (Coil, 1961), xixn, xxiin, xxviiin, 59n
Colden, Cadwallader D., xxiv
*The Collected Prestonian Lectures 1975–1987* (1988), xvn
College of Physicians and Surgeons, 54, 84
Colombia (nation), 77
Columbia Co., N.Y., 84
Columbia Council, R.&S.M., 85
Columbia University, 2, 54, 84
*Columbia University Alumni Register: 1754–1931* (1932), 2n, 84n
Columbian Encampment, K.T., 85
Commanderies. *See* Knights Templar Encampments
Connecticut: Denby, 55; Oxford, 55, 59; Seymour, 80; Woodbury, 55
consistories: Elmira, 25; Sov. Grand, Cerneau, 86
*The Constitutions of the Free-Masons* (Anderson, 1723), xvi

continental Freemasonry xxii
conventions in presenting text, 110
*Cooke Manuscript* (1410), xv
Copenhagen, 1, 17, 26, 48
cord, 8, 181, 198, 209n
cordon de veuve (widow's cord), 182
Councils, Royal & Select. *See* Royal & Select Councils
covenant for a Scotch Lodge, 103
covenant. *See* vow
Coxe, Daniel xix
"crescent moon-backward gamma." *See* cryptanalysis: mystery digraph
Cromwell, Oliver, 11, 13, 235
cross, 108, 184, 209n, 223
"Cross work," 85; rejected by G.L. of N.Y., 56
Cross, Jeremy L. (1783–1861) Masonic lecturer & Gr. Commander, Cerneau S.C., 26, 56; recruited by Folger to be Gr. Commander, 66
cryptanalysis: artistic variations, 37, 43; assumptions of Bennett, 35; attacks, cipher-text-only, 34, matched-plain-and-cipher, 3, 33; boxed-in symbols, 38; *e* often second letter of word, 38; evolving nature of cipher, 44; of *Folger Manuscript* explained, 33–45; frequency of clusters, symbols, and words, 37; Hebrew letters, 45; high frequency letters, 38; homogeneity of cipher, 35; increased security in stacking, 44; invention of Folger's cipher, 44; "mystery digraph," 39; questions remaining, 44; symbol clusters and words, 35; symbols for $a, e, h, o, r, t, th, u$, 40–41; synthesis of common words, 42. *See also* Folger manuscript; Folger's cipher
Cryptic Councils. *See* Royal & Select Councils
*Cryptologia*, 34
cubical stone, 3, 5, 6, 107, 109, 197
Cushman, James, Masonic lecturer, 85, 87; conferred 33° on Atwood, 59
Cusick, Edward R., 59n
Cyrus Lodge, 76

## D

dagger, 236
de Grasse, Count, 102-B
de la Motta, Emmanuel xxv
decline in Lodges during antimasonic period xxviii
degrees
    Ancient Scotch Master, 19
    Disciple, 184–205
    Fellow, 206–221
    Maître Ecossais, 4
    Master, 222–232
    Scottish Master, 4, 30, 50, 51, 53, 183
deHoyos, Arthur, 237n

# Index

Denby, Ct., 55
Denmark xiii, 1, 17, 48
"Deponens aliena ascendit in unus." (Setting aside alien things, he rises as one.), 8
*La Desolation des Entrepreneurs Modernes* (Travenol, 1747), 11, 181, 182
Deszelus, 78
"Dirigit Obliqua." (He makes the crooked straight.), 6
Disciple's degree, 184–205
Disciple's vow, 190
Discipulus. *See* degrees: Disciple
dismasted ship, 6, 103
Diterlé, E., 28n
"D O" (Dirigit Obliqua.), 6, 221
door, 9, 11, 198
draped rectangle, 9
Drummond, Josiah H., 63n, 78n, 102n, 102-Cn
Duncan, William J., 90n, 91n
Dutcher, Benjamin C., 90

## E

*The Early French Exposures* (Carr, 1971), 181n, 232n
*The Early Masonic Catechisms* (Knoop, 1975), xvin, 232n
*Early Masonic Pamphlets* (Knoop, 1945), xvin
Elmira Consistory, 25
emblems of the degrees, 5
Emmerson, Henry, 18, 21
Emperors of the East and West xxii
Encampments. *See* Knights Templar Encampments
Engel, Alfred, 104n, 105n
Ephesus, 237
Epistle, James' first, 210n
Eureka Chapter, R.A.M., 59, 60
Evans, Joseph D., 72
evolutionary nature of ritual xv
*Explication de la Croix Philosophique* (Chéreau, 1806), 105
*Explication de la Pierre Cubique* (Chéreau, 1806), 105
exposés of Masonry xxvii

## F

Fellow's degree, 206–221
Fellow's vow, 147, 212
Fifth Monarchy, 236
Fireman's Lodge, 30, 84
flag, 236
flag, with lion, 236
floor plan of the Lodge, 8, 9
Folger Manuscript: abbreviations, use of, 19, 103; another copy, 3, 18, 19; broken by Wil Baden, 33; characteristics of writing, 19, 45, 103, 104; cipher, second unused, 104; comparison of Macoy and Supreme Council Books, 20–25; cryptanalysis, 33–45; date of book, 1; description, 2; drawings, a few unexplained, 104; facsimile, 112–177; Gram as source, 17; history of Freemasonry, 11, 235–239; illustrations added, 104; Macoy Book, 18, 19, possibly copied, 18, 20, 25, 104; questions remaining, 31, 32; R.E.R., F.M. not a perfect rendition of, 179; revocation of preface, 1, 29; rituals, sophisticated & complete, 15, 179; Supreme Council Book, 19, 20; symbols, some not deciphered, 179; th, special symbol used, 104; vows, 179; Wilsey's name obliterated, 30; words, 180. *See also* cryptanalysis
Folger, Anna C., 102-G
Folger, Robert B. (1803–1892), xxvi; becomes a Mason, 84; biography, 83–102-G; coadjutors, 47–82; early life, 84; expelled from G.L. of N.Y., 29, 55, 73; fiery-tempered, 100; French language, lack of knowledge of, 12; Grand Lodge of N.Y., troubles with, 55; Grand Lodge offices, 90; Grand offices, Cerneau S.C., 27, 101, 102-F; Hebrew, crude knowledge of, 45; historian, 102; *History*, revision proposed, 102-C, reprinted & disclaimed authorship, 102-D; I.R.A. No. 2, joins, 91, offices in, 90; indirectly confessed historical inaccuracies, 102-C; Latin, possible knowledge of, 45; Masonic activities decrease, 102-C; medical background, 30, 84, 87, Gram's influence on, 47; no respect for Pike, 79; opposed Reuben Walworth, 29; receives 32°, 59, 86–87; revoked preface to *Macoy Book*, 99; suspended from Masonry, 91, again, 97; well-educated, 45
Folger, Robert B., Jr., 102-C
Folger's cipher: abbreviations and special symbols, list of, 107; characters, individual, difficult to distinguish, 105; conventions in presenting text, 110; end-of-line symbol, 110; grouping, variability in, 111; key to, 107, 110, 111; *light*, special symbol used, 202n; mystery digraph, 106; non-linear method of writing, 31, 105, 106; pronouns, 111; special symbols, 111; strength of, 105; symbols, some not deciphered, 179; *th/ tauv* symbol, 44, 106, 107. *See also* cryptanalysis
"Folger's Hygeiangelos" (patent medicine), 93
Foulhouze, James, Gr. Commander, La. State S.C., 5, 28, 29n, 68, 69
France, hauts grades in, xxi
Francken, Henry Andrew xxii

# Index

*Les Franc-Maçons Ecrasés* (Larudan, 1747), 11, 31, 235n; as an intermediate text, 12; passages compared with the *Folger Manuscript*, 12–15
"Fraternal Cryptography" (Morris, 1982), 34
Frederick of the Crowned Hope Lodge, Copenhagen, 26
Frederick the Great xxiii
*Freemasonry in Federalist Connecticut* (Lipson, 1977), xxn, xxviin
Freemasonry, continental xxii
French exposés, 180
French language: Folger's lack of knowledge of, 12; Lodges xx, 26, 27
French Modern Rite, 8
French Rite, 16, 28
French system in the English language, 96
funeral urn, 8
*Die freimaurerischen Geheimschriften* (Engel, 1972), 105n

## G

Gardiner, William S., 67n, 68n, 81n
Gardner, William L., 54n, 90n, 99n
gavel, 108, 179, 194
German language Lodges xx, 26
German Union Lodge, 85
*Geschichte der Freimaurerei in Deutschland*, 7n
*Geschichte und Gebräuche der maurerischen Hochgrade und Hochgrad-Systeme* (Lachmann, 1866), 8n
Giblem. *See* passwords
Gilbert, R. A., 4n
glossary of Masonic terms xxix
gloves, 192; for a lady xvi, 193
"The Gold-Bug" (Poe), xiii
Goodman, Paul xxviiin
Gould, Robert F., xxiin, 66n
Gourgas Supreme Council, 58
Gourgas, J. J. J., xxiii, xxiv, 65, 75n
Gram, Hans B. (1786–1840), father of American homeopathy, 2, 16, 26, 30, 85, 89; biography, 47–52; Folger's medical career, influence on, 47; gravestone, 52; homeopathy pioneer in U.S., 47, 87; introduced to Wilsey, 17; Knight of the Order of St. John, 52; source of rituals, 17, 47; Swedenborgian church, member, 52
Grand Lodges: "Great Union" of N.Y., 62, 63, 94; Hamburg, 75n, 78; Louisiana, 69; multiple in N.Y., 75, 83; New York xix, xxiv, 75, 83; New York, Phillips, 74, 75n; New York, Willard, 74; St. John's, revived, 72, 74; St. John's, schismatic, 30, 62, 94, 97; Vermont xxviii
*The Grand Mystery Laid Open* (1726), 181

*The Grand Mystery of Free-Masons Discover'd* (1724), 180
Grand Orient of France: a model for Atwood, 74; Folger claims authority emanated from, 102-B
Grasse, Count de, 102-B
Gray, John F., 54
Greece, 237, 238

## H

Hahnemann, Samuel, 47; theory of homeopathy, 2
Hamburg Grand Lodge, 75
Harmony Council, R.&S.M., 56
Harrington, James, 14, 236
Harrison, Thomas, 14
Haswell, Nathan B., 67
hat and sword, surrendered, 185
hauts grades xxi, 4, 44, 105
Hays, Edmund B., Gr. Commander, Cerneau S.C., 78, 101, 102; preferred over Folger, 79
Hebrew, 235n: *aleph*, backward, 107; *beth*, 139, 235n; chart of letters, 106; *Europe*, 107; Folger's possible knowledge of, 45; *Jerusalem*, 107; letters scattered through text, 105; letters, meaning of some undetermined, 107; Masoretic vowel points, 106; *mem*, 139, 235; *tauv*, 106; *teth*, 106; use of by Folger, 105–107
Hebrew letters, 45
Herring, James, Gr. Secretary, N.Y., 85; dislike for Atwood, 61
Hibernia Lodge, 60
Hicks, Elias, 87
High Priest, Justin, 237
higher degrees, 236
Hiram Lodge, 53
historian, Folger as, 102
*Historical Reminiscences of Morton Commandery No. 4* (Gardner, 1891), 54n, 90n, 99n
*History of Free and Accepted Masons in New York* (McClenachan, 1892), 91n
*The History of Freemasonry* (Gould, 1889), xxiin, 66n
*The History of Freemasonry* (Mackey, 1906), 11, 12n
*History of Freemasonry and Concordant Orders* (Stillson, 1912), 63n, 102n
*History of Homeopathy* (King, 1905), 50n, 52n, 88n
*History of Independent Royal Arch Lodge No. 2* (Duncan, 1904), 90n
*A History of the Ancient and Accepted Scottish Rite in the United States* (Folger, 1877), 86, 102-A
*A History of the Spurious Supreme Councils* (Gardiner, 1884), 67n, 68n, 77n, 81n
*History of the Supreme Council, 33°* (Baynard, 1938), xxivn, xxvn, 63n, 66n, 87n

# Index

holy places, 238
homeopathy, 2, 88
houpe dentellée, 181, 182
hourglass, 3, 184, 230
Hudson, N.Y., 84
Hund, Baron von xvi, 7
Hygeiangelos, Folger's (patent medicine), 93

## I

I.R.A. *See* Independent Royal Arch Lodge
Illuminati, 237
illustrations and symbols discussed: acacia sprig, 109; altar, 9, 107, 109; blazing star, 3, 109; candelabra, 108; carpet, 3; cord, 181; cross, 108, 109; cubical stone, 3, 109; door, locked, 9; draped rectangle, 9; fire, 8, 107, 108; foot steps, 109; gavel, 109; gavel, 108; hourglass, 3; locked door, 11; Master's carpet, 108, 109, 181; moon with stars, 9; pillars, 11; plan of Lodge, 9; pyramid, 109; rope containing skull, 109; scroll with stars, 109; skull, 109, 182; spear thrown over a fire, 108; stars, 9; steps, 11; steps, seven, 9; stick figures, 108; stone, cubical, 107; swords, 109; tracing board, 181; wreath, 109
illustrations appearing in the *Folger Manuscript:* acacia sprig, 109, 152; *aleph,* 139; altar, 109, 139, 143, 152; *beth,* 139; blazing star, 133, 139, 177; caduceus, 156; censer, 152; coffin, 152; compasses, 147, 156; cord, 120; cross, 109, 147, 152, 156, 177; cubical stone, 135, 177; curtain, 143; dismasted ship, 163; door, 135, 149; fire, 143, 147, 202n; flag, 143, 174; foot steps, 109, 151; gavel, 109; grave(?), 156; heart, 147, 152; hexagram, 174; hourglass, 143, 147, 152, 156; Lodge floor plan, 161; Master's carpet, 109, 136, 151; *mem,* 139; moon, 154; pyramid, 155; scroll, 154; scythe, 156; skull, 154, 156, 174; square, 147; stars and moon, 154; steeple, 151; sword, 143; swords, 135; symbols, unknown, 109; temple, 152; triangular monument, 151; trumpets, 143; urn with fire, 147, 151; wreath, 109
"In initio conciones, quid nomen ord?" (In the beginning of the meeting, what is your order's name?), 180
"In silentio et spe fortitudo mea." (In silence and hope is my strength.), 6
indented tarsel, 181
Independent Lodge, 62, 63
Independent Royal Arch Lodge xix, 80, 90
ineffable degrees. See Scottish Rite, 58
*Information for Members of the Ancient Accepted Scottish Rite* (Folger, 1884), 101n
inner chamber, 223

*Institution of Free Masons* (ca. 1725), 180

## J

Jackson, Andrew xxviii
Jacobs, Abraham, Masonic lecturer: conferred, 32*
on Folger & Atwood, 59, 86; degree peddler, 58
Jakin, 177, 180
James II, King of England, 236
James' first epistle, 210n
Jehovah, 185, 200n, 201
Jerusalem, 237n, 238
Jerusalem Chapter, R.A.M., 2, 17, 30, 50, 85
Jerusalem word, 180
Jesuits, 237
Jesus, 200n, 236, 237
*The Jews and Masonry in the United States* (Oppenheim, 1910), 65n
Jews, admission of, attacked, 102-A
John the Evangelist, 237
John the Forerunner Lodge, 27, 70, 95
John, Gospel of, 112, 143
Jørgensen, Jørgen Vagn, 17n, 26n, 48n, 50n, 88n
Justin the High Priest, 237

## K

key to Folger's cipher, 107, 110, 111
King, William H., 50n, 52n, 88n
kneeling on the square, 189, 213
Knight Beneficent of the Holy City, 4
Knights Templar, 182, 237; prerequisite for, 15*, 94; started in New York xx
Knights Templar Encampments: Columbia No. 1, 85; General Grand, 182; Morton No. 4, 53, 54, 55, 85; Palestine No. 1, 62, 64
Knoop, Douglas xvn, xvin, 232n
knotted cord, 8
"Know thyself." 8

## L

Lachmann, Heinrich, 8n
Lafayette Chapter Rose Croix, 64, 86
Larudan, Abbé, 11, 12, 13, 31, 235n
Latin, Folger's possible knowledge of, 45
Lenox, Mass., 84
level, working tool, 215
"Libre B", St. John's Lodge, Philadelphia xix
light, "blazing and unsteady," 196
lion, sleeping, 14, 236
Lipson, Dorothy Ann xxn, xxviin
locked door, 9, 11, 198
Lodge, floor plan, 8, 9
Lodges: decline during antimasonic period, xxviii; French language xx, 27; German language xx; "nominally York—secretly Scottish," 75

Index

Lodges: American Lodge of Research, 33; Andrew in the East, 93; Atwood No. 208, 76; Benevolent, 60; Cyrus No. 208, 76; Fireman's No. 368, 30, 84; Frederick of the Crowned Hope, Copenhagen, 26; German Union, 85; Hibernia, 60; Hiram No. 10, 53; Independent No. 7, 62, 63; Independent Royal Arch No. 2, 80, 90; John the Fore runner, 27, 70, 95; Minerva No. 371, 31, 50, 53, 88; Morning Star No. 47, 55, 59, 60; Mystic No. 389, 56; New York No. 368, 90; 75; La Parfait Union xix; Pythagoras, 75n, 78; Scottish Rite, 27, 69; Silentia No. 198, 60,; 102-G; Silentia No. 360, 53; La Sincérité, 27, 29, 71, 77; St. John's Independent Royal; Arch No. 8 xix; St. John's No. 1 xix; St. John's, Philadelphia xix; Temple xix; L'Union; Français, 85, 15, 29; York No. 367, 60, 62; Zerubbabel and Frederick of the; Crowned Hope, Copenhagen, 26, 48; Zerubbabel of the North Star, Copenhagen, 26, 30; Zorobabel No. 498, 26, 51
Lowndes, Oliver, 58

M
Mackey, Albert G., 11, 12n, 75n
Le Maçon Démasqué (1751), 11, 181
Macoy Book, 18, 51, 53; Wilsey's name obliterated, 55
Macoy Book. See Folger Manuscript
Macoy Publishing and Masonic Supply Co., Inc., 3, 19, 33, 88
Maître Ecossais degree, 4
Marshall, George E., 69
"Masonic Alphabets" (Voorhis, 1952), 33
Masonic Messenger, 82
Masonic Publishing Co., 31
Masonic Sentinel, 67
Masonry Dissected (Prichard, 1730), xvi n, 181n
Masons, Free and Accepted, 189
Masoretic vowel points
Massachusetts: Lenox, 84; response to antimasonic movement, 60
Master's carpet, 3, 108, 181, 197
Master's degree, 222–232
Master's vow, 147
Master's word, 226
matched plain and cipher attack, 3, 33
McClenachan, Charles T., 91n, 102-En
McLeod, Wallace xvi, 23
mem, Hebrew letter, 139, 235
Memoire à Consulter sur l'Origine du Rite Ecossais Ancient Accepté (Foulhouze, 1858), 29n
Memphis, Rite of xxvi
Minerva Lodge, 31, 50, 53, 88
mirror, 8, 210

mirror ceremony, 103
Modern Grand Lodge working, 180
moon with stars, 9
Moore, Charles W., 75n
Morgan, William xxvii, 54
Morin, Stephen xxii, 58
Morning Star Lodge, 55, 59, 60
Morris, Rob, 33
Morris, S. Brent, 34
Morton Encampment, K.T., 53, 54, 55, 85
mosaic pavement, 181
Mosquera, Gen. Tomás Cipriano de, 77
Mulligan, John W., xxiv
"mystery digraph." See cryptanalysis
Mystic Lodge, 56

N
Nebuchadnezzar, 216
New Jersey
  Trenton, 59, 86
New York xix: Albany xxiii; Batavia xxvii; Canandaigua, 54; Columbia Co., 84; Freemasonry xix; Grand Chapter, R.A.M. formed xx; Hudson, 84; Knights Templar started xx; Lodges, 80% closed, 54; multiple Grand Lodges for, 75, 83; Nyack-on-the-Hudson, 102-G; public displays of Masonry forbidden, 60; Royal & Select Councils started xx; Royal Arch Chapters started xx; schism in Grand Lodge, 1823–1827, 56; St. John's Day parade, 60; State Assembly, 93; Sup. Council jurisdiction limited to, 95
New York Dispatch, 102-C
New York Lodge, 90
New York Medical and Philosophical Society, 51
The New York Red Book (1895), 93n
Nivelleurs, 12, 13, 236
Northern Masonic Jurisdiction xxv, 102-B
Nyack-on-the-Hudson, N.Y., 102-G

O
obligation. See vow
ode to a skull, 182
officers, placement of, 11
"Olosaonian, Dr. Folger's" (patent medicine), 93
Oppenheim, Samuel, 65n
order's name, 180, 217
L'Ordre des Francs-Maçons Trahi (1746), 11, 181
Orient Chapter, R.A.M., 62, 64
Osborne, George L., 95
Oxford, Ct., 55, 59

P
Palestine Commandery K.T., 62, 64
Parchard's History, 236

# Index

La Parfait Union Lodge xix
passwords, 180: Gibboam, 180; Giblim, 180, 181; Giblin, 180, 181; Giblos, 181; Jerusalem Word, 180; Master's word, 226
patent medicine, *Folger's Hygeiangelos*, "Dr. Folger's Olosaonian or All-Healing Balsam" 93
Peacher, William G., 4n
Peckham, William H., 102-D
Pennell, Richard, 91
perfect ashlar. *See* stone: square
Perfection, Rite of xxii
Peterson, Norman D., 16n
Philadelphia, St. John's Lodge, "Libre B" xix
Phillips Grand Lodge, 74, 75
Piatt, William F., expelled with Atwood from Grand Lodge, 61
pig pen cipher, 105
Pike, Albert (1809–1891), Gr. Commander, S.J., 76n, 102; addresses S.C., N.M.J., 102-E; not respected by Folger, 79
pillar: beauty, 210, 229; Boaz and Jakin, 11; broken, 5, 7, 205
*The Pioneers of Homeopathy* (Bradford, 1897), 48n, 50n, 52n
plan of the Lodge, 8, 9
plumb, working tool, 215
Poe, Edgar Allan xiii
Poole, H., xvi
prayers: closing, 233; opening, 233
*Précis Historique de La Sincérité No. 373* (Diterlé, 1955), 28n
preface to *Folger Manuscript* revoked 1, 29
Prichard, Samuel xvi*n*, 181n
*Proceedings of the Ohio Chapter of Research*, 33
pyramid, 109
pyramidal monument, 7
Pythagoras Lodge, 75n, 78

## R

R.E.R. *See* Régime Ecossais Rectifié
Rainsborough, Gen. Thomas, 13, 236
Ramsay's Oration xxi
Randall, Nelson, 71
*La Réception Mystéreuse* (1738), 180
reconstruction of continuous rituals xiii
Rectified Scottish Rite. *See* Régime Ecossais Rectifié
Régime Ecossais Rectifié xxxi, 1, 4, 5, 7, 30, 49, 95; Belgian, 11; Christian basis of, 180; derived from Strict Observance, 7; *Folger Manuscript* not a perfect rendition of, 179; Lodges in Copenhagen, 49
ribbon, blue, 213
Riker, Richard xxiv

Rising Sun Chapter, R.A.M., 56, 59
Rite of Perfection, 58
*Rites and Supreme Councils* (1885), 87n
rites of the Temple, 237
Rites, Masonic: Ancient and Primitive xxvi; Emperors of the East and West xxii; French, 16, 28; French Modern, 8; Memphis xxvi; Perfection xxii, 58; Scottish Rite, *which see*; Strict Observance xxxi, 7; York, 28, 66, 69, 94
*Rituel de Loge de Saint-Jean, 3e Grade*, 5n, 6n, 193n
Rome, 237
rope containing a skull, 109
Rose Croix (R✠) cipher, 105
Rose Croix Chapters: Lafayette, 64, 86
Rose Croix degree, 182
Ross, Peter, 72n, 81n, 86n, 97n
rough ashlar. *See* stone: rough
rough stone, 194, 197
Royal & Select Councils: Columbia No. 1, 85; Harmony No. 8, 56; started in New York xx
Royal Arch Chapters: Ancient No. 1, 86; Eureka No. 22, 59, 60; Jerusalem No. 8, 2, 17, 30, 50, 85; Orient No. 1, 62, 64; Rising Sun, 59; Rising Sun No. 16, 56; Solomon No. 3, 55; started in New York xx; Temple, 86
Royal Arch, prerequisite for Scottish Rite, 94
Royal Arch Lodge, Independent No. 2, xix, 80, 90
Runkel, Ferdinand, 7n

## S

St. Clair, Ward K., 3
St. John, Order of, Gram a member, 52
St. John's Grand Lodge, schismatic, 30, 62, 94, 97; defections from, 76; revived, 72
St. John's Independent Royal Arch Lodge xix
St. John's Lodge, N.Y., xix
St. John's Lodge, Philadelphia xix
Saynisch, Lewis, 26, 51, 89
schismatic St. John's Grand Lodge, 30, 94, 97
Scotch Lodge, covenant for, 103
Scotch Master. *See* Scottish Master
"Scotticism," 81
Scots Ritus, 4, 234
Scottish Master, 4, 19, 30, 50, 51, 53, 183; vow, 169
Scottish Rite, 16, 58, 59: Ancient, *Free*, and Accepted, 27; authority asserted over other rites, 71; chartering of Lodges, 27, 30, 69, 70, 71, 94, 95; compared with York Rite, 28; control over York Rite, 75; inherent authority over Lodges, 69; Lodges, R.E.R. rituals possibly used in, 29; Rite of Perfection xxii; subservience to York Rite, 66, 94
scroll with stars, 109

# Index

Second Atwood Supreme Council, 96
*Le Secret des Francs-Maçons* (1744), 181
seven steps, 9
Seymour, Ct., 80
Seymour, Harry xxvi, 102-D
ship, dismasted, 6
Shute, J. Raymond, 4
"Sic transit gloria mundi." (Thus passes the glory of the world.), 192
Sickels, Daniel, 69
"sign and word," 107
Silentia Lodge, 53, 60, 102-G
Simons, John W., Gr. Secretary, N.Y., 68, 69, 70
Simpson, Sampson xxiv
La Sincérité Lodge, 27, 29, 71, 77
skull, 109, 184, 209n, 230; ode to, 182
sleeping lion, 14
Smith, Henry M., 17n, 48n, 88n, 89n, 93n
Solomon Chapter, R.A.M., 55
Solomon's Temple, 239
Southern Jurisdiction xxiii, xxiv, 59
Sovereign Grand Consistory, Cerneau, 86
Speth, G.W., xvin
square stone, 3, 5, 6, 197, 221
square, working tool, 215
*A Standard History of Freemasonry in the State of New York* (Ross, 1899), 86n, 97n, 72n, 81n
star, blazing, 3, 109, 181, 209n
stars, scroll with, 109
*Statement of Proceedings Relative to Grievances Existing in the Grand Lodge of the State of New York, and the Reasons for Reviving St. John's Grand Lodge* (1853), 72n, 97n
steeple, 7
steps: five, 211; of the temple, 11; seven, 9, 225; three, 189
stick figures, 108
Stillson, H. L., 63n, 102n
stone: cubical, 3, 6, 107, 109; rough, 194, 197; square, 5, 197, 221
Strict Observance xvi; emblems, 7; Rite of xxxi; transformed into Rectified Rite, 7
substitution cipher xiii
*Supreme Council Book. See Folger Manuscript*
Supreme Councils: dozen seen by Folger, 83; one in every state, favored by Foulhouze and Atwood, 80; superiority rejected by American Masons, 76
Supreme Councils: "Ancient Council," 102-F; Bideaud xxiv, 86; Cerneau, 4, 27, 58, 59, 63, 102-B; Charleston xxiii; Charleston, xxiv; Gourgas, 58; Louisiana State S.C., 68, 69, 74, 76; Northern Hemisphere, 64, 66; Northern Masonic Jurisdiction xxv, 102-B; Second Atwood, 96n;

Southern Jurisdiction xxiii, xxiv, 59; State of New York, 67; Thompson-Folger, 84; Union of, 1867, 102-B
Swedenborgians, 52
sword, 188, 189, 209n; circle of, 192; hat and, surrendered, 185
"A Synoptical History of all of the Supreme Councils" (McClenachan), 102-E*n*

## T

Tardy, John G., 58, 59
tasselled cord, 181
*tauv*, Hebrew letter, 44, 106, 107
Temple Chapter, R.A.M., 86
Temple Lodge xix
Temple rites, 237
Temple, Solomon's, 239
temporal sign, 181
"Ternario formatur, novenario dissolvitur." (It is formed by three, dissolved by nine.), 8
tessellated border, 181
textual analysis, 23
*th*, cipher digraph, 40
"thick darkness," 186
Thompson, Hopkins, 102-E
Thompson-Folger Supreme Council, 84
tick-tack-toe cipher, 105
Tisdall, Fitz Gerald, 79n, 97
Titus, Emperor of Rome, 238
toast by Folger, 25
Tompkins, Daniel D., xxiv
tools, Masons' working, 215
*Towards a Christian Republic* (Goodman,1988), xxviii*n*
tracing board, 181
Travenol, Louis, 181
Trenton, N.J., 59, 86
"Tria formant alienum deponent et ascendit in unum." (Three things form an alien thing, they set it aside, and it rises into one.), 7, 151
triangular monument, 7, 8
*The Two Earliest Masonic Manuscripts* (Knoop, 1938), xv*n*

## U–V

L'Union Français Lodge, 85, 15, 29
Union of 1867, of northern S.C.s, 102-B
union, chain of, 201
Unkart, Edward, 78
urn, funeral, 8
Vatet, Eugene, 78
Vaughn, William Preston xxviii*n*
veil, 210
veil of the tabernacle, 181, 198

Index

Vermont xxviii
Voorhis, Harold van Buren, 18, 33, 56n, 80n
vow: Ancient Scotch Master, 4, 169, 183; Disciple's, 190; Fellow's, 147, 212; Master's, 147; Scotch Lodge, covenant for, 4, 103; Scots Ritus, 4; Scottish, 234
vowel points, Masoretic, 106

W

Walker, Wendall K., 91n
Walworth, Reuben H. Chancellor & Gr. Master, N.Y., 29, 72, 96, 97
War of 1812 xix
Washington, George, 83
water, 184
*The Whole Institutions of Free-Masons Opened* (1725), 180
widow's cord, 182
*The Wilkinson Manuscript* (ca. 1730–1790), 181, 232n
Willard Grand Lodge, New York, 74
Willermoz, Jean Baptiste xxxi
Willets, Charles W., 95
Williberts Architects, 236
Willis, William, 90
Wilsey, Ferdinand L. (1797–1860), 16, 88; biography, 53–55; vocational history, 54, 55; final illness, 55; first U.S. patient treated by homeopathy, 53; introduced to Gram, 17; medical career, 54; name obliterated in *Macoy Book*, 55
Wirt, William xxviii
Woodbury, Ct., 55
words. *See* passwords
working tools, 215

X–Z

York Lodge, 60, 62
York Rite, 66, 69; compared with Scottish Rite, 28
*The "Yorkshire" Old Charges of Masons* (Poole, 1935), xvi*n*
Zerubbabel, 238
Zerubbabel and Frederick of the Crowned Hope Lodge, Copenhagen, 26, 48
Zerubbabel of the North Star Lodge, Copenhagen, 26, 30
Zorobabel Lodge, New York, 26, 51, 89

*Page 255*

[This text appared in the original printing]

COLOPHON

# The Folger Manuscript

Dr. S. Brent Morris, cryptoanalysist of this volume, is a mathematician for the United States Department of Defense and holds a Ph.D. from Duke University. He is a well known and respected Masonic author who currently serves as book review editor of *The Scottish Rite Journal*. Dr. Morris, a Fellow of The Philalethes Society, delivered the 1983 Lecture of the year for that organization. Among his many Masonic publications is the widely read *Masonic Philanthropies: A Tradition of Caring*. Brother Morris resides in Columbia, Maryland and is a member and Past Master of Highland Park Lodge No. 1150 in Texas.

Sixteen hundred copies of this limited edition were manufactured by Pantagraph Printing and Stationery Company of Bloomington, Illinois.

The text paper is sixty pound basis ivory Sycamore Offset vellum made by Cross Pointe Paper Corporation. The book covers are made of Holliston Sturdite over board and stamped in gold.

This volume, issued by The Masonic Book Club, was selected and prepared by Robin L. Carr and Fred Dolan.

# Related Titles from Westphalia Press

Ancient Mysteries and Modern Masonry: The Collected Writings of Jewel P. Lightfoot, Edited by Billy J. Hamilton Jr.

Jewel P. Lightfoot. Former Attorney General of the State of Texas. Past Grand Master of the Masonic Grand Lodge of Texas. From humble beginnings in rural Arkansas, he worked to become an educated man who excelled in law and Freemasonry. He was a gentleman of his time, well-known as a scholar, public speaker, and Masonic philosopher.

Essay on The Mysteries and the True Object of The Brotherhood of Freemasons
by Jason Williams

This isn't a reprint of a classic. It's a new rendition with new life breathed into it, to be enjoyed both by the layperson trying to understand the Craft and Masonic scholars taking a deeper dive into the fraternity's golden years—when the concepts of liberty and equality were still fresh.

Female Emancipation and Masonic Membership: An Essential Collection
By Guillermo De Los Reyes Heredia

Female Emancipation and Masonic Membership: An Essential Combination is a collection of essays on Freemasonry and gender that promotes a transatlantic discussion of the study of the history of women and Freemasonry and their contribution in different countries.

Freemasonry, Heir to the Enlightenment
by Cécile Révauger

Modern Freemasonry may have mythical roots in Solomon's time but is really the heir to the Enlightenment. Ever since the early eighteenth century freemasons have endeavored to convey the values of the Enlightenment in the cultural, political and religious fields, in Europe, the American colonies and the emerging United States.

## Masonic Myths and Legends
### by Pierre Mollier

Freemasonry preserves the teachings of a primitive Judeo-Christian gnosis. In order to better understand these legends and myths and their significance, Pierre Mollier has studied their origins and attempted to find their sources.

## Exploring the Vault: Masonic Higher Degrees 1730–1800
### by John Belton and Roger Dachez

The study adopted a forensic approach to the available evidence, and the discoveries exceeded expectations. The book details their 'archaeological finds' and offers a novel perspective on the development of the Higher Degrees during the eighteenth century.

## Étienne Morin: From the French Rite to the Scottish Rite by Arturo de Hoyos and Josef Wäges

All extant Masonic records have been consulted and using this meta-data, a comprehensive reconstruction emerges, revealing that Étienne Morin was a founding masonic figure in Saint Domingue and creator of his own high degree system, that operated for a time as a defacto Grand Lodge.

## The Impact of Freemasonry on the Secular and Liberal Discourse in Mexico
### by Guillermo De Los Reyes, Translated by Bradley L. Drew

In this thought-provoking book, De Los Reyes argues that Freemasonry, through its lodges, played a decisive role in shaping Mexico's national thought, contributing to the creation of a liberal and secular State and fostering anticlerical sentiments among the laity that endured well into the twentieth century.

## The French Rite: Enlightenment Culture
### Cécile Révauger, Editor

This book, focused on the French Rite, covers the founding principles of the Enlightenment and their influence on the birth of modern Freemasonry as we know it today. The authors revisit the fundamental values of the Enlightenment, from a rational approach to religious tolerance and cosmopolitanism.

## The Great Transformation: Scottish Freemasonry 1725-1810
### by Dr. Mark C. Wallace

This book examines Scottish Freemasonry in its wider British and European contexts between the years 1725 and 1810. The Enlightenment effectively crafted the modern mason and propelled Freemasonry into a new era marked by growing membership and the creation of the Grand Lodge of Scotland.

## Getting the Third Degree: Fraternalism, Freemasonry and History
### Edited by Guillermo De Los Reyes and Paul Rich

As this engaging collection demonstrates, the doors being opened on the subject range from art history to political science to anthropology, as well as gender studies, sociology and more. The organizations discussed may insist on secrecy, but the research into them belies that.

## Freemasonry: A French View
### by Roger Dachez and Alain Bauer

Perhaps one should speak not of Freemasonry but of Freemasonries in the plural. In each country Masonic historiography has developed uniqueness. Two of the best known French Masonic scholars present their own view of the worldwide evolution and challenging mysteries of the fraternity over the centuries.

## Worlds of Print: The Moral Imagination of an Informed Citizenry, 1734 to 1839
### by John Slifko

John Slifko argues that freemasonry was representative and played an important role in a larger cultural transformation of literacy and helped articulate the moral imagination of an informed democratic citizenry via fast emerging worlds of print.

## Why Thirty-Three?: Searching for Masonic Origins
### by S. Brent Morris, PhD

What "high degrees" were in the United States before 1830? What were the activities of the Order of the Royal Secret, the precursor of the Scottish Rite? A complex organization with a lengthy pedigree like Freemasonry has many basic foundational questions waiting to be answered, and that's what this book does: answers questions.

### A Place in the Lodge: Dr. Rob Morris, Freemasonry and the Order of the Eastern Star
### by Nancy Stearns Theiss, PhD

Ridiculed as "petticoat masonry," critics of the Order of the Eastern Star did not deter Rob Morris' goal to establish a Masonic organization that included women as members. Morris carried the ideals of Freemasonry through a despairing time of American history.

### Brought to Light: The Mysterious George Washington Masonic Cave
### by Jason Williams MD

The George Washington Masonic Cave near Charles Town, West Virginia, contains a signature carving of George Washington dated 1748. This book painstakingly pieces together the chronicled events and real estate archives related to the cavern in order to sort out fact from fiction.

### Dudley Wright: Writer, Truthseeker & Freemason
### by John Belton

Dudley Wright (1868-1950) was an Englishman and professional journalist who took a universalist approach to the various great Truths of Life. He travelled though many religions in his life and wrote about them all, but was probably most at home with Islam.

### History of the Grand Orient of Italy
### Emanuela Locci, Editor

No book in Masonic literature upon the history of Italian Freemasonry has been edited in English up to now. This work consists of eight studies, covering a span from the Eighteenth Century to the end of the WWII, tracing through the story, the events and pursuits related to the Grand Orient of Italy.

# westphaliapress.org

www.ingramcontent.com/pod-product-compliance
Lightning Source LLC
Chambersburg PA
CBHW072145100526
44589CB00015B/2098